'When reading this hugely relev[...] amongst its many merits, one that shines through is that the advice and suggestions are supremely practical and achievable. Whilst many laudable books give aspirational guidance, Sonia's excellent book on wellbeing gives you the opportunity to pause and consider aspects of your practice that could be tweaked to ensure that you remain at your very best, healthy and well-prepared to work with children in the early years.'

– *Fred Lacey, clinical psychotherapist and supervisor, and education and nurture consultant*

'Sonia Mainstone-Cotton's book is essential reading for anyone working with children, from the baby room to secondary school, from new starter to experienced manager or head teacher. She has brought together a collection of practical and inspirational ideas for promoting the wellbeing of staff in a way that is easy to read and easy to implement.

Whilst Sonia sensitively acknowledges the emotional and physical strain of working with children, she writes positively, compassionately and optimistically about the benefits of looking after yourself and your staff. This book is a rare combination of uplifting and useful.'

– *Kathy Brodie, author, consultant and host of the Early Years Summit*

'This is an excellent companion to Sonia's previous book *Promoting Young Children's Emotional Health and Wellbeing*, and isn't just a book for early years practitioners, although it will be hugely valuable for colleagues working in the early years. It is a book for life, for all of us in education and beyond. It is full of profound wisdom – an honest, compassionate book with clear, helpful ideas to enable us all to develop both our individual and inter-related journeys of wellbeing.'

– *Ruth Ferguson, specialist senior educational psychologist, Brighter Futures CIC*

Promoting Emotional Wellbeing
in Early Years Staff

by the same author

Promoting Young Children's Emotional Health and Wellbeing
A Practical Guide for Professionals and Parents
Sonia Mainstone-Cotton
ISBN 978 1 78592 054 7
eISBN 978 1 78450 311 6

of related interest

Developing Empathy in the Early Years
A Guide for Practitioners
Helen Garnett
ISBN 978 1 78592 143 8
eISBN 978 1 78450 418 2

Performance Management in Early Years Settings
A Practical Guide for Leaders and Managers
Debbie Garvey
ISBN 978 1 78592 222 0
eISBN 978 1 78450 507 3

Building Your Early Years Business
Planning and Strategies for Growth and Success
Jacqui Burke
ISBN 978 1 78592 059 2
eISBN 978 1 78450 319 2

How to Be a Great Leader in Early Years
Jennie Johnson
ISBN 978 1 84905 674 8
eISBN 978 1 78450 180 8

British Values and the Prevent Duty in the Early Years
A Practitioner's Guide
Kerry Maddock
ISBN 978 1 78592 048 6
eISBN 978 1 78450 307 9

Promoting Emotional Wellbeing in Early Years Staff

A Practical Guide for Looking after Yourself and Your Colleagues

Sonia Mainstone-Cotton

Jessica Kingsley *Publishers*
London and Philadelphia

First published in 2018
by Jessica Kingsley Publishers
73 Collier Street
London N1 9BE, UK
and
400 Market Street, Suite 400
Philadelphia, PA 19106, USA

www.jkp.com

Library of Congress Cataloging in Publication Data
Names: Mainstone-Cotton, Sonia.
Title: Promoting emotional wellbeing in early years staff : a practical guide for looking after yourself and your colleagues / Sonia Mainstone-Cotton.
Description: Philadelphia : Jessica Kingsley Publishers, [2017]
Identifiers: LCCN 2017030074| ISBN 9781785923357 (alk. paper) | ISBN 9781784506568 (eISBN)
Subjects: LCSH: Emotional intelligence. | Child development. | Child psychology.
Classification: LCC BF576 .M245 2017 | DDC 152.4--dc23 LC record available at https://lccn.loc.gov/2017030074

British Library Cataloguing in Publication Data
A CIP catalogue record for this book is available from the British Library

ISBN 978 1 78592 335 7
eISBN 978 1 78450 656 8

Printed and bound by CPI Group (UK) Ltd, Croydon, CR0 4YY

With thanks to Clare, Fred, Ruth, Rachel and Iain for reading through the chapters and advising me. Thanks to Keith, Louise, Wendy and Rachel for sharing your experience and ideas. Thanks to the Nurture Outreach team and the staff I work with in schools, you have all taught me the importance of wellbeing in staff.

Contents

Introduction   *9*

Chapter 1 Physical Wellbeing   17

Chapter 2 Emotional Wellbeing   35

Chapter 3 Mental Wellbeing   53

Chapter 4 Spiritual Wellbeing   69

Chapter 5 How We Support Colleagues   83

Chapter 6 Managers   97

Conclusion   *117*
Resources for Wellbeing   *119*
Index   *121*

Introduction

I first became really interested in wellbeing when I went on a study trip to an early years setting in Denmark in 2012. I loved the way the children and staff spent lots of time outdoors, how their time was unrushed, how they followed the children's interests without a multitude of government targets and expectations to meet. This really got me thinking about how good this was for both the children and staff's wellbeing and how different this was to what I was seeing in the UK.

In 2016 I wrote the book *Promoting Young Children's Emotional Health and Wellbeing: A Practical Guide for Professionals and Parents.* One of the chapters was on adult wellbeing. After writing that book my publishers and I realised this is such an important subject that it needed its own book.

One of my jobs is as a nurture support worker; I work for a small team in Bath called Brighter Futures. I am part of their Nurture Outreach service, supporting children, mainly 4-year-olds who need additional support in their transition to school. In this role I support children who often have a low wellbeing and find the transition to school very challenging. An essential part of the role is supporting the teaching assistants (TAs) and teachers who work each day with the children. The TAs and teachers are all doing an incredible job, one that is often hugely challenging and has a huge impact on their wellbeing. This role has taught me so much about the importance of having a good wellbeing, the importance of staff taking care of themselves and of staff having high-quality support. On most visits I ask staff members about how they are, how they are taking care of themselves, how they are looking after their wellbeing.

I firmly believe if we are going to help children to have a good wellbeing then we need to be in a good place ourselves. We know that children are affected by how we feel, what we say and how we behave. To really help the children we are working with, we need to first stop and look at ourselves and think about how we are, how good our wellbeing is.

The NHS website[1] (2006) has a wellbeing survey you can take; it is a simple survey but quite a useful tool. I would suggest filling this in before you carry on reading the book.

The World Health Organization's concept of wellbeing includes:

- physical wellbeing

- mental and emotional wellbeing

- social wellbeing

- spiritual wellbeing.

In 2015 there were two surveys of teachers and early years staff; they found that 79 per cent of teachers were considering leaving the job due to stress (Espinoza 2015) and 59 per cent

---

1   www.nhs.uk/tools/documents/self_assessments_js/assessment. html?XMLpath=/tools/documents/self_assessments_js/ packages/&ASid=43&syndicate=undefined.

of early years staff were also considering leaving the job due to stress (Crown 2015). These are very alarming statistics. These statistics indicate to us that the wellbeing of staff is not in a good place and this will inevitably be affecting the children.

Definitions of wellbeing

As part of researching this book I looked at several definitions of wellbeing; one that I came across and really liked was from New Zealand, the Maori philosophy of health called *hauora* (TKI n.d.).

Hauora links

Physical wellbeing (called *taha tinana*) is linked to the body: how the body grows, our development, the ability to move and physically caring for self.

Mental and emotional wellbeing (called *taha hinengaro*) is linked with thinking, acknowledging thoughts and feelings and dealing with these constructively.

Social wellbeing (called *taha whanau*) is linked to family relationships, friendships, feeling that you belong, being compassionate and caring and having social support.

Spiritual wellbeing (*taha wairua*) is linked to how individuals have values and beliefs that influence how they live, looking for meaning and purpose in life, having self awareness and a personal identity. For some spiritual awareness is linked to a religion, for others it is not.

Wellbeing is currently a real buzzword, we hear about it in relation to work, children, young people and health.

There are lots of websites now with suggestions about wellbeing. The charity Mind now talks about wellbeing in a lot of its publicity material rather than using the term mental health, which is interesting. I was told by a Mind worker that more people respond to information about wellbeing than information about mental health.

One important source for information on wellbeing is the NHS (2016), who developed a five-step plan to mental wellbeing. These steps include:

- connecting

- being active

- learning

- give to others

- be mindful/take notice.

An important element of thinking about wellbeing is considering what helps to protect our wellbeing, thinking about the protective factors that contribute to good wellbeing. The Scottish government[2] has produced a really useful set of guidelines and suggestions of protective factors that help promote good wellbeing. Below is a list of the protective factors it recommends to safeguard the wellbeing of individuals:

- feeling safe

- self-determination

- being resilient and having problem-solving skills

---

2   www.gov.scot/Publications/2005/11/04145113/51151.

- feeling in control

- having people you can confide in

- accessing social networks

- financial security

- engaging in meaningful activities and roles

- engaging in creative pursuits

- spirituality.

Actions for change

Take some time to look at the above list and think about how many of these protective factors you have in place.

Are there things you need to address, work on or put in place?

In my research for this book I found a few books on wellbeing for teachers, but at the point of writing this there was almost no literature about wellbeing and early years staff. Working with young children can be a very rewarding job, but it can also be incredibly challenging, stressful and exhausting. As educators, we are in a position to make a profound difference in a child's life, and that is amazing. However, as adults, we need to be in a good emotional and physical space to be able to do that. We need to find ways to look after ourselves; we need to put in place strategies that support us. My fear is that many early years practitioners and teachers are forgetting to look after their own wellbeing. This book will offer some ideas and suggestions on how we can start to do this. Many of the ideas are simple and they are often things we already know, but they are also things that we can easily forget.

Outline of the book

My hope is that you can read this book either as a whole or as individual chapters. Each chapter works on its own with ideas and suggestions. This book explores six different topics and ways we can think about our wellbeing. These include physical wellbeing, looking at what we eat and drink, how much sleep we get and physical exercise. The chapter on emotional wellbeing looks at stress and the impact that it has on our body and mind, reflecting on what we can change and influence. It looks at the importance of practising self-compassion and using emotional language ourselves. The chapter on mental wellbeing explores the need to keep our brains active and engaged, through learning, involvement in the arts, engaging in new experiences and professional development. The chapter on spiritual wellbeing explores what spiritual wellbeing is; it looks at the importance of experiencing stillness and silence and having a rhythm to our lives, as well as using mindfulness and yoga. Chapter 5 on supporting colleagues recognises that we all have a part to play in supporting one another and offers practical ideas on how to do this. The final chapter is aimed at managers – recognising that managers can have a huge influence on staff wellbeing. This chapter offers practical ideas and suggestions taken from managers and head teachers. My hope is that this book will give you some ideas and recommendations; it will encourage you to think and reflect on your practice and encourage you.

References

Crown, H. (2015) 'Nursery workers consider leaving profession due to workload.' Accessed on 27/1/17 at www.nurseryworld.co.uk/nursery-world/news/1154397/nursery-workers-consider-leaving-profession-due-to-workload.

Espinoza, J. (2015) 'Stress pushing teachers to leave profession figures show.' Accessed on 27/1/17 at www.telegraph.co.uk/education/educationnews/11480108/Stress-pushing-teachers-to-leave-profession-figures-show.html.

NHS (2016) 'Wellbeing self-assessment.' Accessed on 5/2/17 at www.nhs.uk/Conditions/stress-anxiety-depression/Pages/improve-mental-wellbeing.aspx.

TKI (n.d.) 'Well-being, hauora.' Accessed on 19/1/17 at http://health.tki.org.nz/Teaching-in-HPE/Health-and-PE-in-the-NZC/Health-and-PE-in-the-NZC-1999/Underlying-concepts/Well-being-hauora.

Chapter 1

Physical Wellbeing

Physical wellbeing is about how we ensure our body is fit and healthy. We know that the impact of ill health can have a massive influence on our mental wellbeing. In this chapter, I am going to look at how we can focus on our physical wellbeing and, through doing this, hopefully also help our mental wellbeing.

Food and drink

There is a great emphasis now on the need for children to eat healthily. We know from research and our own experience that children are unable to function and learn to their best ability if they don't have breakfast at the start of the day, or if the breakfast they eat is sugary (Garner 2015). I know many schools who now provide children with breakfast, either through breakfast clubs or by teachers and TAs bringing in breakfast for individual children. This is brilliant and vital, but how good are the adults at eating breakfast in the morning?

In my last job I worked for a children's charity; we had a variety of breakfast options in the office kitchen, along with tea, coffee and herbal teas for staff to help themselves to. Out of the team's petty cash, bread for toasting and butter along with tea, coffee, herbal teas and milk were provided, and we all brought in different spreads and breakfast cereals for each other to share. The manager who started this (which was then continued by another manager) recognised that many of the staff were in a rush to get to work, and they worked better once they had eaten. The NHS website has some simple ideas and recipes for an easy and healthy breakfast.[1]

Do you eat lunch?

Lunch was the meal I used to skip most often, or if I did eat lunch, it would be at my desk while working, or in the car while visiting settings/families. In my old team, this was the norm; there was a culture of not having lunch and not taking a lunch break. Not that it was frowned upon – it was just that we rarely did it. In the last 3 years that we worked together, with a different manager, we made an effort to eat lunch together, usually after a team meeting once a month. I am now self-employed and one of my roles is working in a variety of schools as a nurture support worker. Since becoming self-employed, I have become quite strict with myself about going home at lunch time and eating. I am fortunate that all the schools I work in are within a 10-mile radius of where I live. My current job is no less stressful than my last, in fact it is probably more stressful, but I feel that I deal with the stress a lot better and I am sure that is helped by stopping each day, eating well and having a proper lunch break.

---

1   www.nhs.uk/Livewell/loseweight/Pages/Healthybreakfasts.aspx.

The effect nutrition has on mental health

Recent evidence in the field of nutrition has been finding that good nutrition is hugely beneficial for our mental health. We know that the guidance is to eat at least five portions of fruit and vegetables a day, and some evidence is showing that this should be raised to seven.[2] There is growing research and evidence looking at the link between anxiety and the health of gut bacteria. The gut produces a large number of neurotransmitters: these are chemicals that communicate information through the body and the brain. One of the neurotransmitters that affects our happiness is serotonin and around 90 per cent of serotonin is made in our gut (Kelly 2017). There is growing evidence to show that if we have a healthy gut this can help with anxiety. Rachel Kelly (2017) has written a book offering ideas, suggestions and recipes on how to eat food that will help with our mood. At the back of the book she has a list of food she describes as 'good mood' foods. A small example of some of these is:

- avocados
- blueberries
- chamomile tea
- kale
- marmite
- sweet potato
- spinach
- dark chocolate.

---

2   www.nhs.uk/news/2014/04April/Pages/Five-a-day-should-be-upped-to-seven-a-day.aspx.

Questions for practice and reflection

- Do you have time to eat breakfast? If you don't, or dislike eating first thing, could you take breakfast into work with you?
- Do you take a lunch break? I know this may not always be practical every day, but could you set yourself a target of having a lunch break two or three times a week?
- Do you eat with colleagues? This can help to ensure you take a lunch break.
- How much fruit and veg do you eat?
- How much thought do you give to the food you are eating and how that is making you feel? Is this something you need to look at and readdress?

Food that makes you feel good

There is a lot of important writing about eating healthily and the link between this and good physical wellbeing. I agree this is vital. I eat healthily, my weight is good for someone of my age and size, I eat a balanced diet, but I also believe it is okay sometimes to eat food that can be less good for you. That is what I liked about Rachel Kelly's book – she recognises the need for occasional comfort eating and has recipes for this. I like eating cakes, and I love chocolate. In my old team, I had a chocolate drawer in my desk. The team knew that if anyone was having a rough day, or a difficult moment, there was chocolate available for them as a comfort in my drawer. I am aware that this is not a healthy way to live every day – turning to chocolate every time something goes wrong – but I also believe it is okay to enjoy this in moderation. I have recently been reading about *hygge* (Wiking 2016). *Hygge* is a Danish word for the feeling of having warmth, comfort and wellbeing. Wiking describes how a cake is an important part of *hygge*; I thought this was brilliant as most of the teams, schools and nurseries I have worked in had one important factor in common: the sharing of cakes! There is something about eating cake, particularly when it has been home baked, that feels good for our wellbeing. It can help us to feel nurtured; it can help us feel wanted. One friend of mine is a children's centre manager; she regularly bakes cakes for her team at team meetings. This is one way she shows her staff they are valued, and she is appreciative of their work. I spoke with a range of friends who work in challenging jobs, either supporting people, education or caring. They all said that cake was an essential part of their team life; they talked about how cakes being provided helped them to feel supported, noticed, comforted. The other key factor people talked about was the act of sharing food together and how positive that was. One friend is a TA in a primary school, and her daughter who attends the school bakes a cake each week for the staff room. Another friend is a nurse on a dementia ward, and she described how the staff often bring in cakes for the patients and have a tea party with the patients. I love these ideas; to me, they feel very life affirming.

Questions for practice and reflection

- Do you share cakes in your place of work?
- Why don't you take in a cake or something else that would be a treat for your next team meeting/staff meeting?

Sleep
How much sleep are you getting?

Often staff who work with children tell me that there are times when they find it very hard to sleep. Thoughts and worries are often whirring through their minds; they often find themselves ruminating over things that have occurred in the day. We know that lack of sleep can leave people feeling tired and irritable, making it difficult to concentrate and make decisions.

Neurologist Judy Willis (2014) suggests teachers spend more time than most people worrying and thinking about the day they have had, and the tasks that are ahead of them, and this often impacts on their sleep. She suggests that on average teachers get 6 hours of sleep a night, whereas the average person needs around 8 hours of sleep. Sleep enables us to have clear minds and create memories. Willis proposes that in the last few hours of sleep, around the sixth to eighth hour, our brain releases neurochemicals that stimulate memory connections. It is during the sixth to eighth hour of sleep that the brain is often working on creative problem- solving, helping us to wake with ideas and solutions to problems.

Suggestions for good sleep

Guidance taken from the NHS[3]:

- Have a regular bedtime routine.

- Make sure your bedroom is a restful environment, think about the lighting, temperature and noise.

---

3   www.nhs.uk/Livewell/insomnia/Pages/insomniatips.aspx.

- Ensure that you have a comfortable bed.

- Think about what you are drinking and eating before bed. The recommendation is that you don't eat just before you go to sleep.

- Avoid caffeine/energy drinks in the evening. Drinking alcohol before bed can make you sleepy initially but will often disrupt your sleep. You could try drinking herbal tea, such as chamomile tea, before bed.

- Avoid smoking before bed – nicotine is a stimulant.

- Try to relax before you go to sleep, for example, read a book, have a warm bath, use a mindfulness meditation.

- If your mind is full of worries and concerns, write them down before you go to bed.

- If you wake in the night and cannot go back to sleep, the recommendation is to get up and do something relaxing until you feel sleepy, then go back to bed.

Other things that work for me:

- I have made a sleep spray that I spray on my pillow each night when I am struggling with sleep. You can buy these, but I have made my own. I use the following recipe:

Aromatherapy sleep spray recipe

- 10 ml of sweet almond oil or another base oil (you can buy this from health food shops)

- 10 drops of essential lavender oil

- 10 drops of essential chamomile oil

Pour into a small spray bottle. Spray onto your pillow each night, or add a few drops to your bath before you go to bed.

For more information about making your blends and the precautions you need to take, have a look at the Woodland Herbs website.[4]

Rest

Rest is different to sleep: the *Oxford English Dictionary* (2017) definition of rest describes it as 'to stop work, to be inactive and recover strength or health'. Often busy people find it very hard to rest, to slow down and stop. In my previous book *Promoting Young Children's Emotional Health and Wellbeing* (Mainstone-Cotton 2017), there is a chapter titled 'Un-rushing and stillness'. This chapter explores how we enable children to slow down, take rest, enjoy being in the moment. However, we can only teach this to children if we know and practise this ourselves. I think as adults we often believe we should be aware how to rest, but I am not sure this is always true. I think rest can fall into three categories: rest of the body, rest of the mind and rest of the spirit or soul. My husband has a very physical job: he is a letter carver and is often cutting into stone. Rest for him often needs to be physical. For myself, my job uses a lot of thinking, compassion and emotional nurturing of others: I often need rest of the mind and the soul. I asked 25 people what they did for rest; their responses are below:

- read

---

4   www.woodlandherbs.co.uk/acatalog/base_oils_for_aromatherapy.html.

- listen to music

- knit

- lie in my hammock in the garden in the sun

- watch films

- eat cake

- sit with a cup of tea and watch trashy TV

- walk

- swim

- be outside

- garden

- cook

- cleaning

- eating/drinking nice food and drink

- listening to podcasts in the dark

- wallpapering

- having coffee with friends

- singing.

Questions for practice and reflection

- Think about what you do for rest, are there any ideas above that you can try?
- Are you getting enough rest? If you're not, how could you fit in more opportunities to rest?

Exercise

Before I started this book I carried out a small research project. I asked adults who work with children to fill in a questionnaire about their wellbeing and work. I had 95 replies to this questionnaire. One of the questions was 'What do you do in life which helps you feel good about yourself?' The most popular answer: 28 per cent of people said they spent time doing some form of exercise. Exercising is known to increase the endorphin levels in our body, this is a chemical that triggers positive feelings in our brain; research also suggests that exercise can help to improve self-esteem, sleep quality, energy levels, and reduce stress and depression.[5]

Despite these encouraging reasons to exercise, a study by the British Heart Foundation (Watson 2015) found that half of all British adults never exercise, which puts Britain's fitness level among the lowest in Europe. The NHS[6] website has guidelines on how much exercise adults should take, with suggestions on what this could be, they recommend around 150 minutes a week.

Swimming is my chosen exercise; I swim every morning Monday to Friday at my local community pool. I started 5 years ago with the aim of losing some weight and getting fitter. I have grown to love swimming; I feel I can be totally myself, I love the rhythm of the activity, I enjoy the way my body glides through the water, I relish the sense of freedom

---

5   www.nhs.uk/Livewell/fitness/Pages/Whybeactive.aspx.

6   www.nhs.uk/Livewell/fitness/Pages/physical-activity-guidelines-for-adults.aspx.

it gives me. My morning swim feels life-giving and life-enhancing; it helps me to feel really good about myself.

A good friend of mine, Jenny Baker (2017), discovered 2 years ago that she had breast cancer. Jenny is a runner; she runs marathons. When Jenny learned about her cancer she asked her oncologist about continuing to run; the advice was that as long as she could run, she should continue. Jenny ran to each of her chemotherapy appointments – it was her way of pulling back some control from what the cancer was doing to her; it helped her to maintain her identity. Later Jenny wrote a book about this experience. For her, running was a powerful, life-enhancing way to improve her wellbeing during a tough time of her life.

Questions for practice and reflection

- Are you exercising regularly?
- If you're not, think about what you could do – what exercise do you enjoy or, if not enjoy, could you tolerate?
- Is there an exercise you could do with friends? Exercising with others can sometimes make it easier.
- Does your workplace have a link with a local gym or exercise class? Could you encourage your manager to make a connection? This might be a boost to the whole team.
- How could you fit exercise into your life? Is there time for this at the weekend? Do mornings work for you? Or is there a class you could attend one or two evenings a week?

Environment

I believe the environment we are in is also essential to our physical and mental wellbeing. The spaces we are in can make a big difference to how we feel. There are some classrooms that I spend time in that look and feel overly cluttered, with masses of visual stimulation. I have also been in nursery rooms that are small, with limited natural light; they feel dark and cold. These spaces can often feel overbearing; they are not a calming space to be in. In contrast, I have been in classrooms and nursery areas that feel light, airy, with space to move and limited visual stimulation. The environment makes such a difference to the children's wellbeing and the staff's wellbeing. Some examples of excellent physical spaces are from Reggio Emilia; this is a small northern town in Italy. Since the 1940s they have been developing a unique way of educating pre-school children, and part of their identity is the emphasis and thought they give to their environment. The environments in Reggio are very spacious, airy and light; they also have lots of natural objects in their spaces. For some ideas and examples, do an internet search for Reggio Emilia classrooms. Also in the UK Elizabeth Jarman (2007) focuses on the environment and how we can create good learning spaces for children. She advocates decluttering, avoiding busy floor coverings and minimising displays on the walls. I believe this not only helps the children but also the staff.

We don't always have the ability to make significant changes to our environment; you may work in a school or nursery with limited space, lacking in natural light. However, there are things we can do that will help the environment. You may spend 7 or more hours in the room you work in;

this is a lot of time if your environment does not help you to feel calm and happy. Even the simple introduction of a vase of flowers in the room can make a difference to how space feels and how staff and children feel.

Questions for practice and reflection

- How does your classroom/nursery room make you feel?
- Is your space too cluttered? Is it full of things you don't need or use?
- Could you make better use of storage?
- How much is on the walls and hanging from the ceiling? Are they serving a purpose?
- Do you use fabrics and cushions to soften the acoustics?
- Do you have natural objects in your space?

Being outdoors

In Japan there is a growing practice called *Shinrin-yoku*. In English this means forest therapy. This is about people spending time in forests; it is viewed in Japan as a preventive therapy, as a way of counteracting *karoshi*, which means death from overwork (Williams 2017). The effects of being in forests have been measured with hundreds of people by Chiba University researchers. Their research showed that a casual walk in a forest caused a 12.7 per cent decrease in the participants' cortisol levels and a 103 per cent increase in parasympathetic nervous activity (relax state) (Miyazaki 2012). The Japanese culture recognises not only the healing effect of being in forests but also the impact that being in green spaces, being outside in nature, has on wellbeing. As an early years practitioner I regularly suggest to people that we need to enable children to have more time outside, and I was very influenced by Richard Louv's (2010) suggestion of nature defect disorder in children. I also think this is really relevant for us as adults. I am currently writing this in the evening, after spending an afternoon outside in my garden. Today is an early spring day with a full day of sunshine, the first in weeks. I know in myself I feel the happiest and most relaxed I have felt all week.

We need to give time to thinking about our physical wellbeing, considering how we physically take care of ourselves and how we can get enough sleep and rest. By giving attention to these aspects of our physical life, we are being kind and compassionate to ourselves.

Routine

Routines can be really important in helping our physical wellbeing: the small things such as making a coffee, taking a shower each day, having a bath before you go to bed, or attending a yoga class once a week are important parts of our day and week. I love drinking coffee and I have become a bit of a coffee snob! We grind our own coffee beans and I buy the beans from a local roastery. The daily routine of scooping the beans, smelling them, grinding the beans and then making the coffee is a simple act, but it is a moment that brings me joy each time. Another important routine in my life is I meet my friend Clare for a coffee every Saturday morning and then I buy my coffee beans from the local market. These two acts have become an important part of my weekly routine, they make me happy, they help me feel connected and they improve my wellbeing. In the role of educator/key worker/carer we can sometimes take on the stress and trauma of the children we are working with; this can leave us feeling stressed, anxious and depressed. Louise Bomber (2011) describes this as secondary stress or trauma. One of the earliest signs of secondary trauma, or depression, is when we abandon our regular routines and those things that make us feel good. We need to be especially aware of this.

Questions for practice and reflection

- What are the routines you have that make you feel good?
- Are you aware of times when you have dropped these routines due to stress, being overworked, etc?
- Are there new routines you could introduce that would help your wellbeing?

References

Baker, J. (2017) *Run for Your Life: How One Woman Ran Circles Around Breast Cancer*. London: Pitch Publishing.

Bomber, L. (2011) *What About Me? Inclusive Strategies to Support Pupils with Attachment Difficulties Make it Through the School Day*. Kings Lynn: Worth Publishing.

Garner, R. (2015) 'Children who eat breakfast before school twice as likely to perform well in tests.' Accessed on 20/1/17 at www.independent.co.uk/news/education/education-news/children-who-eat-breakfast-before-school-twice-as-likely-to-perform-well-in-tests-a6736496.html.

Jarman, E. (2007) *Communication Friendly Spaces*. London: The Basic Skills Agency.

Kelly, R. (2017) *The Happy Kitchen: Good Mood Food*. London: Short Books.

Louv, R. (2010) *Last Child in the Woods*. London: Atlantic Books.

Mainstone-Cotton, S. (2017) *Promoting Young Children's Emotional Health and Wellbeing: A Practical Guide for Professionals and Parents.* London: Jessica Kingsley Publishers.

Miyazaki, Y. (2012) 'Nature therapy Ted Talk.' Accessed on 25/3/17 at https://www.youtube.com/watch?v=MD4rlWqp7Po&list=SP629FCC64F4B98E D5&index=27.

Oxford English Dictionary (2017) 'Definition of rest.' Accessed on 14/2/17 at https://en.oxforddictionaries.com/definition/rest.

Watson, L. (2015) 'Half of all British adults never exercise.' Accessed on 15/2/17 at www.telegraph.co.uk/news/health/news/11607408/Half-of-all-British-adults-never-do-any-exercise.html.

Wiking, M. (2016) *The Little Book of Hygge: The Danish Way to Live Well.* London: Penguin.

Williams, F. (2017) *The Nature Fix: Why Nature Makes Us Happier, Healthier and More Creative.* London: WW Norton & Company.

Willis, J. (2014) 'Teachers guide to sleep and why it matters.' Accessed on 27/1/17 at https://www.google.co.uk/amp/s/amp.theguardian.com/teacher-network/teacher-blog/2014/nov/11/good-night-teacher-guide-sleep.

Chapter 2

Emotional Wellbeing

Stress

Our emotional wellbeing is just as important as our physical wellbeing. In the introduction to this book, I talked about how stress is a primary reason for many teachers and early years staff wanting to stop working in the profession. Stress can have a devastating effect on our physical wellbeing and mental wellbeing. Stress can lead to panic attacks, heart palpitations, chronic pain, migraines, stomach problems, depression and memory loss. When we feel stressed our body is releasing cortisol and adrenaline; this is the body's way of dealing with a threat – in our brain stem we are going into 'fight or flight' mode. If we continue to release high levels of these hormones, this can have an adverse impact on our health. The mental health charity Mind[1] has a useful website with a list of signs of stress and how this can affect us. It also has a list of ideas on how to manage stress, these include:

---

1 www.mind.org.uk/information-support/tips-for-everyday-living/stress/signs-of-stress/#.WLkyJ7Gcb3A.

- *Recognise the triggers to your stress.* By identifying them, this can help you to be more aware and can help you think of solutions to help.

- *Organise your time.* Making lists can help you feel more on top of things. Think about which is the best time of the day for you. For example, are you a morning person or a late evening person? When are you most alert and most able to do things and deal with tasks?

- *Take breaks.* Don't try to do too much in one go.

- *Address some of the causes of your stress.* There may be some actions you can take to alleviate or help with the stress you are experiencing.

- *Accept the things you can't change.* There are things we have no control over and we can not change. Sometimes by realising this and accepting this, it can lower our stress levels.

Stress can also be contagious (Devon 2015): we all know how a very stressed colleague can have an impact on the stress levels of the rest of the team. Also, the stress levels and anxiety of the children we work with can similarly affect our stress levels; we can take on secondary stress, where we pick up on the stress of the person we are working with and experience this stress ourselves (Bomber 2011). Being mindful of this can help us to think about whether it is our stress we are feeling or someone else's stress, and then we can take appropriate action.

Circle of concern and influence

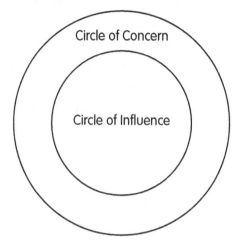

One useful exercise we can do when we are feeling overwhelmed by what is happening is called the circle of concern/circle of influence. This was created by Stephen Covey (2013). The diagram shows what this looks like.

The outer circle is the circle of concern; in here you label all the things that concern you. The inner circle is the circle of influence; in here you write down the things you can influence and have some control over. This can be a useful tool to help think about what things you can change, and have some control over. It can help give you ideas about how and what you spend your emotional and physical time and energy on. Covey[2] describes being proactive as taking responsibility for our lives: by being proactive we can decide how we behave and act and the choices we make. He proposes that *proactive* people focus and work on the issues within

---

2   http://uthscsa.edu/gme/documents/Circles.pdf.

their circle of influence and this will, in time, increase their circle of influence. Whereas, *reactive* people have a tendency to neglect those areas they have control and influence over; they focus their attention in other places, which they have no control over, their circle of influence then decreases.

The Maudsley[3] has a checklist for mental wellbeing; one of its categories is around enhancing control, within this it suggests:

- Individuals have a feeling of control over their lives; this includes being able to set and work towards goals and being able to influence and shape your own circumstances.

- Having a belief in yourself and your potential.

Actions for change

Take some time now to draw a circle of concern and influence.

Have a look at what is in your circle of influence. Are you spending time focusing on these areas? Are there things in here you could give some more time and focus to?

There are practical actions we can take when we are stressed, which will help our emotional wellbeing. The rest of this chapter will explore these.

---

3   www.maudsleyinternational.com/media/16152/mental_well_being_checklist.pdf.

Animals

Many people find keeping pets a good stress relief. We know that hospitals and hospices now have dogs visiting patients. Research has shown petting animals can increase the hormone oxytocin, which helps us to feel good and it can decrease the stress hormone, cortisol. Several of the people who responded to my research on wellbeing mentioned walking dogs and spending time with their pets as a good way to help their wellbeing. This is not just related to keeping cats and dogs – we keep guinea pigs. Our current guinea pig adores being stroked; she has been a brilliant stress relief for my teenage daughters while they have been taking exams. If I have had a hard day at work I will often come home and sit with the pig, and she immediately calms me.

Being self-compassionate and using kind words

Over the past few years as I have researched and reflected on emotional wellbeing I have been drawn to the ideas and practices that we can carry out to be kind to ourselves. Brené Brown (2015) talks about the need to be kind to ourselves: the need to recognise when we are struggling and finding life hard, and to be gentle with ourselves. Kristin Neff (2011) also speaks about the need to develop self-compassion. I find these ideas liberating. All too often we are quick to criticise ourselves, to judge ourselves harshly. Over the past few years, I have tried hard to practise self-compassion and kindness to myself, and I encourage the staff I work with to also try this.

The way we can put this into action and improve our emotional wellbeing is by, first, recognising when we are feeling stressed, anxious or worried. Kristin Neff (2011) encourages us to speak out loud what we are feeling, acknowledge it and say kind words and be compassionate to ourselves. She proposes that by soothing our pain we are helping to release oxytocin. Oxytocin can contribute to reducing the feelings of fear and anxiety and counteract cortisol. Over the past year I have started to use the emotion language I use with the children I work with, on myself, usually in the car, on my own. I will often speak out words such as 'Sonia, it is okay to feel worried and scared, but you can get through this'. By using kinder words, by acknowledging to ourselves when life is feeling hard, this is a good starting point to begin to change the scripts we tell ourselves and to help improve our emotional wellbeing.

Comfort ourselves

We all know how powerful touch can be; in my nurture work I often gently stroke a child's arm or rub their back if I can see they are feeling distressed. This can also be calming for ourselves. Kristin Neff (2011) proposes that if we are feeling stressed, anxious or self-critical, we can give ourselves a hug, or gently stroke our arm or hand, showing ourselves some care, love and tenderness. Or if others are around and you feel awkward about this, imagine hugging yourself. She suggests being loving and kind to ourselves can act as a soothing, calming influence.

Having an emotional vocabulary

In my book about promoting young children's emotional wellbeing (Mainstone-Cotton 2017), I have a chapter on emotional vocabulary. In my role as a nurture consultant, I use emotional vocabulary and emotion language all the time with the children I support. Having an emotional vocabulary and a good emotional intelligence is vital for our wellbeing.

An emotional intelligence helps us to understand our emotions and feelings and how to manage them. Just as we use emotional language with children to help them know what they are experiencing, it is important that we use this emotional intelligence and language to explain to others and acknowledge to ourselves how we are feeling and why. In Brené Brown's research (2017) she found the average number of emotions people can identify in themselves and named three. The three were happy, sad, annoyed. She proposes we need to have an emotion granularity, where we can recognise the subtle differences in our feelings and emotions. She proposes that as adults we need to be able to identify around 30.

Actions for change

How many emotions can you name and identify? As a quick exercise you are unlikely to get to 30 and that is okay!

We know that for years in the UK talking about how we felt was seen as a social taboo. Thankfully this is now changing, and as a society, we are talking more about mental health, our feelings and emotions. However, we can still find it hard sometimes to be honest about how we are feeling. How often do people ask 'How are you?' and we reply 'Fine', even when we are feeling awful. The Mental Health Foundation website has some guidance on how to talk about feelings.[4]

Are you kind to yourself?

One question I regularly ask the staff I work with is, 'What are you doing to be kind to yourself?' I asked this one week to a teacher just before the half term break – she was particularly stressed, she had a little boy in her class with very complex needs, and he expressed this through some very challenging behaviour; the impact of this was catching up on her, and she looked exhausted. When I asked the question she looked

---

4   www.mentalhealth.org.uk/your-mental-health/looking-after-your-mental-health/talk-about-your-feelings.

quite shocked and said she didn't know – she had lots of work to do, reports to write and lessons to plan, she hadn't thought about anything else. We discussed what she enjoys doing, what makes her happy and she said baking. She decided that each day of the holiday she would bake something different. When we came back to school I asked how the week had been, she said she felt good, she got the work done, she had a lie in each morning and did some baking each day. Her main comment was the very decision to do something that made her feel happy and to be kind to herself helped her to feel more in control and calmer, she also said her husband was thrilled about all the baking!

What do you do to be kind to yourself?

I asked this question on my questionnaire for staff, some of the popular answers were:

- run
- swim
- walk my dog
- knit
- crochet
- paint
- sing in a choir
- cook
- yoga
- mindfulness

- spend time with friends

- spend time with family

- read

- eat well

- garden.

Actions for change

Have a look at the list and see if any of these would work for you. It doesn't matter what you do, but the very act of deciding today 'I am going to do…to be kind to myself' is a powerful act.

Living in a state of happiness

There is an increasing amount of research into the impact happiness has on our wellbeing. Anthony Seldon (2015) has written a book on this subject: he was a head teacher of Wellington College and implemented lots of ideas to increase the happiness and wellbeing of his pupils and staff. He proposes that happiness is not dependent on what we have or what we gain, but that we experience happiness by living wisely, by being in relationships with other people and treating others as equals. Seldon is involved in setting up a movement called Action for Happiness.[5] Their aim is to help people to be happy about their lives and recognise the things they can do to help make this happen. They have ten keys or

---

5   www.actionforhappiness.org.

actions that they recommend people can take to be happier. These are:

1. giving – doing things for other people

2. relating – be connected with other people

3. exercising

4. being aware – living mindfully

5. learn and try out new things

6. have a sense of direction or goals you are setting yourself

7. be resilient

8. think about what makes you feel happy

9. acceptance and feeling okay about who you are and what you can do

10. think about what gives your life meaning – are you part of something bigger?

Actions for change

Have a look at the list and think about what you do. You might want to pick out one or two and work on these.

Choosing joy

I believe that finding joy is an act we can choose to engage in. So often it is easy to think that joy is something that people have when they are in a job they love, they have money – all is well for them. However, joy can be something that we choose to engage in. The Henri Nouwen Society[6] proposes that every moment of our life we can choose to find joy; this is not to negate from difficult, painful times but to recognise that we can still find joy in moments of deep hardness. It is often so easy to get stuck focusing on negative thoughts, feelings and actions. The challenge is to look for the joyful moments. For me this is particularly important when we are working with children who present with challenging behaviours and lives. The children I support through my nurture work can at times present with sad stories and difficult lives, which can lead to very challenging behaviour. It is so easy to get stuck in the problems, in the moments that have gone wrong, and forget or not notice the glimpses of joy. To choose to see the moments of joy takes a very purposeful and mindful decision. The moment of joy might be the child who managed to sit for 5 minutes or the child who was able to self-regulate rather than hit out. One way of practising an intentional act of finding joy is through taking time at the the end of each day and asking the question, 'Where did I find joy today?'

Being thankful, expressing gratitude

Another writer on happiness is Sonya Lyubomirsky (2007), who is a professor of psychology at California University. She specialises in research around happiness. From her research, she has found a key component to people being happy is intentional activities. One example of this is practising gratitude. Her research has shown people who regularly

---

6   http://henrinouwen.org.

practise an attitude of gratitude are happier. Some examples of how to do this are:

- *Keeping a gratitude journal* – either daily or weekly, write down a few things that you are grateful for that day or week.

- *Practising gratitude in the moment* – this is about being aware in the moment of what you are grateful for and stopping to notice and acknowledge this. If you have faith, this may be a time when you stop and thank God for the beauty of the buzzard you have just seen, or you may just stop and acknowledge to yourself how grateful you are for the flowers you have grown, etc.

- *Take photos/draw/express the things you are grateful for in creative ways* – one year I did this by taking photos on my phone. Each week I would photograph something that I felt grateful for.

- *Express gratitude to another person* – I try to do this each time I have been working with a child in my nurture work. At the end of the session I will thank them for the time we have had playing together; I will pick out one thing I particularly enjoyed. This is partly about boosting the self-esteem of the children I work with, but it also helps me to find something positive from our session. This is important in helping me to remain positive about the work.

Actions for change

Spend a moment thinking about the things you have to be grateful for.

What has happened over this past day or week that you are grateful for? Are there ideas here that you could work on?

Relaxation

In Chapter 1 on physical wellbeing, I wrote about rest and how we need to take rest. Relaxation and rest are often seen together and impact both our physical and our emotional wellbeing. We need to ensure we are intentionally taking the time to relax; often this can be one of the first things we drop when we are busy and becoming stressed. In the previous chapter, I listed ideas for ways you can take rest; there is a growing recognition of the benefits of using meditations to help you relax. I will explore this more in Chapter 4 on spiritual wellbeing. The website of the Mental Health Foundation[7] has a podcast wth a guided meditation aimed at helping people to relax. This is worth trying.

Being with others

There has been an increasing amount of research about loneliness and the impact this has on our mental health and wellbeing. Jo Griffin (2010) suggests that loneliness is not about being alone but is a 'subjective experience of isolation'

---

7   https://www.mentalhealth.org.uk/podcasts-and-videos/mindfulness-10-minute-practice-exercise.

over an extended period that can lead to mental health difficulties. We can feel alone even when people surround us or we live with others. What is important is the quality of the close relationships we have: if we are living in a relationship with lots of conflicts or that is toxic, this can be more damaging to our wellbeing and mental health than being alone. It is not about the number of people we have around us but the quality of the relationships. We need people who we can be honest with, who believe in us and support us, and for whom we do the same. New research shows that if we have enriching and good quality relationships we are less likely to have mental health problems and it can help us to live longer (Mental Health Foundation 2016).[8]

Sometimes an early warning sign of depression is when we become isolated and can't face spending time with other people. We all need people around us whom we can trust, be ourselves with, talk to, have a laugh with. However, this takes time and effort, and when we are feeling overworked and exhausted spending quality time with others can be one of the first things we let go. In Chapter 1, I wrote about how important routines can be: regularly being with others can be part of our intentional routine. If you're living with other people, for example, in a shared house or with a partner, this does not always mean you are spending intentional time with other people. Parents with young children often comment they can not remember the last time they spent quality time with their partner – organising babysitters, having the energy and/or the money to go out can feel and be

---

8   https://www.mentalhealth.org.uk/publications/relationships-21st-century-forgotten-foundation-mental-health-and-wellbeing.

too much. The danger is that this can become habit forming, and you can reach a point where you have forgotten how to spend quality time together. My children are now 17 and 19; one has left home for university, and the other will soon be moving on too. Over the past few years my husband and I have made a real intentional effort to do things together, so much of our life has been with the girls. We didn't want it to become a major shock to our marriage when they both left home, and we were left with one another not knowing how to spend time together. We mostly go to art exhibitions, go to the cinema, go for walks, but these are things we need to agree to set time aside for and intentionally do – in our busy lives they don't just happen. The other important routine I have, as I mentioned previously, is seeing my friend Clare for a coffee every Saturday morning. This is such an important part of my weekly routine: it has been in place for years, Clare and I have shared many important moments in our lives, I know that Clare is there for me no matter what and I for her. If I have a tough week, just knowing I am seeing Clare on Saturday makes me smile and feel glad.

Questions for practice and reflection

- Who do you have in your life that you can spend time with, who supports you and accepts you for who you are?
- Do you need to be more intentional about spending time with people?

Your one wild and precious life

A few years ago I discovered the poet Mary Oliver (1992). She has a poem called 'The Summer Day'; you can hear her reading the poem on YouTube.[9] In the last lines of the poem she poses a question about how people will use their precious life.

I love this question. For me, it is a question of hope, a question of encouragement. When we are feeling stressed, overwhelmed or unhappy, we can feel powerless and hopeless. However, this question can act as an encouragement. I doubt for many of us the answer is to work harder. Your answer may be to find more joy, to discover new places or simply to spend time with those you love.

Actions for change

Spend some time as you finish this chapter thinking about the question that Mary Oliver poses. What is your plan?

References

Bomber, L. (2011) *What About Me? Inclusive Strategies to Support Pupils with Attachment Difficulties Make it Through the School Day*. Kings Lynn: Worth Publishing.

Brown, B. (2015) *Daring Greatly: How the Courage to Be Vulnerable Transforms the Way We Live, Love, Parent and Lead*. London: Penguin Books.

Brown, B. (2017) *Rising Strong as a Spiritual Practice*. Podcast. Accessed on 11/07/17 at www.soundstrue.com/store/rising-strong-as-a-spiritual-practice-2.html.

Covey, S. (2013) *The 7 Habits of Highly Effective People*. Electronic Edition. New York: Rosetta Books.

---

9   https://www.youtube.com/watch?v=16CL6bKVbJQ.

Devon, N. (2015) 'To improve the mental health of young people, we should start by tackling stress among teachers.' Accessed on 3/3/17 at https://www.tes.com/news/school-news/breaking-views/improve-mental-health-young-people-we-should-start-tackling-stress.

Griffin, J. (2010) 'The lonely society.' Accessed on 3/3/17 at www.mentalhealth.org.uk/sites/default/files/the_lonely_society_report.pdf.

Lyubomirsky, S. (2007) *The How of Happiness: A Practical Guide to Getting the Life You Want.* London: Piatkus.

Mainstone-Cotton, S. (2017) *Promoting Young Children's Emotional Health and Wellbeing: A Practical Guide for Professionals and Parents.* London: Jessica Kingsley Publishers.

Mental Health Foundation (2016) 'Relationships in the 21st Century.' London: Mental Health Foundation. Accessed on 12/10/17 at https://www.mentalhealth.org.uk/publications/relationships-21st-century-forgotten-foundation-mental-health-and-wellbeing.

Neff, K. (2011) *Self Compassion: Stop Beating Yourself Up and Leave Insecurity Behind.* New York: Harper Collins.

Oliver, M. (1992) *New and Selected Poems. Volume One.* Boston, MA: Beacon Press.

Seldon, A. (2015) *Beyond Happiness.* London. Hodder and Stoughton.

Chapter 3

Mental Wellbeing

Mental wellbeing is about how you use and engage your brain – being involved in activities that stimulate your thinking your curiosity, your creativity. Often this is about the ways that you do this outside of your job. The charity Mind[1] suggests that continued learning though life engages our minds and this enhances our self-esteem. Recent research has shown the benefits of engaging your brain and how this can help against dementia.

Reading

Reading is an essential way in which I help my wellbeing. I love to read; my reading tastes are broad, I am usually willing to read anything. For me reading is a way to switch off from the thoughts and tasks that are usually filling it; reading allows my brain to think of something else. Research shows that almost 4 million adults in the UK never read for pleasure (Flood 2013). There is research to show that reading can increase our emotional intelligence by helping

---

1   https://www.mind.org.uk/workplace/mental-health-at-work/taking-care-of-yourself/five-ways-to-wellbeing.

us understand a broad range of viewpoints (Bury 2013). Reading can help to keep the brain active: through reading we often create mental images, these stimulate the neural pathways. The research has also found that reading for 30 minutes a week can increase our health and wellbeing; some studies suggest it can improve self-confidence and help with sleep.[2]

Reading for learning is also important. We learn new ideas and find out about new practices through reading. It is an obvious statement that reading for learning is essential; however, when we are busy, reading for learning can often be lost. I have always tried to read broadly around subjects I am working on and interested in. During the summer months when I worked for a children's charity, and we were often quieter in our work, I was able to take some reading days. Similarly, now as a nurture consultant, I am not in schools in the holidays, so I always use the summer holidays to read at least two or three books on the subject of attachment or brain development, trauma or something similar, which helps to inform and enhance my practice. In the nurture team I work in, we have all recently read a book by Bessel Van der Kolk (2015) about trauma and its impact on the body. We discussed the book, and reflected on how this informed our work and the children with whom we were working. It was a useful way to learn, discuss, reflect and share thoughts.

Learning

Being engaged in ongoing learning, or lifelong learning as it is often called, is recognised as an important part of

---

2   www.bbc.co.uk/guides/z86jhv4.

enhancing wellbeing. The Skills You Need website[3] suggests that lifelong learning is about having a positive attitude to learning both professionally and personally. It suggests that lifelong learning can help us to gain a better understanding of the world around us and it can help to improve the quality of our lives by boosting our self-esteem, helping us to be less risk averse and more open to change.

Professional development

As part of your professional development ongoing learning is an important way to develop. Every organisation should have ways to help its staff develop and learn – this could be through in- house training or sending staff on training days. Other ways could be through encouraging staff to engage in further reading and share the learning from this in a team meeting. I did some research with practitioners to hear the ways they develop their ongoing learning. Their examples were:

- reading books and articles
- using webinars
- using online training
- attending courses organised locally
- sharing practice in the team
- listening to podcasts.

---

3   https://www.skillsyouneed.com/learn/lifelong-learning.html.

There is now a growing range of high-quality training you can access online, often for a low price. Kathy Brodie[4] had an early years summit in 2017, which involved interviews with 16 early years professionals on the subject of personal, social and emotional development; this is a high-quality training resource. The interviews can be bought through her website; she also has other training you can access through her web pages. There are also many other early years trainers and consultants who have training and podcasts on their websites.

Learning through other practice

Throughout my professional life, I have been fortunate to see, observe and learn from other practice. For me this is a really good way of extending learning, reflecting on my practice and learning new skills and ideas. I have been very fortunate in the many roles in my career to have opportunities to visit other charity teams, nurseries, children's centres and schools. I have spent many hours shadowing other workers and observing practice. I have also been fortunate to observe practice in Reggio Emilia, Denmark, Sweden and Romania. Through visiting other schools or nurseries, you can step out of your role and see how other people do the role. There may be some ideas and practices you are not keen on, but you will also see ideas that inspire you. In my last role for a children's charity, I supported settings in how they listen to children and help them to embed this in their practice. I was able to share ideas from other schools and settings, but

---

4   www.kathybrodie.com.

I also encouraged staff to go and see for themselves. I know that sometimes this can be a challenge with staff ratios and cover, etc., but for teachers, if you have planning, preparation and assessment (PPA) time, why not consider using that once or twice a term to visit another school? As nursery workers, you could ask your supervisor if you could visit another nursery as part of your professional development. Contact the school or nursery you would like to visit and see if they would be happy to host you for a visit; someone from their setting could come over and see yours in return. In my current role as a nurture worker we spend time throughout the year shadowing our colleagues, which gives us the opportunity to learn from one another. This may be another possibility for you in your workplace: to shadow one of your colleagues.

Learning through conversations and sharing practice with one another

One important area of learning, which is free, is conversations with colleagues and other practitioners. Having open dialogue, the space to ask questions, be inquisitive, curious and reflective about our practice, helps us in our development. I have been really fortunate throughout my career to work in teams that encouraged discussion, questioning and debate about practice. In all the teams I have been a member of, we have had space in team meetings to discuss practice, to learn from each other. There are now also many online groups that enable conversation, questions and dialogue. I am a member of a few early years Facebook groups: this can be a really useful platform to ask a question, hear other people's views, learn about other's ideas. We know children are curious, open and want to learn. As practitioners we need to be the same. We need to continue to seek out ways to learn and develop.

Questions for practice and reflection

- How do you engage in ongoing learning? As a setting do you have copies of the relevant professional magazines and, if you do, do you read them and discuss what you have read?

- Do you set yourself a target to try and read a professional book, maybe three or four a year (of course, by reading this you have read one!)?

- Are you using the internet to engage in groups that link with your job, for example, teacher groups or early years workers? There are so many out there now. There are also many people who write blogs, for example, teachers, early years workers, social workers and counsellors.

- Do you access training? This may be through your local authority, training that your employer buys in or online training. It is worth setting yourself a target each year of how many training opportunities you would like to engage in. This can act as an encouragement/reminder and an intentional act.

- Do you have a slot on the team meeting agenda to discuss practice and ideas?

Learning outside of work

This can be wide and varied, from learning a new language, learning to play an instrument or learning new creative skills. For me, it is about engaging in opportunities that are different to my work role or that allow me to try something and learn a new skill. This spring I have been learning more about what I can make from foraging. After a study trip to Denmark around 7 years ago, I became fascinated with foraging and what we can eat and make from the weeds that are in my garden and around the lanes where I live. I have found some foraging people whose blogs I now follow. I have had great delight in trying out some of the ideas, not all successful! However, the process of finding nettles, plantain, etc. and then making something with it engages my brain; I am learning new skills, and it feels very creative and quite playful. I have been thrilled with some of the things I have made: nettle and wild garlic salad is delicious, wild garlic bread is amazing, nettle cordial was less of a success, and dandelion salve for tired muscles is a brilliant wellbeing discovery. For me, the important aspect of this is the enjoyment I get from it, the pleasure derived from making something from weeds is very simple and is helping my mental wellbeing.

Life outside work/volunteering

Often when we are busy it is hard to think about volunteering, or it can be challenging to find the time and space to engage in volunteering. The Help Guide website[5] for promoting mental health suggests that volunteering can help to reduce stress, engage you mentally and help to give you a sense of purpose. This links with the happiness research I talked about in Chapter 2. Volunteering can link you with other people with similar interests; it can also help you to learn new skills that may go on to be useful in future careers.

Over the years I have been involved in different voluntary roles. I have been a trustee for a young people's charity. I have been a governor and chair of governors. Recently I have been advising and supporting a small charity working with young adults with learning disabilities around participation practice. Without a doubt some of these roles have taken a lot of headspace and time, but they have also all been hugely rewarding. I learnt so much from each of the roles and there were lots of moments where I could see I was making a real difference, and that was hugely satisfying. It is worth thinking about whether you could volunteer. I have one friend who is a Brown Owl, which she loves; I have other friends who are involved in community gardening projects, volunteering

---

5   https://www.helpguide.org/articles/healthy-living/volunteering-and-its-surprising-benefits.htm.

at National Trust properties, run local youth or children groups – there are many, many ways to volunteer. The Do-it Trust website[6] shows you a range of volunteer opportunities in your local area.

Creativity

In my last book around children's wellbeing (Mainstone-Cotton 2017) I have a chapter on how important creativity is for children's wellbeing. I explore how as practitioners we need to feel comfortable about creativity ourselves to be able to encourage children in being creative. For many years I did not see myself as a creative person – I can't draw or paint, and I am not musical. However, I am married to a very talented artist and, over the years, I have learnt from him that creativity is more than drawing, painting, etc. Creativity is also about how we view the world; we make creative choices all the time, for example, how we decorate our houses, how we dress, the colours we put together, etc. Around 10 years ago I learnt to felt with wool fibres; this is a very creative process. Learning to felt was liberating, the felted pieces I make are very abstract, it is mostly about experimenting and playing with colours and fibres. I have used felting since in my work, but it is mostly something I choose to do that is stimulating, engaging and separate to work.

Many people find creativity is a good way to stimulate their mind, but also find it a release from work and stress. Research shows that engagement in the arts can enhance wellbeing and help to promote resilience. There are now

---

6   https://do-it.org/opportunities/search.

many programmes that promote health and wellbeing, linking hospitals, GP surgeries and community settings with art programmes. The National Alliance for Arts, Health and Wellbeing[7] supports and leads in this area in the UK. Many people say that being involved in the arts helps them to feel good; often people comment that being involved in creative things is good for their soul. Research in the area of the arts and wellbeing shows how participating in the arts can have an impact on prevention of poor mental health and can help with the prevention and treatment of illness (Devlin 2010). In the research I did before I started writing this book, many of the people I questioned talked about being involved in creative opportunities as a way of helping their wellbeing. Examples that people gave were:

- being in a choir
- drawing
- painting
- taking photos
- knitting
- crocheting
- playing an instrument
- dancing
- writing.

---

7   www.artshealthandwellbeing.org.uk/what-is-arts-in-health/national-alliance-arts-health-and-wellbeing.

Questions for practice and reflection

- How often do you engage in creative opportunities?
- Have a think about the creative things you do, or maybe have done in the past. Is now the time to start engaging in these again?

Cultural engagement

In my role as a trainer, I often encourage settings to think about how they help children to engage in cultural activities. I live in a village just outside Bath. This is a beautiful city, and we are privileged to have many cultural opportunities and, as residents of Bath, we can access many of these for free. However, I am aware that many children I have worked with in the city have never visited the Roman Baths, the Victoria Art Gallery, the Costume Museum, all of which are on our doorstep and free. I encourage staff to think about how they help children to learn about and engage in cultural opportunities. As professionals, we need to open this up to children as many parents are not doing this. However, as I mention in the section on creativity, I believe we need to be confident as adults and actively engage in cultural opportunities ourselves – we are then in a position to inspire and share this delight with children. There are so many ways to engage in cultural opportunities. This could be through visiting art galleries, exhibitions and museums, watching films, going to the theatre, attending concerts and poetry readings or visiting gardens and houses – these are all brilliant ways to engage and extend our thinking. Research in Norway[8] has found that participating in a wide range of cultural activities can have a positive effect on mental wellbeing; it can also help with anxiety and depression. A research project in the UK found that people reported having lower levels of anxiety and increased wellbeing after viewing art (Fujiwara and MacKerron 2015). They rank the engagement of cultural activities in relation to the effect on them making people feel happy. Their findings were:

1. theatre, dance and concerts

2. singing and performances

3. exhibitions, museums and libraries

4. hobbies, arts and crafts

5. listening to music

6. reading.

In the UK we have excellent museums and art galleries, many of which are free.

Questions for practice and reflection

- When did you last engage in a cultural experience?
- Are you aware of the local galleries, museums in your area?
- Could you consider looking at what is on in your local area and diarying in a time to visit?

---

8   www.nhs.uk/news/2011/05May/Pages/cultural-activities-wellbeing. aspx.

New experiences

Some people thrive on trying new things, going to new places, having new experiences. I am less of that sort of person: I am quite cautious and can be anxious at trying out new opportunities. However, I am aware that engaging in new experiences can be good for our wellbeing, so I intentionally try to do this, sometimes! Being involved in new experiences can engage our minds, it can stop us from becoming bored and stuck. It can help open up new possibilities and opportunities, which we may discover we love. Often trying something new enables us to grow and develop.

Sometimes what stops us trying something new is fear; fear can be so powerful and holds us back. Brené Brown (2013, 2015) explores how we need to dare greatly and be brave and strong by trying out new experiences and putting ourselves in positions that sometimes make us feel vulnerable and scared. She suggests we need to learn to engage with our feelings of vulnerability and fear, and through this we can become stronger. From my experience, choosing to write was a scary new experience. When I first became self-employed I decided to start writing a blog.[9] This was partly a way to process and reflect my role as a nurture worker. The act of writing and putting it into a public arena felt incredibly frightening. I felt unconfident about my writing ability; I was aware that I have some dyslexic traits and I knew that I had been told in the past that my writing style was too colloquial. The message in my head was that no one wanted to read what I had to write; I felt extremely vulnerable. However, I decided that it didn't matter if people read the blog, I hoped the process of writing

---

9   https://soniamain.wordpress.com.

would be a useful reflective process for me and improve my writing skills. A year later my blog was seen by an editor in a publishing company, and they asked me to write my first book. I still have moments of fear: when the first book came out, I was worried no one would buy it. Now, a year on, I am finishing my second book, I have learnt to love the process of writing, I still blog, mostly weekly, and I now write articles for various magazines and online organisations. By putting myself in a vulnerable position, by being brave and trying something new, I discovered a new love, a new experience that I enjoy.

Question for practice and reflection

- Is there a new experience that you have been thinking of trying but have been fearful to give a go? Maybe now is the time to step out and try it.

References

Brown, B. (2013) *Daring Greatly: How the Courage to Be Vulnerable Transforms the Way We Live, Love, Parent and Lead.* London: Penguin.

Brown, B. (2015) *Rising Strong.* London: Penguin.

Bury, L. (2013) 'Reading literary fiction improves empathy, study finds.' Accessed on 2/6/17 at https://www.theguardian.com/books/booksblog/2013/oct/08/literary-fiction-improves-empathy-study.

Devlin, P. (2010) 'Restoring the balance: The effect of arts participation on wellbeing and health.' Accessed on 4/6/17 at: www.artsforhealth.org/resources/VAE_Restoring_the_Balance.pdf.

Flood, A. (2013) 'Four million adults in UK never read books for pleasure.' Accessed on 2/6/17 at https://www.theguardian.com/books/2013/feb/14/4-million-uk-adults-never-read-books.

Fujiwara, D. and MacKerron, G. (2015) 'Arts Council England: Cultural activities, art forms and wellbeing.' Accessed on 4/6/17 at www.artscouncil.org.uk/sites/default/files/download-file/Cultural_activities_artforms_and_wellbeing.pdf.

Mainstone-Cotton, S. (2017) *Promoting Young Children's Emotional Health and Wellbeing: A Practical Guide for Professionals and Parents.* London: Jessica Kingsley Publishers.

Van der Kolk, B. (2015) *The Body Keeps the Score: Mind, Brain, Body and the Transformation or Trauma.* London: Penguin.

Chapter 4

Spiritual Wellbeing

Spiritual wellbeing is an area that is often overlooked, but I think it is an important aspect of our lives. Spiritual wellbeing is about feeling connected, feeling part of something bigger than us. Brené Brown (2017) suggests spirituality is about recognising we are connected to one another by a power greater than ourselves; she suggests the essential part of that connection is in the feeling of love and belonging. In her research on wholehearted living, those people with the best wellbeing were engaged in spiritual practices.

For some, spiritual wellbeing is about engaging in religious practices: this may be through prayer, attending places of worship or reading holy books. For others, spiritual wellbeing is about contemplative practice outside of a religious practice. There is growing evidence that spiritual practices are linked with an increase in better health and wellbeing. Examples of some contemplative practices are:

- meditation (mindfulness meditation is mentioned in more detail later in this chapter)

- prayer

- yoga

- journaling.

I am going to explore some different examples of spiritual wellbeing that can be used whether you have a faith or not.

Finding stillness and silence

I think an important part of nurturing our spiritual wellbeing is through finding stillness and silence – having times when we can be still and encounter silence. This can be very rare in our busy, noisy lives.

Several years ago I read lots about silence and finding silence. One of the books that really had an impact on me was by Sarah Maitland (2009) – *A Book of Silence*. In my previous book (Mainstone-Cotton 2017) I wrote about helping children to encounter times of stillness and silence. This is really important for children: their lives are so often full of noise, activity – if we can help them from a young age to enjoy moments of stillness and silence I believe we are giving them a great gift. However, to do this as adults we also need to be able to encounter silence and stillness ourselves. Silence and stillness can be difficult, it can lead to people feeling uncomfortable and awkward; many people seek out ways to fill the silent spaces.

I have learnt to love silence. I enjoy the quietness of the house first thing in the morning when no one is up; I love my daily swim, for me, this is a time of silence – the time in the pool is a precious time of quiet. Each Sunday morning I walk around the community meadow at the back of our house – again this is my time for quietness and silence. Of course, there is never really complete silence around, there are sounds in the pool of the gentle splashing, and walking around the meadow I can hear birds singing. However, it is silence from the noise we encounter so much in our lives. I feel that the times of quietness and silence enable me to think, to reflect, to slow down. Our lives are so often full of noise, from traffic sounds around us, music, radio, TV, etc. We are often surrounded by lots of noise all day and when we work with children this can be really intensified in our workplaces. Research shows that lots of noise can have a negative impact on our health; it can lead to high blood pressure and cause people to feel increasingly stressed (Gregoire 2017).

I have a friend who runs and teaches on a degree course; he takes a week out each year to go on a retreat,[1] sometimes this is part of an organised event, for example, staying in a monastery on a week's silent retreat, other times it is taking himself away for a week. He recently went for a week to the Isle of Mull, where he camped, went offline and spent the week in the solitude of the Scottish island. He describes this as giving him headspace. I know it is not possible for everyone to find a week to go away and be in silence, but the practice of intentionally putting time aside to be in quiet, to switch off devices, can be very liberating and therapeutic.

Finding silence through being outside and encountering nature

Maitland (2009) describes how she first encountered enjoying silence through gardening, being outside, in nature. She describes gardening as working with silence, not just being silent, and makes the link between how plants grow silently and how we can work with them silently. For many,

---

1 http://jonnybaker.blogs.com.

being outside in nature can give them a new perspective, it can give them the space to think, see things differently. Ian Adams (2013) links this with the biblical teaching of how being outside and paying close attention to the natural world around us can help us to see things in a new way and give us a new perspective. I have a friend who swims every day in the sea; she lives in Cornwall and swims all year round. For her the swimming is a mindful act. Karen suffers from depression and anxiety, she has found the daily rhythm of swimming and noticing what is around her has helped her mental health. She photographs[2] her daily swims and sells beautiful prints of her photos.

Actions for change

When was the last time you encountered silence and stillness? Do you have times in your day or week when there is silence? If not, could you try this and put some time aside? Some ways you could find silence:

- For 15 minutes turn off radios/TV/music and sit. Notice what you can hear.
- Go outside for a walk in a park, the countryside or the coast (if it is near). Turn off all technology and notice what you can hear. There will be sounds, but they will be different to what you normally encounter.
- Run a hot bath, turn off all technology, shut the door and find some quiet and space.

---

2   www.snappingoutofit.co.uk.

Being grounded

There is a practice called grounding or earthing; this is about literally feeling the ground and being connected to the earth. This is about walking barefoot; it is a very mindful practice, by doing this you become aware and mindful of the earth, the ground, the space you are walking on. If you walk barefoot you immediately slow down, as you are much more aware of what you are walking on. During the summer months, I often walk around the community meadow on my Sunday morning walks, barefooted, really noticing the feel of the grass, the earth. Also, being on a beach how often are you drawn to taking your shoes off, feeling the sand, the pebbles, the coldness of the sea? This can be such a mindful experience. When we are feeling stressed we can often feel desensitised to what is around us; walking barefoot engages our senses, it can help to reconnect us to the space we are in. This is an exercise that works well with children, particularly children who are highly stressed and tense. I often find that exercises which work with the children I work with also work for the adults who care for them.

Finding a rhythm to your life

In Chapter 1, I wrote about the importance of routine and how often one sign of being overly stressed is when we lose that routine. Of similar importance to routines is finding the rhythm for our lives; for me this is more than a routine, this is about self-nurturing, this is about doing things that are not just the routines we have to do, for example, making sandwiches the night before for work/school. Rhythm in life is about doing things daily that make us feel good, that connect us, that enable us to feel good.

There are a few rhythms that I have: swimming Monday to Friday morning and walking around the meadow on a Sunday morning. If I am on holiday and I can't swim, then I will walk each morning around the area we are staying in. These are very simple but I know they are life-giving to me. Nicole Wolf[3] suggests on her blog that having a regular rhythm and practice helps to anchor you and helps you to recognise when your life is beginning to go off balance.

I asked a group of family, friends and colleagues what rhythms they had. Their list is below:

- First cup of coffee/tea in the morning in my special mug.

- Shower first thing in the morning, no matter how bad I feel, that will help me.

- A cold shower at the end of my shower, to help me feel awake and alive.

- Reading to my children last thing at night.

- Daily swimming in the sea.

- Yoga every day.

- Cooking the evening meal, I love this act.

- Mindfulness practice every day.

- Writing daily in my journal.

- Spending 10 minutes praying at the start of each day.

---

3   http://nicolewolf.com/find-your-rhythm-through-a-daily-practice.

Mindfulness

Mindfulness practice has a long history in Buddhism and Christian contemplative practice; it is also used as part of yoga, tai chi and other non-faith-based meditation practices. Mindfulness is about being in the moment, noticing, recognising, being present to what is around us and what is going on in our heads and inside our bodies, and noticing our breathing, noticing the breath as we breathe in and breathe out.

Mindfulness practice helps us to focus on the breath in the body; a mindfulness meditation is not about clearing the mind, but instead recognising what thoughts are going through our mind and coming back to noticing the breath (Willard 2010).

Noticing our breathing

Often when we feel stressed and anxious our breathing can become very quick and shallow–this is called overbreathing. Using mindful practices can help us to slow our breathing, and it can help us to concentrate on our breath. When we exhale more oxygen than we inhale, this helps to reduce the overbreathing, it slows down the heart rate and can help us to relax. The 7/11 breathing technique is a helpful tool to help us focus on the breath.

7/11 breathing

Step 1
Get comfortable and sit down if you can.

Step 2

Breathe in through your nose and count to seven. Imagine the air is reaching all the way down to your diaphragm so your stomach gently pushes out with the breath.

Step 3

Breathe out through your mouth for a count of 11.

Repeat as many times as you need to help feel calmer and more relaxed. If you find it hard to do 7/11, try 5/7. The aim is to breathe out for longer than you breathe in.

A fun alternative to 7/11 breathing is using bubbles. I use this with children a lot. Take in a deep breath and blow out slowly through the bubble wand. It works in the same way as 7/11 but is more fun!

Shauna Shapiro[4] (2017) gave a TED Talk about mindfulness in which she refers to Harvard research showing that the mind wanders on average 47 per cent of the time. Shapiro explains how mindfulness trains the mind to be here, to be in the present moment. By practising this regularly, we can help our brain to grow and develop this. Shapiro has carried out lots of research around the benefits of mindfulness; she suggests that mindfulness is about kind attention to ourselves, not judging ourselves.

There are many useful tools and courses that teach mindfulness. There will be mindfulness courses being taught in your local area or you could buy books that teach you about mindfulness; there are also mindfulness apps and podcasts you can use. The first time I was introduced to

---

4   https://www.youtube.com/watch?v=IeblJdB2-Vo.

mindfulness I attended an 8-week course that used a book by Dr Mark Williams (2011) On the Mental Health website[5] they have a 10-minute mindful meditation podcast led by Dr Mark Williams that you can access for free. Some schools run mindfulness sessions for their staff and others pay for staff to go on mindfulness courses.

Examples of different mindfulness practices

Mindfulness practice is not just about breathing meditations, but also about noticing, being in the moment. There are many different mindfulness practices you can use: the website mindful.org[6] has a list of ideas of mindful practices. One mindful practice I use a lot is my daily swim and also walking. Mindful walking is about noticing what is around us, instead of rushing to get to the end destination, noticing and enjoying the journey we are on. My Sunday morning walk around the community meadow is often a mindful walk. This walk is about noticing the changes in the meadow; I love noticing the changes throughout the year from the bare trees to the new leaves, the wild flowers growing back each year, the return of the moths and butterflies in the summer months and then conkers in the autumn. Adam Ford (2011) describes how he once realised on a walk that one reason to be here is to notice and delight in what we see around us; he suggests we do that by mindfully walking.

---

5 https://www.mentalhealth.org.uk/podcasts-and-videos/mindfulness-10-minute-practice-exercise.

6 www.mindful.org/mindfulness-practices-from-mindful-women.

Using a labyrinth

Labyrinths are a circular path; they are an ancient practice of 'circling to the centre', with links back to 4000 years. Labyrinths are a one-path design in a circle shape, with one entrance and exit. Labyrinths are often used as a meditation tool or a prayer tool; they are sometimes described as walking prayer or a walking meditation.[7] You can find labyrinths in some churches, cathedrals, retreat centres, schools and universities, and some public spaces. A list of some labyrinths in the UK can be found on the Pilgrim Paths website.[8] Some people also use finger labyrinths as a meditation tool; again these are described on the Pilgrim Paths website. A photo of one my husband[9] carved is below.

---

7   https://sacredwalk.com/guidelines.

8   https://www.pilgrimpaths.co.uk/page21.html.

9   http://iaincotton.co.uk.

Yoga

Yoga is an ancient philosophy that has existed for thousands of years. Yoga does not require you to have a belief or faith: for some yoga is a spiritual practice,[10] for others it is a form of exercise with meditation. Yoga connects the mind, the body and the breath, and helps to focus on what is happening inside the body and mind; it has an emphasis on being mindful in the moment and noticing (Lee 2014). There is a growing amount of research to link mental health benefits with yoga; it is thought to help reduce stress and depression and bring about a calmness (Khoshaba 2013). Yoga is being taught in many secondary schools; recognising the benefits it has for young people's mental health, an organisation called Teen Yoga[11] has been set up to train adults to teach yoga to young people and, through this, increase the mental health of our youth. In some schools teachers attend these lessons alongside the young people. In other schools weekly yoga lessons are also run for the staff, recognising the benefits it has for staff wellbeing. There will be many yoga classes in your area that you can attend.

Journaling

Some people use journaling as a tool for improving their wellbeing. This can be used as a reflective tool, to help you write down feelings, thoughts, concerns. Helen Cepero (2008) suggests that journaling is a way to bring your life into 'sharper focus'. Some use this as a spiritual practice

---

10   www.teenyoga.co.uk/2017/02/yoga-vs-christianity-among-parents.

11   www.teenyoga.co.uk.

and find it helps them to feel closer to God; some use it as a way to write a letter to God, using it as a prayer. For others it is not a spiritual practice, but it helps their wellbeing and enables them to empty what is in their mind and let go of the things that are clogging up their thinking. Capero suggests that journaling is about allowing yourself the freedom to write what is on your mind and in your heart and not to worry about the style of writing, how it looks, whether it is grammatically correct, etc. I have used journaling on and off over the past 20 years. Sometimes I have used it as Lent practice and reflection, other times I have used it when life has felt very hard. I used it throughout the period I was made redundant and started as a self-employed person. I found it hugely beneficial during this time.

Some suggestions for journaling:

- Buy a notebook. I like to have a notebook that looks beautiful, expressing that my writing is something of worth.

- Make sure you have a pen or pencil with your journal that you can use.

- Set aside a time in the day when you will journal; this may be first thing in the morning or last thing at night, or a different regular time.

- Have your journal in a place where you are going to remember to fill it in. I have mine by the side of my bed.

Community

At the beginning of this chapter, I mention that spiritual wellbeing is about feeling part of something bigger. Community is a really important part of this: knowing that you are part of a group. There are many examples of these: faith groups, cycling, running, swimming groups, reading groups, choirs, drama, etc. By being part of a group you are actively engaging with others; people notice when you are not there. Being part of a community gives you a sense of something bigger than you. One of the signs of stress and depression is when we start to pull away from people when we find being with others very hard. At the end of the book is a list of organisations who can provide advice around mental health.

References

Adams, I. (2013) *Running Over Rocks: Spiritual Practices to Transform Tough Times.* London: Canterbury Press.

Brown, B. (2017) 'Rising strong as a spiritual practice.' Audio. Accessed on 18/6/17 at www.soundstrue.com/store/rising-strong-as-a-spiritual-practice-2.html.

Cepero, H. (2008) *Journaling as a Spiritual Practice.* Madison, WI: InterVarsity Press.

Ford, A. (2011) *The Art of Mindful Walking Meditations on the Path.* London: Leaping Hare Press.

Gregoire, C. (2017) 'Why silence is so good for your brain.' Accessed on 12/4/17 at www.huffingtonpost.com/entry/silence-brain-benefits_us_56d83967e4b0000de4037004.

Khoshaba, D. (2013) 'Take a stand for yoga today: Yoga's positive benefits for mental health and well being today.' Accessed on 20/4/17 at https://www.psychologytoday.com/blog/get-hardy/201305/take-stand-yoga-today.

Lee, C. (2014) 'Yoga 101: A beginner's guide to practice, meditation and the sutras.' Accessed on 20/4/17 at www.yogajournal.com/meditation/yoga-questions-answered.

Mainstone-Cotton, S. (2017) *Promoting Young Children's Emotional Health and Wellbeing: A Practical Guide for Professionals and Parents.* London: Jessica Kingsley Publishers.

Maitland, S (2009) *A Book of Silence.* London: Grants Books.

Willard, C. (2010) *Child's Mind: Mindfulness Practice to Help Our Children Be More Focused, Calm and Relaxed.* Berkeley, CA: Parallex Press.

Williams, M. (2011) *Mindfulness: A Practical Guide to Finding Peace in a Frantic World.* London: Piatkus.

Chapter 5

How We Support Colleagues

When I started writing this chapter and the research about the subject, I was struck by how much is written on 'how to deal with difficult colleagues' or 'how to challenge the colleague who is annoying you'. However, it is quite hard to find information about how to support colleagues. I believe this is a really important subject and one that we can all reflect on. Brother Roger from Taize[1] suggested that if we have a peaceful heart, this makes life beautiful for all around us, recognising we can all have an impact on other people's wellbeing. Roffey (2016) suggests that teachers and education staff's wellbeing is affected by three things: what we do for ourselves to look after our wellbeing, the sociopolitical climate (which we may have no influence over) and social connections – the relationship we have with those around us. Our relationships with the people we work with can have an enormous impact on our wellbeing.

---

1   www.spiritualityandpractice.com/quotes/quotations/view/31259/spiritual-quotation.

Picking up on the stress around us

In Chapter 2, I wrote about the impact other people's stress can have on us, how we sometimes take on the stress of other people and how we need to be mindful of that. In the workplace, the relationship with our colleagues can be critical to our mental health. We have all heard of workplaces where there is a culture of bullying and mistrust. If this occurs in places of work where we work with children and young people, it will often go on to impact the children. I can think of several schools where there is an issue of bullying with the children, and there is also a problem of bullying in the staff team.

Supporting one another

As individuals in a team, we all have a responsibility for how we support our colleagues. When we are feeling stressed and overwhelmed ourselves, thinking about other people can sometimes feel too much. However, there is evidence to show that if we consider others and do something for another individual, this is beneficial to our mental health. The charity Mental Health Foundation[2] has produced a booklet offering ideas and guidance around this. They suggest that thinking about others and helping other people can benefit our mental health by triggering positive physiological changes in our brains that are associated with happiness, and this is often followed by a period of feeling calm. Of course doing too much for other people and not thinking about your

---

2   https://www.mentalhealth.org.uk/publications/doing-good-does-you-good.

mental and physical health is not good either; we need to get the right balance.

Supporting colleagues doesn't need to be complicated or involve significant gestures. Often the small things make a real difference, examples of these could be making a cup of tea for someone when you can see they are tired or stressed, taking on another person's playground duty if they are having a difficult week or bringing flowers to the office.

I asked friends and colleagues for examples of how they or others supported and offered support in their workplace. Some of their examples were:

- handing out sachets of hot chocolate to colleagues who look particularly harassed

- sharing food once a week

- sending cake into school once a week

- having a sense of humour and fun

- giving each other a 5-minute break when we can see it is getting hard

- taking the lunch shift for a colleague

- taking on the closing-up shift for a colleague

- thanking staff for their time.

Roffey (2016) gives examples of how one school sends out a weekly newsletter: on the front page is a thank you to different members of staff in the school community; they get noticed and thanked for something they have done that week. This includes all members of the school community from teachers, senior leaders, lunch time staff, cleaners, caretakers. I know from my experience it feels good when someone I work with notices what I do and thanks me, or tells me how much they appreciated the work. It makes me feel good.

Another way of supporting one another can be through peer supervision or peer reflection groups. This is a good opportunity to support one another in a team; it gives you time to reflect and think about your practice. I know some schools that use this. In the nurture team I work with we use a solution-focused reflecting team model,[3] which is a useful tool, allowing a person in the team to bring forward a challenge or an issue arising from their work, and giving them the space to talk, think, reflect and have ideas and input from colleagues. It is a very simple and effective way to support one another.

Checking that colleagues are okay

When we work with children and young people, sometimes we can be dealing with highly emotive, stressful situations. It is vital that we have people we can check in with, who are ensuring that we are okay. In one school I worked with two reception class teachers each had a very traumatised child they were working with. The children often expressed themselves by screaming, shouting, throwing, kicking, biting, etc. This was very tough and stressful to manage. Both these teachers were brilliant at looking out for each other and checking in with one another each day, checking the other

---

3   http://sfwork.com/solworld/downloads/SFRTeamPrimer02.pdf.

person was alright and offering a space to be listened to. I think this made a massive difference to their wellbeing.

In some roles where you are not school or nursery-based, but travel to and from work with children and young people, it is not always so easy to notice when your colleagues are struggling. In some roles, for example, social workers or support workers, you may not go back to the office at the end of the day, or you may not have an office base. In these situations it is vital that your team has a good system for offering support; this may be a manager who is on call out of hours each day, or you have a system where you check in with other colleagues.

When a colleague notices and recognises that you have been working in a challenging situation, it can make such a difference to your wellbeing. By managers or members of the team checking that you are okay, acknowledging the stress of the situation, these simple gestures can help you to feel looked after, supported and listened to.

Regular checking in with someone else

I am self-employed and, although I work within a team, I mostly work on my own and meet with the team once a month and with my supervisor for regular supervision. I am aware that when you mostly work on your own it is easy not to be very mindful about the hours you are working, the stress you are experiencing, and it can be hard to stop and take a rest. I have a good friend who is also self-employed and a lone worker; he works in schools as a children's counsellor. We message each other every Thursday; this is often our day when we are not in a school. We check in with how the other person is, telling them a little about our week and asking the other person what are they going to do that day that will bring them some rest or what are they going to do that will make them happy. This is our way of holding each other accountable for looking after ourselves, it is our way of looking out for one another, and it works for us.

Questions for practice and reflection

- Is there anyone in your workplace who checks you're okay? If not, could you set this up with a colleague, so you are supporting one another?
- Do you ask colleagues how they are?

Developing a culture of compassion

We can probably all think of work environments where it can feel toxic, where there is a bullying culture, and staff feel constantly judged. This, in turn, can lead to a culture of bickering and backstabbing. In contrast to this, there are work environments where there is a culture of compassion, understanding and believing that everyone is working to the best of their abilities. Karen Armstrong (2011) refers to how she learned from Rabbi Albert Friedlander the importance of loving yourself and how this is essential if you are to go on to love others and be compassionate to others, that if you don't love yourself, you are unable to love others.

Letting go

We know that when we are feeling stressed and overwhelmed by work and life, we can be more easily hurt by other people's words and actions. It can become very easy to hang on to the pain caused and feel resentful. Also, when we are in a challenging, stressful work environment, it is easy to feel resentful about the demands of work, the type of work, and not feeling valued enough. Holding on to resentment can cause us difficulties in our bodies and mind; it can lead to a rise in blood pressure and the stress hormones. The online *Mindfulness* magazine has 11 suggestions on how to let go and forgive (Goldstein and Goldstein 2017), some of their suggestions include:

1. Understand about forgiveness, that it is something we can choose to do to release ourselves from the pain of the stress it can bring.

2. Give yourself permission to acknowledge the pain you are experiencing.

3. Name the experience and how you feel (this links with the self-compassion and emotion language in Chapter 2 on emotional wellbeing).

4. Let out the pent up feelings; this might be through writing or talking to others.

Language that we use in the workplace

This is about the culture of words in your workplaces. Education, health and social care settings are notorious for using acronyms within the workplace. I have worked with teams from schools, nurseries, children's centres, church teams, health teams and social services teams, and they all have their own language, acronyms and meanings behind words. This can feel incredibly intimidating to visitors or new team members.

Actions for change

It is worth taking a moment to think about the language in your team. How inclusive is it? Is it clear to visitors or new members of the team?

Celebrating each other and your work

How often do you celebrate each other in your team? This may be buying a card for a member of staff on their birthday or celebrating each other's achievements. When I was working with my old team, and I achieved my MA, the team celebrated by buying me cake and flowers. This was a lovely gesture and helped me to feel valued.

The friend who I check in with weekly asked me at the end of the spring term what I was doing to celebrate the work I had done that term. I have found this is a helpful question: at the end of the term we can be so exhausted and desperate for a holiday, our head can be full of the things that have been hard, and we can so often forget to recognise and celebrate what has been good. Some schools and nurseries go out for a drink at the end of a term; some go for a meal. If you work in a nursery that is open all year, the year doesn't fall into terms for you; other than the national holidays or bank holiday weekends, there isn't a natural break. I know of some nurseries that take the time to celebrate their work by going out for a meal together two or three times a year.

The question of how to celebrate the work we achieved is a really important one.

Actions for change

How do you celebrate achievements in your workplace? Here are some ideas:

- Go out for a drink at the end of term.
- Manager buys cake for staff team at the end of term/year.
- Team day – a day to come together, do an activity together, eat together (in my old team we would go for a walk and have a picnic).
- Celebrate each other's birthdays/achievements, for example exams passed, weddings, etc.

Discovering more about your team

Spending time together as a team, away from team meetings or direct work, can be very beneficial to helping develop a team culture. I mentioned how some teams go out for a drink or lunch together. However, there are also other ways that do not involve spending money, as this can be prohibitive for some people. Some examples are:

- Have a team bring and share lunch once a month or once a term.

- Organise a book club for the team over lunch time.

- Go for a walk together after work.

Some find it useful to discover the personality types in their team. By understanding the personality types of the team, it can help you to gain a better understanding of the strengths and weakness of the group and can lead to a compassionate understanding of one another. There is a free online test based on Myers–Briggs that I have used called 16 personalities.[4] There is a lot of value in spending time as a team gaining a greater understanding of one another.

Practising acts of kindness with colleagues

There is a growing recognition of the importance of sharing acts of kindness. There is a website – random acts of kindness[5] – set up for ideas and inspirations around this. This has examples of really simple ideas such as:

- Find ways to compliment people today.

- Send an email to a colleague thanking them for something they have done.

- Tell someone's manager what a great job they have done.

- Leave flowers in the staff room.

For centuries, religious leaders, writers and philosophers have suggested that to be happy we need to be kind and compassionate to others. More recently Lyubomirsky (2007)

---

4   https://www.16personalities.com.

5   https://www.randomactsofkindness.org.

developed some research around this. She proposes that by carrying out acts of kindness you can begin to view yourself as a compassionate and considerate person; this can raise your optimism and confidence and can improve the way you see yourself. Also, being kind to others can trigger a chain reaction – it can encourage others to be kind also. We know this can be so with children and it is just the same with adults. It can just take one person in a team to start intentionally being kind to others, practising acts of kindness, and this can start to change a culture and workplace environment.

Some other ideas of acts of kindness:

- buying or making a smoothie for someone who is run down

- buying cake

- taking people out for coffee

- buying chocolate

- making up a nurture bag for people (see below for ideas)

- passing on a book

- sending emails to thank staff, tell them what a good job they are doing

- sending postcards to people, telling them how much you appreciate them

- leaving Post-it® notes with a word of thanks on their desk

- sharing food at lunch time

- buying flowers for the office/nursery/staff room

- spending time to listen

- offer to do a job for someone/take
  on some of their workload

- if people want it – physical contact, for
  example, a hug or stroking their arm

- smiling at people

- helping people to arrive well – notice them,
  ask how they are, take time to listen.

Questions for practice and reflection

- How could you practise acts of kindness to others in your team?
- Could you try some of these today or this week?

Nurture bags or buddy box

One of the things I have developed over the past few years is a nurture bag. This is something simple, a gift that you make up for someone who you know needs a bit of nurturing. This would be a great thing to make for a colleague. Your bag will be made up uniquely for the person you have in mind. I made one for my daughter when she went to university; hers had warm socks, chocolate, a small bottle of my homemade raspberry vodka, a comforting book, a stress oil blend and hand lotion. I also made one recently for a close friend who was dying; hers had hand lotion, a book of poems, warm socks, chocolate and a calming oil blend. The aim of these bags is to show the person that you know them, you care for them and recognise they need some nurturing at the moment. There is a website set up that can send out a buddy box,[6] which is a similar idea. It sends out a package monthly, quarterly or as a one-off. There is also a teacher who set up a scheme whereby teachers or educators can sign up and are linked to a buddy and send them a buddy box once a term. This is called the #Teacher5adayBuddyBox.[7]

References

Armstrong, K. (2011) *Twelve Steps to a Compassionate Life*. London: The Bodley Head.

Goldstein, S. and Goldstein, E. (2017) *Let it Go: 11 Ways to Forgive*. Accessed on 23/3/17 at www.mindful.org/let-go-11-ways-forgive.

Lyubomirsky, S. (2007) *The How of Happiness: A Practical Guide to Getting the Life You Want*. London: Piatkus.

Roffey, S. (2016) *Teacher Wellbeing: Five Ways to Help Each Other*. Accessed on 30/3/17 at http://growinggreatschools.com.au/teacher-wellbeing-five-ways-to-help-each-other.

---

6   https://www.blurtitout.org/buddybox.

7   https://teacher5adaybuddybox.wordpress.com.

Chapter 6

Managers

Managers have an important role in thinking about and looking after the emotional wellbeing of their staff. We all know of many stories where managers create a bullying and toxic environment. However, this chapter is going to focus on positive ways a manager can support their staff. Managers are in a brilliant position to make a difference. If your staff have good wellbeing they are in a great position to enhance the wellbeing of the children they are working with; they are also able to flourish and meet their full potential, which is good for both them and the workplace. We know that poor wellbeing of staff can lead to staff having increased sick leave, being dissatisfied with the job, working less well and often staff leaving.

In the world of business, the talk is about building staff's emotional resilience; this is about staff being able to succeed personally and professionally while working in a highly pressured, continually changing and fast moving work environment. I think that describes the role of working with children. There is a Tool Kit on the Mental Health website[1]

---

1   https://www.mentalhealth.org.uk/publications/emotional-resilience-toolkit.

with ideas and suggestions from business that gives ideas to promote staff's emotional resilience. The ideas are from business but many of them are just as relevant to education settings and charities.

Starts with you

To be able to help your staff to have good wellbeing you need to have good wellbeing yourself. This book is full of practical ideas on how we can look after ourselves individually; hopefully, you have read these and are using some these on yourself. In my experience, so often the people who are leading and managing can have some of the lowest wellbeing.

Before you start reading the rest of the chapter, take a moment to think about your own wellbeing. Just as when we are on an aeroplane we are told we need to put the oxygen mask on ourselves before we support others around us, I would suggest you do the same now. Take a moment to think about your wellbeing, maybe try out the NHS wellbeing survey[2] or think about the following questions.

---

2   www.nhs.uk/tools/documents/self_assessments_js/assessment. html?XMLpath=/tools/documents/self_assessments_js/ packages/&ASid=43&syndicate=undefined.

Questions for practice and reflection

- How are you feeling today, calm or stressed? Optimistic or pessimistic?
- How are you sleeping? Do you get enough sleep? The recommendation is that the average person needs 8 hours of sleep a night (Willis 2014).
- Are you eating well? Do you eat breakfast and take a lunch break?
- Do you exercise? If you do, is it enough?
- At the end of the day and week are you stopping and relaxing, switching off, taking time to relax?
- What do you do that helps you to relax? Do you do this enough?

Your staff team

How is the wellbeing of your staff? Do you know? Their wellbeing will be affected by many different aspects of life – their personal lives, family, home lives – but their work lives will have a big impact. You cannot influence or change their home and personal lives, but you can affect their work lives. Dabell (2016) suggests the wellbeing of staff should be top of the agenda of head teachers (I would extend this to managers of any organisation, particularly those who work with children and young people).

A good place to start thinking about the wellbeing of staff and how you can enhance this is to do a survey or audit. You can find these online; there are organisations where you can buy in their services or you could write your own.

The charity Education Support Partnership[3] recommends some questions you could use.

They are (where appropriate use a scale of 1–5):

- How stressed do you feel?

- Do you feel you have enough support in the workplace?

- Are you able to manage your workload?

- Do you have someone you can go to if something is wrong?

- Would counselling be helpful to you?

- What do you like about your job?

- What do you dislike about your job?

The charity offers a service to work with you and your staff team on a positive workplace survey.

It is too easy to presume we know the needs of the staff team, but without asking them and consulting them, we don't know. A wellbeing audit will give you a sense of the needs of your team; it can help to provide information on training and development that is needed. Of course, if you are going to take the time to do a wellbeing audit, you need to act on the findings, you need to respond to staff quickly, tell them what you are going to do, and if possible put in some immediate changes.

Some immediate changes you could introduce are:

---

3   https://www.educationsupportpartnership.org.uk/staff-engagement-wellbeing.

- Look at how many meetings you have – are they all needed? Could they be shorter?

- Add staff wellbeing to your team agendas, talk about it openly, without judgement. Get staff to take it in turns to lead a wellbeing activity. This ensures it is relevant on the agenda and not tokenistic.

- Provide free coffee, teas and milk and sometimes cake!

- Engage someone in the team to lead on wellbeing (this doesn't negate your responsibility but recognises the importance of wellbeing).

- Thank staff for the work they do.

- Smile at staff. Notice them at the beginning of the day. We make an effort to welcome the children we work with at the beginning of the day; in the same way, notice and welcome your staff at the beginning of the day.

- Notice when staff have done something well and praise them.

- Set up a buddy or mentor system in the workplace.

- Provide a comfortable and welcoming staff room – somewhere where staff can eat away from their desk/classroom.

- Communicate well – you need to get the level right, not too many emails or texts but make sure everyone knows what is happening. One way is to do a team briefing or email on a Monday morning.

- Ask staff for their ideas/thoughts.

- Provide information about counselling services or provide a mental health support package.

- When you know staff have had a very challenging day, check in with them, ask how they are.

- When staff are off ill, when they return ask them how they are.

I spoke with friends and colleagues, who are a mixture of managers, teachers, nursery workers, head teachers, children's centre workers and social workers. I asked for their three main ways to promote wellbeing with staff. Their answers were:

- Give out cards at the end of each term, thanking staff for their work.

- Managers acting in the way they want their staff to act, for example, asking for help when overwhelmed, collaboratively working.

- Provide regular supervision, which can facilitate appropriate targets and support, and authentic feedback on performance.

- Communicating well, keeping everyone in the loop.

- Providing a yoga class or mindfulness class for staff once a week.

- Ask after people – show an interest in their lives.

- Acknowledge people when they arrive at work each day, giving them a chance to arrive well and leave behind the stresses of the morning routine.

- Remember birthdays and significant events.

- Provide a comfortable and inviting staff room or communal room.

- Provide interesting continued professional development (CPD).

- Encourage staff to take a proper break each day, away from their desk/classroom.

- Provide drinks for staff.

- Making sure the manager/head teacher is available to speak to, have an open door policy.

- Allow staff to go to their own children's events, for example, nativity plays.

How well do you know your team and the roles they are doing?

As a manager how well do you know your team? And what understanding do you have about the role they are doing? Finding out about your team members and being genuinely interested in who they are as individuals can help staff to feel valued. When staff feel valued this helps their wellbeing. Also, by having a true understanding of the staff roles and the rigours of the job, you are in a better position to offer support and insight to staff. Some of the best managers I have encountered are those who are still in touch with the direct practice of working with children and families. I can think of many head teachers and nursery managers who still spend time teaching or working with a group of children; within the voluntary sector, I have worked with managers who regularly continue to work directly with both individual children and groups of children. Often the managers who have direct contact with children are in a better position to be able to understand the challenges of the role. Managers need to be genuinely curious about and interested in the work their staff are doing. Being involved in direct practice can give managers an opportunity to demonstrate that interest and curiosity. Also by participating in some direct experience managers are in a good position to develop a culture of openness and honesty about the challenges and difficulties of the role; they are able to speak from a place of experience. Observation can also be a really useful tool in helping you to understand the work your staff do. Observation can be peer or manager. Where settings have this as part of the ongoing learning of the whole team, it is a welcome part of development. In one of my old teams we used video observations of our work with the children and we watched these as a team. It was a really useful tool to help us reflect about our work.

Questions for practice and reflection

- When was the last time you spent time doing the role of your staff?
- Do you have a regular time when you are teaching/running a group/working with children? If you don't, could you put this into your schedule and diary? Maybe once a term or once a month or weekly.

Strategies to help staff manage stress

In Chapter 2, I talk about stress and the impact that can have on our bodies and our minds. I offer a few suggestions for managing stress. One big cause of stress in schools, early years settings and children's centres is linked to workloads. As managers, it is important that we are aware of the workload and the strain this can put staff under. Here are some ways you can help with this:

- Give a good amount of notice and send a reminder of when work needs to be completed, for example, dates of when reports or monitoring needs to be in.

- At times that are particularly busy in the year cut back on meetings, for example Christmas, end of term, report writing time.

- Discuss stress levels in meetings, be open about it and acknowledge what is causing the most stress currently, and together as a team think about strategies to reduce this.

- Encourage staff to leave the building at a reasonable time. I know of one school where the head closes the school at 5pm twice a week and tells staff to go home.

- Model good practice and wellbeing to your staff. Don't send emails late at night, this could give out the message that you are working late and expect them to be.

- Have in place a support system for staff who are becoming ill through stress. This may be a telephone counselling support scheme, information about talking therapies, link to a counsellor or health practitioner they can talk to.

- Can you eat together regularly? I know of one nursery where staff have breakfast together each Monday morning and tea each Friday evening. This is their way to start the week and end the week well.

Environment

Think about the working environment your team are in. Does the environment encourage wellbeing? Is there natural lighting? Is there a comfortable place staff can take time out away from their desks, time away from the children and eat lunch? Having a space that is comfortable to sit in, away from the work space is an important part of providing for staff wellbeing. It encourages staff to take a break from their work; it gives the message to the staff that you value them. I have been in nursery staff rooms that are tiny and overly cluttered. Having a cluttered staff room can leave staff feeling they are unable to rest.

You may be really limited for space, but there could still be things you can do to make the space more inviting. One friend works with teenagers in supported lodging; there is no space in their building for a staff room, but they do have a kitchen that they use with clients. They have put a table and chair beside the window, put a table cloth on the table and a vase of flowers; they have a sign to go on the door when it is busy and being used. This simple act has enabled the staff to have some time away from their desks and clients, time to eat lunch and take a short break in a nicer environment. It has encouraged the staff to take regular lunch breaks.

I understand that in some workplaces it is very hard to put in a staff room; in a pre-school that works half days from a church hall staff will not have time or space for a break. However, in these spaces, there are still ways you can nurture your staff and look after their wellbeing, one way may be through providing free tea, coffee and biscuits or fruit.

Questions for practice and reflection

- Do you have a staff room and, if so, what do your staff think of it?
- If you don't know, ask them. Have a think together about how it could be improved – this does not necessarily mean spending money.
- If you don't have a staff room, is there a space you could develop?

Support for staff

Have you developed a culture in your team that encourages honesty, where staff can ask for help and not be judged for that? Team meetings can be a place where staff can share what is going well or what is a challenge. As a manager, you can create an honest and supportive atmosphere rather than one of shame and competition. You could have staff wellbeing on the team meeting agenda; use this opportunity to check in with people, have honest conversations about workloads and stress loads. In my old team, we would often take time at the beginning of the meeting to go around and give a quick catch up about our work and how we were. We would all be honest about how we were feeling; it was a safe environment to do this. Some schools and nurseries set up a mentor system where all staff are given a colleague to mentor and support them, where they can express concerns, difficulties and ask questions without feeling ashamed or that they arc failing.

When new members of staff start work, what induction scheme do you have? A good induction scheme for new staff and supply staff helps to answer questions, inform them of polices, etc., but it should also give them the opportunity to learn about the job without being thrown in at the deep end unsupported.

Supervision

Supervision is an important way to support staff. Supervision is a fairly new introduction for early years settings; it became a requirement for all early years settings by the Department for Education in 2012. In education it is almost unknown – a few schools are now recognising the benefits and putting it in place. Within much of the voluntary sector supervision has been in place for many years. Supervision is a space where you can talk through aspects of the job, where you are accountable for your work, where you can be supported, have space to reflect and be offered guidance and at times be challenged (John 2012). Supervision is also the means to manage safeguarding and ensure staff feel supported around managing risk.

My experience of supervision in the voluntary sector, for example, children's charities, is that it is coming from a place where it is recognised that staff are often working with some complex social and psychological issues with the children and young people, and there is a need for staff to have regular support around this. This is now very similar for teachers and TAs in schools, many of whom are working daily with children who have complex behavioural, social and psychological challenges. Supporting these children is incredibly challenging, Bainbridge and Westergaard (2014) were involved in a supervision pilot in the Diocese of Kent with schools. They found that many school staff are emotionally drained and it is having a detrimental effect on the emotional wellbeing of staff. They propose that staff working with children and young people in education settings should have access to quality supervision. They suggest that supervision enables staff to:

- use reflection to develop good practice

- be supported in managing the psychological and emotional impact of their work

- recognise, acknowledge and address stress levels.

Bainbridge and Westergaard (2014) recommend that staff in education settings are able to meet with an independent supervisor two or three times a term.

I have been a supervisor, and I have been supervised for most of my working life. A good supervisor checks out at the beginning of the session how the staff are by asking the simple question, 'How are you today?' and being genuinely interested. This allows the staff member to be honest and allows the supervisor to get a feel at the beginning of the meeting for the wellbeing of the staff. In my current role as a nurture consultant, all of our team offer supervision to the staff we support, recognising the needs of the children they are supporting are very high, which has a great impact on staff. Unfortunately, for some, supervision is a place where they feel they are being criticised or having more demands put on them; that is not the role of supervision. Supervision needs to be a two-way listening and communication process, with both supervisors and the supervised having space to speak and be heard.

Questions for practice and reflection

■ Do you have supervision in your workplace? Is it a place where staff can be honest and open with their feelings and emotions?

■ If you have supervision, how do you ensure it is not just taken up with issues from work? Do you ask after your staff's wellbeing? Do you ask staff what they are doing to be kind to themselves?

■ How do you encourage staff to be honest about how they are feeling and what is happening for them at work?

Staff development

What is in place to help your staff develop? We know that CPD is really important for all staff: hearing new ideas and developing our practice enable staff to learn and enhance their work. Often CPD can be one of the first areas that is cut, particularly in these hard times of increasing budget cuts. Funding for CPD can be challenging, but there can be creative ways around this. For example, sharing training events with other settings, encouraging staff to visit other schools and nurseries to see and learn from their practice, setting up learning hubs where staff with expertise in the setting share their knowledge and learning with colleagues, as well as buying in trainers or sending staff on training.

Messages from managers

For this chapter I spoke with four managers. One was a nursery manager, two were ex head teachers and one a manager in a children's charity. I wanted to hear from them about their ideas on how to support staff wellbeing.

The early years manager, Wendy Baker,[4] has had years of experience managing nurseries and being an area manager. Wendy now supports nurseries and managers as an early years trainer consultant. I asked her for her top tips. They were:

- Believe in your staff.

- Never give up on your staff.

- Be there for your staff by being an effective listener.

- Communicate effectively.

The two head teachers I interviewed, Louise and Keith, are two people I have known for a long time and I have a huge amount of respect for their practice. Their tips were:

- Be consistent in how you lead and manage.

- Create a culture in school where it is
  okay to say 'I am finding this hard'.

- Believe and trust your staff.

---

4   www.wendybaker.guru.

- Cultivate a culture that is non-judgemental. This comes from the top.

- Protect your staff; don't pass the pressure onto your staff.

- Publicly celebrate success.

- Thank staff.

- Provide activities to support wellbeing, for example, buy in specialist supervision or Indian head massage at lunch times.

- Publish dates at the beginning of the year, for example, sports day, reports, etc.

- Where possible accommodate staff requests, for example, to attend their child's nativity plays, graduations. Remember birthdays.

The children's charity manager, Rachel, had some really useful probing questions. Rachel was my manager for several years.

- What would you like to role model to staff?

- Is how you are in work reflective of this?

- How do you avoid being caught in the trap of feeling that you are indispensable?

- How do you ensure that what you are doing today is needed to do a good enough job rather than necessarily a perfect job?

- How do you role model that you are taking time for yourself?

All four spoke about the importance of believing and trusting in your staff. Trusting staff to get on and do their job and not micromanaging them will help their wellbeing. In the way we know it is important for us to believe in children and to have faith that they are capable and full of potential, we also need to have faith in our staff. I know that my manager believes in my ability to be a good nurture worker, and that is important. That helps me feel good about myself and my role; it also enables me to work at my best ability. Lack of trust in staff can create a toxic environment.

Support for development

All of your staff and yourself need to have opportunities to grow and develop. An essential part of being a leader is offering staff opportunities, liaising and planning with them about their learning and development needs. It is good practice to plan each year the learning and support each member of staff needs for the year ahead. In this time of budgets cuts, staff development can be one of the first areas to be cut. I would suggest this should be one of the last areas to be cut. You need your staff to be growing and developing, you need your staff to be motivated and inspired, and staff development can assist with this. Cultivating and encouraging staff development needs to be encouraged and led from the top. Many schools and early years settings now take part in action research projects. These can be an excellent way to develop practice and learning for individuals and teams. Action research focuses on improving learning, which can help you to enhance your practice (McNiff and Whitehead 2010). Engaging in action research can be a creative way of helping staff extend their learning and practice without being costly.

Where do you get support?

While speaking to the managers, I was particularly aware that it can be a very lonely position. When it is your business, or you are the head teacher, who supports you? Head teachers have the chair of governors. I believe a critical role of being a chair of governors is to support the head teacher and check on their wellbeing; however, this does not always happen. For schools and nurseries the local authority may offer you support, or for church schools, the education team in the diocese may offer support; however, with the changes in local authorities and the introduction of academies and multi-academy trusts, the role of the local authorities is changing. In some areas head teachers get support from one another, but again this is not always the case. I think it is an important question to finish this chapter with: who supports you? Some head teachers and nursery managers now pay for an outside person to meet with them once or twice a term, to listen to them, support them and check on their wellbeing. Other managers and head teachers have support from other people in their position. It is important that as a manager you have someone supporting you.

Questions for practice and reflection

- Take a moment to think about what support you have. Is this something you could improve? Is there someone you know and trust who you could approach to support you? This may be another head teacher or nursery manager, who you could have a reciprocal arrangement with.

References

Bainbridge, A. and Westergaard, J. (2014) *Supporting Teachers in Their Role: Making the Case for Formal Supervision in the Workplace.* Accessed on 7/5/17 at www.consider-ed.org.uk/supporting-teachers-in-their-role-making-the-case-for-formal-supervision-in-the-workplace/.

Dabell, J. (2016) *Protecting Your Staff Wellbeing.* Accessed on 1/5/17 at www.headteacher-update.com/best-practice-article/protecting-your-staffs-wellbeing/145302.

John, K. (2012) *Supervision Part 1: Equipped to Lead.* London: Nursery World.

McNiff, J. and Whitehead, J. (2010) *You and Your Action Research Project,* third edn. Abingdon: Routledge.

Willis, J. (2014) 'Teacher's guide to sleep – and why it matters.' Accessed on 27/1/17 at https://www.google.co.uk/amp/s/amp.theguardian.com/teacher-network/teacher-blog/2014/nov/11/good-night-teacher-guide-sleep.

Conclusion

Through this book, I have explored the importance of why we need to have good wellbeing. We are in a privileged position working with children: we are able to make a difference to their lives. However, to be able to do this well we need to give time, thought and attention to looking after ourselves.

I hope this book has given you practical ideas and suggestions that you can try out. I have been really privileged in my role as a nurture worker to support, guide and work with some fantastic teachers and TAs in reception classes. Through this work I have seen how important it is to look after our wellbeing. I firmly believe by making small steps towards taking care of ourselves we are in a better position to make a great difference to the lives of the children with whom we work.

I hope you enjoy trying some of these ideas. Maybe that will be through eating some cake, smelling the roses and/or having a hot bath. But remember, you are important, your health is important and you need to take care of yourself.

Resources for Wellbeing

Mental Health Foundation
Mental health charity

www.mentalhealth.org.uk

Mind
Mental health charity

www.mind.org.uk

Sane
Mental health charity

www.sane.org.uk/home

Index

absenteeism 97
acceptance 45
Action for Happiness movement 44–5
activities
    for emotional wellbeing 43–4
    for exercise and fitness 26–7
    and learning opportunities 59–60
    for rest and relaxation 24–5
    trying new things 65–6
    see also contemplative practices;
        cultural activities
Adams, I. 72
adrenaline 35
animals 39
anxiety
    and cultural activities 64
    and diet 19–20
    and nature encounters 71–2
    and sleep 22
    see also stress
Armstrong, K. 88
aromatherapy sleep spray 23–4
art galleries 63–4
arts-based activities 61–4

Bainbridge, A. 109
Baker, J. 27
Baker, W. 111
baking 21
barefoot walking 73
beauty in nature 47
being grounded 73
blog writing 65–6
    see also journaling

Bomber, L. 29, 32
book clubs 92
Book of Silence, A (Maitland) 70
breakfast 17–18, 106
breathing techniques 75–7
Brighter Futures (Bath) 9–10
Brodie, Kathy 56
Brother Roger from Taize 83
Brown, B. 40, 65, 69
buddy boxes 94–5
buddy systems 101
bullying 84, 88
Bury, L. 53–4

caffeine 23
cakes and cake baking 21, 85, 93
cats 39
celebrations 90–1
Cepero, H. 79–80
children, trauma and stress impacts 32
chocolate giving 19, 20–1, 93
choirs 62
'circle of concern and influence'
    (Covey) 37–8
classrooms 28–9
clutter 28
colleagues
    challenging 83
    kindness towards 92–4
    feeling stressed 84, 86, 87
    support for 83–95
comfort eating 20–1
communication, managers–
    staff 101–2

community projects 60–1
compassion and kindness
    for colleagues 92–4
    examples of 93–4
    for self 40, 42–4
contemplative practices 69–81
    earthing and being grounded 73
    finding stillness and silence 70–2
    forms of 69–70
    importance of life's rhythms 73–4
    journaling 79–80
    mindfulness 75–8
    using a labyrinth 77
    and yoga 79
continuing professional development
    see professional development
control, and stress 37–8
cortisol 30, 35
counselling services and
    schemes 102, 105–6
Covey, S. 37–8
creativity 61–3
Crown, H. 10–11
cultural activities 63–4

Dabell, J. 99
dance 62
decluttering 28
Department for Education 108
depression, early signs 32, 49–50
Devlin, P. 61
Devon, N. 36
diet 17–21
    breakfasts 17–18
    and comfort eating 20–1
    lunch 18
    and mental health 19–20
    see also food and drink
Do-it Trust website 61
dogs 39

early years staff
    considering leaving
        profession 10–11
    impact of stress 10–11, 86–7
    self-compassion 40, 42–4
    supporting colleagues 83–95
    taking on secondary stress 32, 84

workloads and stress 99–
        100, 105, 106–7
    see also managers and management
earthing 73
Education Support Partnership 100
emails 105
'emotional granularity' (Brown) 41–2
emotional intelligence 41–2
    and reading 53–4
emotional resilience 45, 97–8
emotional wellbeing 11, 35–51
    being joyful and happy 44–6
    control enhancing measures 37–8
    expressing gratitude 46–8
    having an emotional
        vocabulary 41–2
    identifying feelings 41–2
    recognising priorities 51
    and relationships 48–50, 83–4
    relaxation and rest 48
    and self-compassion 40
    and stress 35–6
    use of touch 41
endorphins 26
environmental factors 28–9, 30–1
Espinoza, J. 10–11
exercise 26–7, 45
    and mindfulness 77

Facebook 57–8
feelings 41–2
'flight or fight' responses 35
Flood, A. 53
flowers in rooms 29, 92, 94
food and drink 17–21
    eating to feel good 20–1
    'good mood' choices 19
    importance of lunch 18
    nutrition and mental health 19–20
    provisions for staff 101, 103
    sharing 21, 90–1, 93
foraging 59–60
Ford, A. 77
forest therapy 30–1
forgiveness 89
Friedlander, Albert 88
friendships, finding time for 31–2
Fujiwara, D. 64

gardening 71–2
Garner, R. 17
giving 45
goals 45
Goldstein, E. 89
Goldstein, S. 89
gratitude 46–8
  thanking others 47, 85–6, 92, 93–4
Gregoire, C. 71
Griffin, J. 48–9
groundedness 73
gut bacteria 19

happiness 44–8
  activities and actions 45
  being joyful 45–6
  being thankful 46–8
  and supporting others 84–5
hauora (philosophy of health;
    New Zealand) 11
head teachers 114
Help Guide website 60
Henri Nouwen Society 46
hobbies 62
hygge 20–1

induction schemes 108

Jarman, E. 28
John, K. 108
journaling 79–80

karshi (death from overwork) 30
Kelly, R. 1920
Khoshaba, D. 79
kindness
  examples of 93–4
  for self 40, 42–4
  to colleagues 92–4

labyrinths 78
language use 89–90
learning 45
  practice-based 56–8

and professional development
  55–6, 103, 110–11, 113–14
and reading 53–4
Lee, C. 79
leisure activities
  for emotional wellbeing 43–4
  for exercise and fitness 26–7
  and learning opportunities 59–60
  for rest and relaxation 24–5
  trying new things 65–6
  see also cultural activities
Lent 80
letting go 89
lifelong learning 54–5
  and professional development
    55–6, 103, 110–11, 113–14
  shared practice 57–8
  work-based 56–7
loneliness 48–9
  and management 114
Louv, R. 31
lunches 18
Lyubomirsky, S. 46–7, 92–3

MacKerron, G. 64
McNiff, J. 113
Mainstone-Cotton, S. 24, 41, 61, 70
Maitland, S. 70, 71
managers and management 97–115
  general staff support
    measures 107–8
  getting to know staff 103–4
  importance of own wellbeing 98–9
  introducing positive changes 100–3
  making environmental
    changes 106–7
  recognising staff wellbeing 99–100
  staff development 110–11
  strategies for stress
    management 105–6
  supervising staff 108–10
  support for 114
  support for staff development
    113–14
  tips and advice 111–13
Maori wellbeing philosophy 11
marathon running 27

Maudsley mental wellbeing
checklist 38
meditation 48, 69
and breathing 75–7
and mindfulness 75–8
tools for 78
mental health, and nutrition 19–20
Mental Health Foundation
42, 48–9, 84
Mental Health website 77, 97
mental wellbeing 11, 53–66
and creativity 61–3
cultural engagement activities 63–4
learning and professional
development 54–8
non-work orientated learning 59–61
and reading 53–4
trying new experiences 65–6
mentors 101, 108
Mind 12, 35, 53
mind wandering 76
mindfulness 75–8, 102
podcasts and courses 76–7
Miyazaki, Y. 30
museums 63–4

National Alliance for Arts, Health
and Wellbeing 62
'nature deficit disorder' (Louv) 31
nature and green spaces 30–1, 77
being grounded 73
finding stillness and silence 70–2
Neff, K. 40–1
neurotransmitters, and nutrition 19
new experiences 65–6
new staff members 108
NHS
five-step plan for mental
wellbeing 12
healthy eating advice 18
sleep advice 22–3
wellbeing survey 10, 98
noise 70–1
nursery rooms 28–9
nurture bags 94–5
Nurture Outreach services 9–10

observations in the workplace 104
online groups 57–8
outdoors 30–1
oxytocin 39–40

panic attacks 35
peer reflection groups 86
peers
celebrating with 90–1
getting to know 91–2
shared learning experiences 57–8
support for 83–95
personality types 92
pets 39
physical wellbeing 11, 17–32
and environmental factors 28–31
and exercise 26–7
and nutrition 17–21
and rest 24–5
and routines 31–2
and sleep 22–4
Pilgrim Paths website 78
practice-based learning 56–7
prayer 69, 78
professional development 55–6,
103, 110–11, 113–14
practice-based 56–7
shared experiences 57–8
Promoting Young Children's
Emotional Health and Wellbeing
(Mainstone–Cotton) 24, 61, 70

reading 53–4
reflective tools 79–80
Reggio Emilia (Italy) 28
relationships 48–50
finding time for 31–2, 49–50
manager–staff 99–104
and routines 31–2
supporting colleagues 83–95
and wellbeing 83–4
relaxation 48
aromatherapy sprays 23–4
see also rest
religious practices 69, 72, 80
resentfulness 89

resilience 45, 97–8
resources for wellbeing 119
rest 24–5
retreats 71
rhythms in life 73–4
Roffey, S. 83, 85
role models 112
routines 4, 31–2, 49–50, 73–4
to improve sleep 22–3
running 27

school classrooms 28–9
Scottish government, guidelines to
safeguard wellbeing 12–13
secondary stress 32, 84
Seldon, A. 44–5
self-compassion 40
self-employment 18
serotonin 19
shadowing colleagues 56–7
Shapiro, S. 76
shared learning 57–8
Shinrin-yoku (forest therapy) 30–1
silence 70–2
skills development 55–6
sleep 22–4
lack of 22
tips and suggestions 22–3
smiling 101
smoking 23
social wellbeing 11
solution-focused team models 86
spiritual wellbeing 11, 69–81
being grounded 73
encounters with nature 71–2
finding stillness and silence 70–2
forms of contemplative
practices 69–70
importance of rhythm in life 73–4
mindfulness and breathing 75–8
reflective tools and
journaling 79–80
using a labyrinth 78
yoga 79
staff development see learning;
professional development
staff illness 97, 102

staff requests 103, 112
staff rooms 101, 103, 106–7
stillness 24–5, 70–1
stress 35–6
impact on teachers 10–11, 86–7
management of 36, 105–6
other peoples 84, 86–8, 99–100
recognising in staff 99–100
recognising triggers 36
resentment vs forgiveness 89
secondary 32, 84
and workloads 99–100,
105–6, 107–8
stress hormones 30, 35
stress relief
being self-compassionate 40
pets and animals 39
taking control 37–8
supervision 86, 102, 108–10
supporting colleagues 83–95
celebrating events and
each other 90–1
developing a culture of
compassion 88
examples of 85
getting to know colleagues 91–2
introducing nurture bags 94–5
letting go 89
making regular checks on 87–8
practicing kindness 92–4
recognising need for 86–7
watching language use 89–90
swimming 26–7, 72, 74
and mindfulness 77

teachers
considering leaving
profession 10–11
impact of stress 10–11, 86–7
see also managers and management
team meetings 57–8, 101
teams
getting to know 91–2, 103–4
personality types 92
and solution-focused approaches 86
supporting colleagues 83–95
see also managers and management

Teen Yoga 79
thanking others 47, 85–6, 92, 93–4
time management 36
    prioritising relationships 49–50
    prioritising wellbeing routines 31–2
TKI n.d. 11
touch 94
    and comfort 41
toxic environments 88
trust 113

Van der Kolk, B. 54
volunteering 60–1

walking
    and being grounded 73
    with colleagues 92
    and mindfulness 77
    and silence 70–1
Watson, L. 26
wellbeing
    audits of 99–100
    descriptions and definitions 11–14
    emotional aspects 11, 35–51
    forms of 11
    guidelines for 11–12
    impact of other people on 83–4
    Maori philosophy 11

mental aspects 11, 53–66
physical aspects 11, 17–32
protective factors 11–12
and relationships 83–4
resources 119
spiritual aspects 11, 69–81
Westergaard, J. 109
Whitehead, J. 113
Wiking, M. 20–1
Willard, C. 75
Williams, F. 30
Williams, M. 77
Willis, J. 22, 99
Wolf, N. 74
Woodland Herbs 24
workload management
    99–100, 105, 106–7
workplace cultures 88
    and bullying 84, 88
    use of language 89–90
workplace environments 28–9, 106–7
World Health Organization,
    on wellbeing 10
worry see anxiety
writing 65–6
    reflective journaling 79–80

yoga 79, 102

CPI Antony Rowe
Eastbourne, UK
January 07, 2025

Contents

Dramatis personae   ix

Family trees   xii

1. Where are you from?   1

2. The colour of love in post-war Britain   11

3. Growing up mixed: From the mid-1950s
    to mid-1970s   44

4. When British meant white: Singapore
    1934–45   63

5. An ambivalent belonging   97

6. Empire and Enlightenment   130

7. The fantasy of empire   163

    Epilogue   183

    Acknowledgements   193

    Bibliography   195

    Notes   199

Dramatis personae

The Roberts family

William Roberts aka Thiruvenkatam: born Mahkarai, Chingleput, 1768; died Madras, 1838. Founder of the Madras Unitarian Church. Married: 1 Name unknown; 2 Mary (1789–1840).

Joseph Roberts: born Madras, 1816, died Madras. Studied at Unitarian College in Manchester and in York, England. William Roberts's second son.

William Roberts Jr: born Madras, *c.*1820, died Madras, 1899, second Pastor of Madras Unitarian Church and third son of William Roberts, the Unitarian church's founder.

Samuel Turnbull Roberts: born Madras, *c.*1845, died Madras, *c.*1893. Clerk in the Madras Public Works Secretariat.

Walter Godwin Turnbull Roberts: born Madras, 1893; married Hilda Weston, 1918; died Singapore, 1965.

Dudley Samuel Roberts: born 1925, Miri, British North Borneo; died Singapore, *c.*1994.

Esmé Helen Roberts: born 1927, Miri, British North Borneo; married Maurice Osler, 1949; died Watford, England, 2019.

Ralph Eustace Roberts: born 1929, Miri, British North Borneo; died Singapore, *c.*2014.

The Weston family

William Robert Weston: born Madras, 1868, died Madras. Married: 1 Susan Amelia Sherman (1875–98), 1893; 2 Lydia Ann Walmsley, 1901.

Hilda Ruth Weston: born Madras, 1897, died Singapore, 1978. Married Walter Roberts. Sister of Mabel, Jimmy, Harry, Marjorie, Ivy, Claude, Noel, Beryl, Lucy.

The other Roberts family

Abraham Roberts: born 1784, Waterford, Ireland; died Bristol, England, 1873. Army officer in the British East India Company, son of John Roberts and Anne Sandys. Married: 1 Indian woman; 2 Isabella Poyntz Ricketts, 1820 (died 1827); 3 Isabella Hamilton Maxwell, neé Bunbury (1830).

Captain Thomas Roberts of Waterford (1778–1855): Abraham's brother.

Frederick Sleigh Roberts: born 1832, Kanpur, India; died St
Omer, France, 1914. Son of Abraham Roberts and
Isabella Bunbury.

The Walmsley family

Joseph Walmsley: born Walton-le-Dale, Lancashire,
England, 1842. Weaver and soldier in the British
army, son of Anne Parson and William Walmsley.
Died 1891, Madras.

Lydia Ann Walmsley: born Madras, 1878, daughter of Joseph
Walmsley and Elizabeth Smith; married William
Weston, 1901; died Rushden, Northamptonshire,
England, 1964.

The Osler family

Charles (Charlie) Hubert Osler: born Bedmond, England,
1907; died Abbots Langley, England, 1974. Married
Hetty Brigginshaw (1908–1985), 1927.

Maurice Charles Osler: born Bedmond, England, 1927;
married Esmé Roberts, 1949; died Hemel
Hempstead, England, 2006.

Audrey Osler: born Hemel Hempstead, England, 1953.

Charles (Charlie) Osler: born Hemel Hempstead,
England, 1955.

THE WESTONS

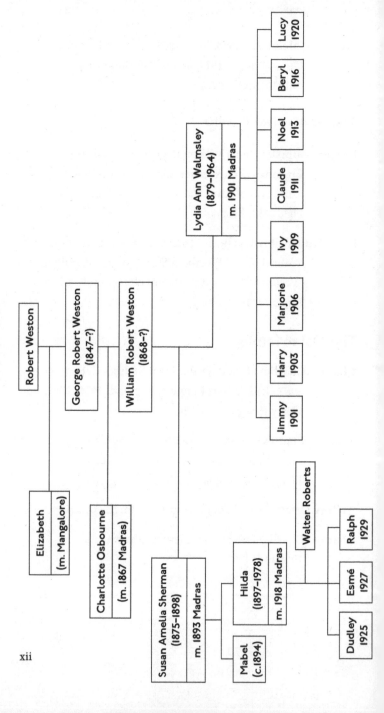

THE ROBERTS

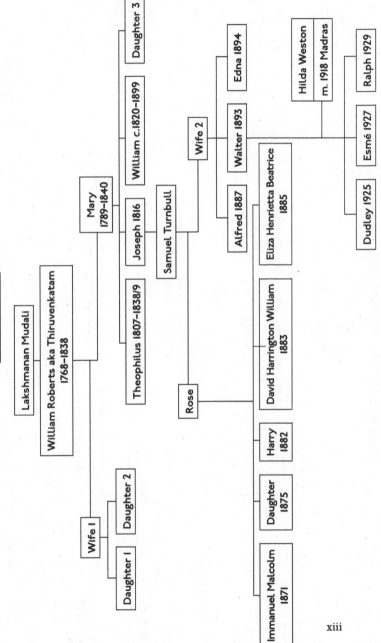

THE ROBERTS OF WATERFORD, IRELAND

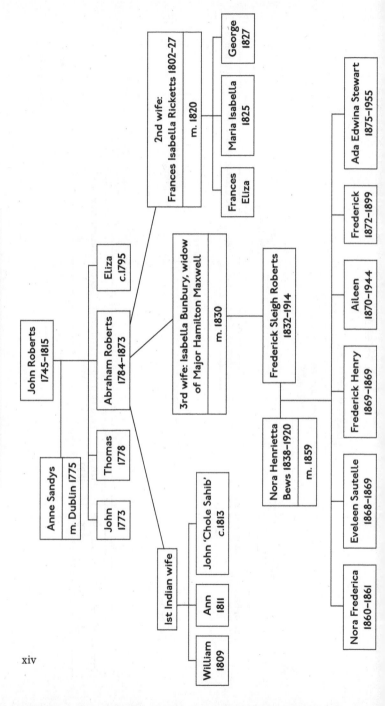

John Roberts 1745–1815 — Anne Sandys m. Dublin 1775

Abraham Roberts 1784–1873

Children of John Roberts and Anne Sandys: John 1773, Thomas 1778, Eliza c.1795

2nd wife: Frances Isabella Ricketts 1802–27 m. 1820 — Frances Eliza, Maria Isabella 1825, George 1827

3rd wife: Isabella Bunbury, widow of Major Hamilton Maxwell m. 1830

1st Indian wife — William 1809, Ann 1811, John 'Chole Sahib' c.1813

Frederick Sleigh Roberts 1832–1914 — Nora Henrietta Bews 1838–1920 m. 1859

Nora Frederica 1860–1861, Eveleen Sautelle 1868–1869, Frederick Henry 1869–1869, Aileen 1870–1944, Frederick 1872–1899, Ada Edwina Stewart 1875–1955

1

Where are you from?

15 July 1949, RMS *Canton*, Singapore: friends saying
goodbye to Esmé as she leaves for England

'Your English is very good. Where are you from?'

While most people in England, where she had migrated
to, were well-intentioned, it didn't feel like a compliment

to a young woman who had grown up in a British colony, Singapore. Of course her first language, English, was good.

Esmé was amazed to discover that in Watford, England, in the 1950s, few people knew just how far the British Empire stretched or that people from colonies such as Singapore, which had been part of the empire for more than 130 years, were British. Her multilingual family originated from Madras (now Chennai), India – which was also under British control, in this case since the early seventeenth century. The language of communication between family members from across the British-governed territories was English.

'Where are you from?' is a question we all ask each other, and get asked, frequently. It may come up in conversations with taxi drivers, when we travel on holiday and at social events. But for us, people of colour, when we are asked this question by white people, it can feel like more than simple curiosity: it tells us that being British is tied to ethnicity, or skin tone, or geographical background. It can feel political, since the assumption (naive or aggressive) is that to be British, you have to be white. Either consciously, or unconsciously, the question is challenging a *right* to belong.

Seventy years after my British/Singaporean mother came to Britain to marry my English father, I still hear the question she was asked, and I'm forced to wonder about the assumptions behind it. 'Where are you from?' remains all too familiar to me and other people of colour living in twenty-first-century Britain and, indeed, anywhere in western Europe, regardless of whether we live in an international city such as Birmingham or Frankfurt, or in a quiet corner of Burgundy. You can confidently claim to be from Halifax or Highgate, Bristol or Brighton, but if you respond, 'I'm from here,' often the questioner won't be deflected or satisfied by your response. They will persist: 'No, where are you *really* from?'

People of mixed heritage may encounter this more frequently than most, for our skin tone, hair texture or clothing are less likely to provide helpful clues to those who feel the need to pigeonhole us. It doesn't matter whether the questioner is acting purposefully or innocently, whether they are malicious or just plain curious, their tone or mannerisms often suggest that our claim to belong is suspect. The effect is to exclude, whether or not that's the intention, and it hits home.

It can feel patronising and, for someone with experience of racism, it is not merely unsettling. It's threatening.

People of colour, whether new migrants or citizens whose families have lived in Europe for many generations, all find strategies to deal with this question, and you're on high alert waiting to see what the next question will be. Are they really interested in you, even if their question is clumsy? Or do they simply want their own judgements or unconscious biases confirmed?

In the mid-1980s, I started work at a large, multicultural secondary school in Birmingham. The white male headteacher asked me where I was from. I could see that he wanted an account of where I was born and where my parents came from. I answered him as briefly as possible, and then asked him where he was from. He was clearly not expecting the tables to be turned. Hopefully, he'll have paused before he asked the same question of another young colleague or student of colour. In any case, it's a good strategy and one that, for me, generally works. But it's tiring to be on the alert or to resort to the aphorism, 'We are here because you were there.'

Because the questions are so potent and because they come from – to be generous – a place of profound ignorance about the British Empire and its past colonising, I decided to take those two freighted questions – *Where are you from? No, where are you really from?* – that plagued my mother all those years ago and continue to bother my brother and me, and ask them of myself. I hope that in finding out the answers, on my own terms, that I also open up questions and provide new insights on Britain's history. Whether or not we trace our families from beyond the shores of Britain, we all deserve a better understanding of the past, and an opportunity to recognise the complexities, far-reaching consequences and contradictions of empire.

So, yes, this is a family history, but it aims to be much more than that. It is the result of my own attempt to inform myself, precisely because I am British, about who I am and where I am from.

I've set out to discover more about my ancestors and have traced my maternal family back through seven generations to mid-eighteenth-century India. Perhaps it would have been simpler to get a DNA test! But, certainly, that wouldn't have provided me with the rich stories of my ancestors that I have uncovered.

The British Empire frames and shapes my family's history and the stories of individual relatives. Whether born in Britain, like me or my father, or in some other distant British territory, like my mother and many other family members, we are part of this same empire, so its ambitions, politics, economics and, significantly, its legacy not only form our backdrop but have also presented both opportunities and restrictions on these same lives. The stories highlight how, for some, life chances are enhanced while, for many, the policies of empire cause suffering and injury. I wanted to know my family history to fill in some of the gaps in my education, but this is not just my history; it elucidates the largely untold history of a nation and of its citizens, both people of colour and white.

My family story is one of migration across every generation, over four centuries, prompted by war, a desire to study, a global economic crisis, a fresh start, love and even child abduction. In fact, I seem to be the first generation still resident in the country in which I was born, and for a long while I thought I was less adventurous than my parents and grandparents. Modern means of transport and my career have allowed me to travel, too – to 'migrate' for several months on extended visits to Japan, China, Costa Rica and the USA; to work in Norway for thirteen years; to travel for shorter projects and work-related activities to more than fifty other countries, across most regions – but I've always come home to the UK.

My childhood experiences and those of various family members across many generations, back to the eighteenth century, in Britain, Singapore, India or Sarawak in present-day Malaysia, uncover a good deal about the country I have grown up in, the place that British journalist Sathnam Sanghera has dubbed 'Empireland', which is Britain.[1] The stories I tell here reveal as much about Britain as they do about the countries of the British Empire. Together, the tales of individuals, dating from the eighteenth century through to the early twenty-first century, demonstrate that it was not India, the oldest imperial territory, that was at the heart of the empire, but Britain itself. India was certainly held to be the 'jewel in the crown' of empire in that it helped support Britain's industrialisation, and brought riches and a life of opulence to its British military conquerors, adventurers and rulers. India may have dominated the imperial imagination, but the real jewel – the place the imperial British loved and admired the most, to which colonial administrators generally retired and which was the true beneficiary of this colonial endeavour – was their homeland, Britain.

In my travels through various archives I found disturbing links between my mother's reception as a migrant in mid-twentieth-century Britain, my own childhood in 1950s, 1960s and 1970s Hertfordshire, and the ways in which the British imposed their will over four centuries on people in the empire they characterised as inferior. Back in the late eighteenth century, my three times great-grandfather was forced, as a young Tamil boy, to flee his family home after his parents were killed and their village destroyed as a result of the struggle between the British East India Company and local Indian rulers to wrest control of the land. He and his family were merely collateral damage. Those who wanted the land and its resources were indifferent to the suffering and inevitable famine they inflicted on people they judged to be of little consequence. The racism and discrimination of twentieth-century Britain echo this old imperial tale. There is a hierarchy of people who matter.

Careless or wilful amnesia has allowed the idea of the British migration narrative to begin in the mid-twentieth century, with people from India, Pakistan and the Caribbean forming the foundation of present-day multicultural Britain. A racist fixation has some twenty-first-century Britons fantasising that people of colour arrived after the Second World War, without any link to the country, to exploit the British welfare state and British hospitality. The truth was portrayed – only partially and in a simplified way – in the opening and closing ceremonies of the Birmingham 2022 Commonwealth Games, where we saw new citizens arrive to help Britain get back on its feet after the Second World War. In this positive and more accurate counternarrative, the newcomers were *invited*, and helped to build up the country's infrastructure and industry in a 'better together' scenario. This promotion of a British multicultural identity, also adopted at the London 2012 Olympics, was designed not only to challenge the racist version, but also to promote positive images of Britain's capital and its second city, and by extension the whole nation, to the world. But this story overlooks the reality of a multicultural Britain over previous centuries. Throughout the age of empire, over four centuries, there have been travels between Britain and India, and between India and other parts of Asia. Like many other Indians, from all social classes – princesses, seamen, ayahs (nursemaids), workers and students – my direct ancestors have been travelling to Britain from India, and returning home again, since the eighteenth century. They also travelled from India to China, France, Singapore, Sarawak and possibly other places I've yet to discover. All were helped by the employment and trading opportunities that a vast empire provided. The myth that everyone was desperate to come just to Britain is patently untrue.

My family are Anglo-Indians, people of mixed Indian and European descent, over many generations. Anglo-Indians always occupied a liminal position in India, sometimes favoured by the British, employed to take on certain roles that suited the imperial administrators. At other times, they were mocked and ridiculed by the colonisers, and found themselves in a vulnerable situation. This was particularly the case in the late nineteenth and early twentieth centuries when, in the face of the Indian independence struggle and in an effort to retain power, the British began making concessions to Indians and excluding Anglo-Indians from certain jobs.

The colonial authorities set out to 'rescue' the mixed heritage children of working-class British soldiers and Anglo-Indian or Indian women, believing them to be doubly vulnerable to vice on account of being from the dissolute working-class *and* having native parents. The story of one such child, Lydia Ann Walmsley, who grew up to marry my great-grandfather, widower William Weston, and acted as mother to my grandmother Hilda, is perhaps the most shocking one I came across.

Anglo-Indian families are known for their adoption of Christianity and Western styles of dress. But those Anglo-Indian individuals who embraced Islam and Indian styles were less likely to feature in the colonial accounts and records of the India Office. One particular ancestor of mine went from Hindu, to Muslim, to Anglican Christian and eventually to Unitarian five generations ago, and he was not unique in searching for a belief system that matched his ideals. Others in the story embraced Islam from a Christian upbringing. Perhaps most interesting is how one of my relations, a man brought up in rural India, drew on the ideas of the European Enlightenment, experiences of revolutionary France and living among working women and men reading radical pamphlets in London, to promote education among the poorest classes in early nineteenth-century Madras, finding a receptive audience among his fellow citizens from varied religious traditions and cultures.

I began with two intriguing family stories, puzzles really, retold in my family. The first, more plausible story was that a direct ancestor, an eighteenth-century-born Indian, was said to have founded the Unitarian Church in Madras.

The second story was sketchy and unlikely. As my mother left for England in 1949, her father told her about a family member buried in St Paul's Cathedral. This turned out to be Frederick Sleigh Roberts, Earl of Kandahar and Waterford and former commander-in-chief of the British Army in India, who died in 1918.

How my family might be related to this Victorian hero, who had fought to preserve and strengthen the British Empire in India, southern Africa and Afghanistan, was unclear. I was even hoping that this story was untrue.

Working back generation by generation, I tried to resolve this puzzle about my family and me. I looked for clues in the records of the India Office at the British Library and other archives; asked naive questions of librarians; pestered family members; studied photographs; searched through family papers; read entertaining and moving letters from family members written in the eighteenth, nineteenth and twentieth centuries; and tracked down anyone in Chennai, India, in the UK, in Ireland and across the globe who might have some answers. This detective work, together with much reading, has led me to some confident – and some tentative – answers to my questions about family, migration and empire.

I don't have all the answers on how the British established

their empire, but I do have some insights into the attitudes and methods used to impose empire and white supremacy across the world, and the impact this had on one community and one family. And in many ways I have found the answer to my question: where are you *really* from? The answer says as much about Britain as it does about me – and that's what I want to share.

Esmé: her second week in England, on honeymoon
with Maurice in Hastings, August 1949

2

The colour of love in post-war Britain

Esmé and Maurice's wedding, 1949

Esmé migrated to Britain from Singapore in 1949 to marry the man she loved.

Following one's heart is rarely listed as a reason for migration but it is often the reason people leave their homeland – as it was for my mother.

She was twenty-two years of age and it was her first lone trip. Born in Sarawak, she had lived for a short while in India, but had been settled in Singapore since the age of seven. This was her first time away from home and family but she was excited to see the place long presented as the mother country. Her newly minted passport, issued at Government House, Singapore, in June 1949, confirmed she was a British Subject and Citizen of the United Kingdom and Colonies. She was planning to marry another citizen of the United Kingdom and Colonies. Esmé was a brown-skinned woman of mixed Indian and European heritage; her fiancé was white from a family long settled in Britain. She had met Maurice Osler two years before in Singapore.

Esmé felt she knew a good deal about the country she was moving to. She had attended Anglican church schools, followed a British curriculum and taken British school-leaving examinations. Esmé and her parents saw themselves as loyal British citizens: her father Walter had volunteered as a member of the Local Defence Corps in the Second World War when Singapore came under attack from the Japanese Imperial Army in 1941. Walter had continued to serve Britain at considerable personal risk after the British surrender to the Japanese, helping New Zealanders among the British Commonwealth forces stranded on the island to escape.

There were no explicit laws banning interracial marriage in Britain or the British Empire in the 1940s (unlike in the

United States, where the last state laws against interracial marriage were finally overturned in 1967 by a Supreme Court ruling).[1] Under British colonial rule, such relationships had, at different times, been encouraged, discouraged, recognised or reluctantly tolerated by the authorities for hundreds of years. From the early nineteenth century, British seaports such as London, Bristol, Cardiff and Liverpool and the colonial cities of Calcutta and Madras were witness not only to interracial marriage, but to established mixed heritage communities.

However, my parents were marrying in 1949 and in the Britain of the immediate post-war period, the colour of romantic love mattered. The government thought that post-war unemployment was going to be partly solved by deportation. From 1945, and throughout the following year, the Liverpool police, working with immigration officials and authorities, forcibly rounded up and removed as many as 2,000 Chinese seamen, returning them to Shanghai, Singapore and Hong Kong even though hundreds of them were married to British women and were accepted members of the local community. They simply disappeared, and many of these women were left believing their husbands had abandoned them and their children. It didn't matter that these merchant seamen had risked their lives to ensure Britain remained fed and fuelled during the war, and might properly have been recognised as war heroes, or that they had married and had children.[2] The British government of the day effectively denied the fellow humanity of these families and, almost worse, for some fifty years the government continued to deny that any deportations had occurred. It wasn't until 2022, after decades of campaigning by the seamen's adult children, that the Home Office finally admitted to the deportations. At last, it was accepted that the authorities' decisions were 'racially inflected [with] Chinese seamen ... characterised sui generis as not merely an employment problem but as members of a criminal underclass'.[3]

Then came the marriage in 1948 of Black African Prince Seretse Khama of Bechuanaland (Botswana) to white Londoner Ruth Williams. It made front-page news in Britain. The marriage became a lightning rod for anxieties and racial prejudices about interracial marriage in Britain. Church leaders gave opinions on both sides, as supporters of the couple and as detractors of interracial marriage, sometimes expressing opposition under the guise of concern for the children of such unions. The marriage generated extensive debate – even in parliament, with some MPs characterising it as 'unfortunate' and against their 'instinctive belief'.[4]

In Singapore and across the empire, as well as in Johannesburg, the political impact of the marriage was met with headlines such as: 'Tribe say yes to white wife', 'Church joins in row over typist', 'Ruth blocks Seretse from Chieftainship' and 'London-born Ruth is only a concubine'.[5] Ruth's characterisation as a typist (she was in fact an insurance clerk for Lloyd's of London) and a concubine, and the way she was presented as the cause of Seretse's problems, show how gender and misogyny intersected with empire. As the marriage was also seen as threatening a key Commonwealth economic partnership between Britain and the emerging apartheid state of South Africa, the poor couple were made to bear a great weight – all because of their love. They were defying the norms on which the nation, and indeed the British Empire, were based. It did not matter that these were the empire's ideals, rather than its rather messier reality.

*

Against this background, my parents fell in love. Their relationship, unlike that of Ruth and Seretse, did not cause a political storm. But like other 'mixed' relationships of that era, it provoked a miscellany of hostility, scepticism and support. Did they understand that the step they were taking, at that time and in that place, was so controversial? My mother later told me they discussed possible challenges that any future children might face in an intolerant society. They both must have witnessed the global political storm the Karma marriage had raised, but it would have been difficult for either to imagine the everyday racism of post-war Britain. Maurice lacked direct experience of it and Esmé, living in multicultural Singapore, had good reason to believe that people of various ethnicities could live together happily. After all, she had grown up with a mix of Chinese, Indian and Eurasian friends.

An uneasy peace

Esmé and Maurice's story begins in Singapore, in the immediate aftermath of the Second World War. Swiftly following the surrender of the Japanese Imperial Army in August 1945, Japanese soldiers and officers were rounded up and interned in local camps. A wave of relief spread across the island now that the turmoil and dangers of occupation were coming to an end, but peace did not come immediately. Esmé recalled how there were skirmishes, and occasional sounds of gunfire on the island, as some local people sought out those they believed to be traitors or collaborators and took revenge.

The British authorities, returning to the highly prized naval port after their ignominious retreat a few years earlier, initially relied on Indian troops, who had not been interned by the Japanese during the war, to keep the peace. (In the early days of the war, the Japanese had hoped to win the goodwill of Indian troops and civilians with the promise of support for Indian independence from British rule.) Esmé and her family, as well as others in Singapore, knew life would not continue as it had been before the war. The island bore the visible signs of bombing and occupation, and people quietly carried the scars of the conflict, some acknowledging them and others denying them, even to themselves.

Eventually, the Roberts family moved back from the countryside to their old home in Sophia Road that had been requisitioned by the Japanese during the occupation, and gradually began to pick up the rhythm of their lives. Esmé's younger brother Ralph, who was twelve years of age when war broke out, now returned to school, but she recognised a pressing need to support her family and took a course in shorthand and typing. She then took a job at Thomas Cook, the travel agent, followed by work for the government of Malaya in Singapore, and later was pleased to secure a better position as secretary to the manager of an insurance company, Legal and General. To the eighteen-year-old, her prospects looked promising: she was finally able to make a serious contribution to the family income, and even purchase new clothes. During the war, Esmé and her mother had managed, between the two of them, with just two dresses good enough for work or to wear outside the house.

Just as her work prospects were improving, Esmé suffered a setback. The middle-aged English manager who had taken her on began to make unwelcome advances. Feeling uncomfortable and extremely vulnerable, she walked out before even receiving that month's salary. But news travelled fast through the Singapore business community grapevine, and almost straightaway the chief clerk to the government, Mr Jaganathan, who knew Esmé from her former government employment, invited her to apply for a post with the Royal Air Force. Soon she found herself each day on the RAF employees' truck travelling out of town to the airbase at Changi to work for a group of non-commissioned officers, and before long she was promoted to senior secretary, working for a wing commander.

An Englishman abroad

My father, Maurice Osler, first travelled from Britain to Singapore in 1947. He was one of a generation conscripted into peacetime National Service, in which young men aged eighteen to thirty were signed up to address a shortage of military personnel.[6] This deficit was made all the more acute when, following Indian independence, Britain no longer had the huge Indian Army, something it had relied on in both world wars, on which to draw. British national servicemen were used to support and maintain Britain's shrinking empire; occupy post-war Germany and Japan; and re-establish and strengthen the country's international power, especially in the Middle East.

Before conscription, Maurice had lived his whole life in a semi-rural area of Hertfordshire, some twenty-five miles from London, moving just two miles from his birthplace, Bedmond, the birthplace 800 years earlier of Nicholas Breakspear, the only English pope, to the neighbouring village of Kings Langley. But aged just twenty, and still not old enough to vote, he travelled first to a training camp at Catterick in Yorkshire, and then nearly 7,000 miles across the globe to Singapore, just one-and-a-half degrees north of the equator.

Maurice was one of the first peacetime conscripts into the army, and served in the Royal Signals. It was the first time he had ever visited Yorkshire, let alone East Asia. Previous adventures had been confined to cycling trips from home, day outings to the seaside at Clacton, or heading a little further afield to Oxford or Cambridge and spending a weekend youth hostelling.

As they travelled, the young men either had their horizons widened or their prejudices about foreigners reconfirmed. For Maurice, it was a unique opportunity to extend his education and understanding of the world as, after war broke out when he was aged twelve, he had stopped going to school regularly thanks to a lack of parental supervision. His father had been conscripted and his mother had taken a job as a conductor on the Green Line buses travelling in and out of London. At the age of fourteen, he officially left school and joined the General Post Office as a telegram boy, later training as a telephone technician. He was an avid reader and among his books were wartime and post-war propaganda booklets ordered by post, covering diverse topics such as Norway's heroic wartime efforts to resist the Nazi occupiers, or Kenya's economy and the contributions of settler colonists. It was through this habit of reading, and taking every opportunity for international travel, that Maurice began to question things taught by teachers who themselves had limited education. Throughout the 1930s, children had been fed a diet of unqualified pride in and loyalty to empire, with songs, parades and dressing up for Empire Day. Much later, in the 1990s, he told me: 'They told us lies in history at school.'

Unlike many National Service conscripts, Maurice found he could make use of his previous civilian training and put his telephone technician skills to the test in Singapore, supporting the work of the RAF at the Changi airbase. His barracks were situated close to the beach and the warm, tropical South China Sea. It was here that Maurice learned to swim. This tranquil, rural setting hid some recent atrocities, for it was close to where as many as 10,000 Singapore residents had suffered summary execution. Mostly Chinese men and boys, their bodies were thrown into mass graves. But these graves were not uncovered until 1962. To Maurice and the other young British servicemen stationed there, Singapore must have seemed an idyllic posting. It was an intense contrast to the green Hertfordshire lanes he knew, and the cold, drab, grey towns of post-war Britain with which most of the young servicemen were all too familiar.

A fine romance

Esmé and Maurice did not meet by chance. Esmé's desk at RAF Changi was situated outdoors on a wide, wooden, first-floor veranda, opposite the other senior secretary, a man. They shared a telephone, on which the RAF officers would call them when their services were required. Opposite the veranda was a building housing the telephone exchange. One day, they found their internal line was out-of-order. A young British serviceman came over to fix it.

It was a meeting contrived by Maurice's co-workers. Maurice had seen Esmé among those alighting from the truck that dropped off civilian workers at the airbase. Shortly after, he spotted her working on the veranda. He was shy and somewhat inexperienced with girls, but his workmates noted his interest in the pretty young woman and so suddenly the internal telephone line was out-of-order and Maurice was sent to fix it. The other senior secretary may have been in on the game, since he later passed Esmé's home address and telephone number to Maurice.

One Saturday evening shortly afterwards, Maurice called Esmé from the NAAFI club in town, asking if he might visit her at home.[7] Esmé's parents knew of the unwelcome advances at Legal and General, and had heard about the out-of-order telephone episode at Changi. They also knew that Esmé, wisely in their opinion, did not wish to date anyone in the RAF for risk of neighbourhood gossip. Although it was known she was working at the airbase, to be seen with a serviceman was likely to damage her reputation. Both the family and the local community were socially conservative. Esmé was no doubt expected eventually to marry someone from their church, or the son of one of her parents' wide circle of friends. Going out alone with a young man was frowned upon and a young woman wanting to get to know someone would normally be chaperoned by a female friend or go out on a double date. Her father, the stricter of the parents, was out, but her mother, Hilda, agreed that Maurice might call at the house. If Maurice needed directions in finding them, he should be careful not to ask for her but for her father, Mr Walter Roberts. As Maurice made his way to Sophia Road, he checked directions with a passer-by. He explained who he was looking for. 'Well, that's me,' came the answer.

Hilda and Walter Roberts quickly grew to like Maurice. His being white was not an issue. Their Christian faith was one in which all ethnicities were accepted, and the church where they worshipped, and their wider circle of friends of varied religious backgrounds, reflected this. As Eurasians, they had close family members of varied skin tones. Esmé happened to be a little darker-skinned than either of her brothers and while Eurasian girls were generally considered more attractive if they were fair-skinned, Esmé was a popular girl who had excelled at school and was always surrounded by friends. Her colouring seems to have been largely irrelevant in 1940s Singapore.

More tricky would have been an inter-faith marriage. Years later, Hilda and Walter's elder son, Dudley, married a Muslim woman and converted to Islam, and that caused his mother much heartache, even though Dudley – not a particularly religiously inclined man – told me that it was all much the same to him and that both religions worshipped the same God. Maurice had not been brought up in a church but had been baptised as a baby into the Church of England. Although he professed to be a Christian, he was also of the opinion that there were many ways to the same religious truth. Maurice was soon writing home to his parents to tell them about the wonderful girl he had met and hoped to marry. His mother Hetty was appalled. First, she wrote to him outlining how such a match was inappropriate and claimed that any future children would never be properly accepted. When this had little impact she persuaded Maurice's aunt, her sister-in-law, also to write. Neither woman made any impression.

Hetty Osler was a strong-willed and determined woman, and Maurice, although a serving soldier, was still a minor, just twenty years old.[8] Hetty's next ruse was to write to his commanding officer requesting, as Maurice's legal guardian, that he be transferred from his post in Singapore. She may have claimed, or at least intimated, that he was in moral danger. This was certainly conveyed to Maurice.

A conversation I had in 2019 with a retired senior naval officer led me to understand that personal relationships between military personnel and local civilian populations remain sensitive matters, even with a time lapse of more than fifty years. Maurice's commanding officer, faced with Hetty's letter, appears to have taken the route of least resistance. Maurice was informed he was being transferred to a new posting in Iraq.

The young couple were clearly distressed. But rather wonderfully, in contrast to Maurice's parents, Esmé's consoled them saying that this was an opportunity for them to reflect on and test the strength of their attachment. They were not formally engaged, but Maurice bought Esmé a silver locket. Maurice left for Iraq and the distance test began.

Maintaining a long-distance relationship at that time depended on letter writing, since international phone calls were prohibitively expensive. Months passed and the letters went back and forth. Esmé left her job at RAF Changi for a more convenient one in town, returning to work for the government. In September 1948, with just a few months of his National Service to complete, Maurice turned twenty-one. He went to his commanding officer and requested a transfer back to Singapore. His request was accepted.

Once Maurice was in Singapore, the couple started talking earnestly about their future. Would their home be in Singapore or the UK? There was clearly work for Maurice as a telephone engineer on the island. He could see out the rest of his National Service in Singapore, be demobbed and begin married life there. Realising that Maurice was not going to back down, his mother Hetty had to re-evaluate the situation; she did not want to lose her son, her only child. If they were going to be married, she insisted that they live in England. She made arrangements to borrow money from a family member, and then offered to pay Esmé's passage to London.

Maurice had pursued Esmé determinedly, and was devoted to her. If Esmé had insisted that they settle in Singapore, there is no doubt he would have remained there even though he had not completed his telephone engineer training, and so might have struggled to secure a good salary and the further training he needed. If the couple opted to spend a few years in Singapore and then move to the UK, there was no guarantee he would be able to pick up the apprenticeship he had begun.

Esmé was kind-hearted and, as she later explained to me, assumed at the time that Hetty's attempts to stop their romance were based on her fear of losing her only son, rather than on any ingrained bigotry. To some degree, Esmé's parents seemed to share this perspective. If she moved to the UK, they would be parted from their daughter, although they would still have their other two children, Dudley and Ralph, nearby. The Roberts family had remained a very tight unit during more than three years of Japanese occupation, when they had gone through extreme hardship together. As a child, Esmé had been separated from her father for a year and a half, while he looked for work and her mother Hilda took the children to stay with her parents in India. Maurice, although he travelled to Singapore and Iraq, had been effectively looked after by the army. Esmé was certainly more experienced in international migration and living in different environments, and having lived through three-and-a-half years of occupation, was perhaps more adaptable. Maybe leaving Singapore also offered Esmé the chance to put the suffering of the occupation behind her. But I am certain Esmé would not have left her parents if she had realised it would be a full sixteen years before they were reunited.

Esmé was particularly protective of her younger brother Ralph, recognising that he was experiencing difficulties in adjustment after the war. But at that time, none of the family fully realised the trauma he had experienced, and could not have anticipated the further trouble he was to encounter during the continuing upheavals in Malaya. A major regret after leaving Singapore was that she had been unable to help her brother.

Much later, when she and I went to Singapore together in the late 1980s, I observed how some of her friends who had remained in Singapore had been able together to come to terms with the disruption and distress of the occupation years; whereas she was away and by herself, and had to reconcile what she saw as lost years, cheated of the education and future career she had hoped for.

After some deliberation, Esmé and Maurice decided he would return to the UK to be demobbed, and she would follow. Esmé's parents took various steps to ensure their daughter would be well cared for in Britain. Hilda's English brother-in-law, Tom, Ivy's husband, was dispatched to check that all would be well for Esmé, beginning married life under her mother-in-law's roof. He reported back favourably. A friend of Esmé, Elsie, and her husband Bill, a former RAF serviceman, who had also met in Singapore, visited Maurice's parents on a charm offensive, presenting themselves as living proof that a 'mixed marriage' could be happy and successful.

Maurice completed his National Service and returned home, while Esmé began her preparations to leave.

A passage to England

Practical arrangements had to be made for the wedding and for travel to the UK, with Esmé needing to apply for a passport and to be vaccinated against smallpox. Together with her mother, she put together a trousseau, a trunk full of new clothes, now freely available to buy in Singapore, though strictly rationed Britain. These included an outfit for going away on honeymoon, and several pairs of silk stockings. Then there were fittings for a wedding dress. Esmé planned the wedding service from Singapore, selecting favourite hymns and readings. Two friends of the bride were to act as witnesses: Elsie, and Geoffrey Abisheganaden, a childhood friend, their fathers also being firm friends. Geoffrey was studying law in London, and he was renowned for his singing voice. His family, like Esmé's, were staunch Christians who had first learned to sing at home as part of their daily family worship.[9] Geoffrey was tasked with performing a solo: the 23rd Psalm, 'The Lord is my Shepherd'. Since Esmé's parents could not be present at her wedding, a decision had to be made as to who would give the bride away. Maurice's uncle, Walter, was asked to stand in for Esmé's father. The two men, at least, shared a name.

A passage was booked on RMS *Canton*, due to depart Singapore on 15 July 1949. Built in Glasgow, the *Canton* was launched in 1938 as a passenger liner, but the following year, when war broke out in Europe, it was converted into an Armed Merchant Cruiser or AMC. The *Canton*, like many of the passengers it was carrying from Singapore, had endured a difficult time during the war, having been attacked by U-boats, partially sunk, repaired and then continued in service. In 1944, the *Canton* was refitted as a troop ship, carrying thousands of soldiers over the next two years, after which the ship was decommissioned and refitted again as a passenger liner. It was given the white and yellow livery of P&O (the Peninsular and Oriental Steam Navigation Company) liners, with a varnished wooden bridge. The ship's capacity was for 298 first-class and 244 tourist-class passengers.

Photographs taken before the *Canton* left port show Esmé surrounded by well-wishers, but she looks strained, as do her parents and brothers. She shared a berth with two other young women, travelling tourist class. It was an almost four-week journey calling at Ceylon (Sri Lanka) and then heading to Europe via the Suez in Egypt. Life on board meant she was rarely alone, but she later told me how lonely she felt. Those twenty-six days on board were undoubtedly a bittersweet time for Esmé. On some nights she cried herself to sleep. She was looking forward to her marriage to the man she loved, but she was leaving behind her parents, family and friends, uncertain as to if and when they might be reunited. Her parents were by this time in their fifties. Both Esmé and her parents deeply regretted they could not be there to see her married. A photo of Hilda taken a few weeks later at a wedding reception shows her looking solemn but composed. Someone has scrawled a message on the back assuring Esmé that her mother is happy and well.

Esmé brought with her a small silver-coloured tin box decorated with the head of an elephant. A memento of her mother, it was not valuable, but important to Esmé as it had already crossed the ocean. Hilda had brought it with her decades earlier when she left India, and had managed to hold on to it throughout the war years, despite the disruption of having to move so many times. Esmé's luggage included two finely carved Chinese camphor wood chests, and she carried with her a number of cards and wedding gifts from friends. She also brought a commendation from her church in Singapore, to serve as an introduction to the church where she was to be married, plus letters of commendation from her employers and certificates confirming her shorthand and typing speeds, for when she began the process of looking for work.

Esmé disembarked in Tilbury, London, on a Monday in August 1949. Maurice had brought a local taxi to the docks to wait for her and bring them back to his parents' home, but the process of disembarkation took some time, as tourist-class travellers were obliged to wait while all the first-class passengers disembarked. The taxi was sent back to Hertfordshire and Maurice eventually escorted Esmé to his parents' home on the train. It had been several months since they had seen each other and a time of great excitement in each other's company.

As Esmé looked out of the train window, nothing was quite as she had expected. Maurice lived close to the Ovaltine factory and in Singapore, when the cinema showed advertisements for the then-popular drink, he had pointed out the picturesque Ovaltine model farm. The factory was nothing like this, and the rows of small, terraced housing seen from the train did not resemble any view of England Esmé had previously encountered. She was incredulous to see how people in England lived. Esmé went to stay with Maurice's parents and he decamped down the road to his aunt and uncle's house to stay with his cousins.

Marriage and motherhood in a strange land

After she arrived, Esmé tried to document her life, sometimes systematically, often a little haphazardly. I know some details of her life not only from stories she told but documents she kept: passports, receipts, certificates, and all manner of notes relating to anything from a piece of jewellery, memento or photograph, to a several-page account of a particular place or event, written at the time or several decades later.

Her first week in England was hectic, if somewhat disorienting, with many people to meet. Maurice and Esmé applied for a special licence so they could be married immediately; Esmé chose flowers for her bouquet; and visited the minister of the church where they were to be married. On the Friday, they went up to London to buy a wedding ring. It was a simple gold band with an engraved orange blossom design, which suited the bride's tiny hands. Esmé was clear she wanted 22 carat gold not 9 carat – regardless of the greater cost – for, after all, she had never had an engagement ring. On the Saturday, five days after Esmé arrived in England, they were to marry in the Hertfordshire village of Kings Langley. Maurice's cousin, Doris, would be Esmé's bridesmaid. Maurice's mother Hetty had ordered the cake and booked refreshments for a reception for forty-two people.

Astonishingly, on the morning of the wedding, Hetty made one last-ditch attempt to put a stop to it. She visited her son at her brother's house, and tried once more to talk him out of the marriage. Doris and her parents were witnesses to this, and Doris, clearly shocked by her aunt's behaviour, later confided what had happened to her close friend, Joan. I don't believe that Esmé ever found out about this unhappy episode.

Joan told me of it more than seventy years later, after both my parents had died. Sadly, it fits a pattern of behaviour and beliefs held by my paternal grandmother, and which I later observed for myself. My grandfather Charlie, by contrast, was soft-hearted and accepting of Esmé. My grandparents were like chalk and cheese. Charlie was a quiet, easy-going and kind man who we much later discovered had witnessed terrible atrocities in Egypt while serving in the army during the Second World War. He would invariably give way under pressure. This meant, of course, that he was unable or unwilling to stand up to Hetty.

Esmé's parents were not the only ones who were concerned for her welfare in England. The minister at the local Baptist village church, where the couple were to marry, took the opportunity to speak to the young women in his congregation about the need to reach out and make her feel welcome. Joan also recalled this talk, and how the minister, Mr Don Metherell, had stressed the need for them to go out of their way to help Esmé settle in. Perhaps he had a sharper insight into what it might feel like to be an outsider than many, for during the First World War, as a pacifist and conscientious objector, he was imprisoned for refusing military service and ostracised by many in the community for his stand. It was said he was tarred and feathered by vigilantes, who were no doubt fired by the wartime nationalist propaganda and all too ready to label a pacifist and a progressive in their midst as a coward.[10]

Despite my grandmother's opposition, my parents were wed on 13 August 1949.

But marrying an outsider, and a woman of colour, was clearly news in late 1940s England, and their wedding was recorded in many local newspapers. Various photos show a curious crowd outside the church, waiting to glimpse the bride, as word had got around the village about Maurice's bride from Singapore. Nearly sixty years later, a man from their village told me that as a boy he had been among those who came to stare. It seems the curious were not disappointed. At a time of post-war austerity and rationing, the bride wore an elegant, long-sleeved, silk wedding gown, tiara, veil and long lace train. (The tiara, veil and train were later borrowed by the groom's cousin and a number of other local brides, and appear in many subsequent wedding photos, but the handsome silk dress was too small for these others to get into it – it remained my mother's alone.)

My parents' marriage was notable, especially in the relatively inward-looking small community of Kings Langley where they came to live. Although less than twenty-five miles from London, it clearly saw itself as separate from the big city. A handful of people commuted to work in London, and so were no doubt regularly exposed to people visibly different from themselves, not necessarily in workplaces where they could get to know them, but on the street and on public transport. But these daily commuters were a small minority, for the area was still at that time semi-rural, with many, like my paternal grandfather, working in factories, but others still employed on the land. Esmé had learned courage and determination in Singapore during the war years, and these qualities were to be important in addressing the challenges that were to come.

I find it hard to imagine the degree of risk that she took, as a young bride. Travel restrictions, both national and international, during the COVID-19 pandemic reminded all of us of how difficult it can be to be separated for an indefinite period from family and friends; of not being able to visit parents or other loved ones, especially when they are sick or dying; of grandparents being separated from grandchildren; or not being able to see a newborn baby. Esmé said goodbye to her parents, brothers and friends in 1949, and it was many years before they were reunited.

It was only in the 1950s that intercontinental air passenger travel became possible and, even then, it remained the pre-serve of the elite and wealthy throughout the decade. Phone calls were not an option and so Esmé, once she was married and settled, communicated with her parents by airmail, which was commonplace across the British Empire since the mid-1930s. I recall that there were generally a few blue airmail letters tucked away somewhere, at home, which were bought postage-paid from the post office, and where the length of any communication was curtailed by the size of the paper. I remember they had to be folded, and when received had to be carefully cut in specific places, so as to keep the pages intact. Throughout the 1950s, 1960s and beyond, airmail was distin-guished from surface mail, letters and packets sent by sea, for which the postage was substantially lower. Surface mail was the common means of sending parcels or large quanti-ties of letters and cards, such as Esmé would have posted and received at Christmas.

Esmé spent the first two years of her married life in her parents-in-law's home. It was a small, two-bedroomed bun-galow; the young couple would not have had much privacy. They were both out at work during the day, and so Maurice's mother did most of the cooking, and at weekends, Esmé, who had never had to cook in Singapore, learned the basic skills from her mother-in-law. I try and imagine how it was for her in another couple's home with a woman who did not think well of her. Hetty's hostility was always brewing just below the surface, but the one time she lost her temper and shouted at Esmé, Maurice stood up to her and she never did it again. Thankfully, after two years, Esmé and Maurice had saved enough money to put down a deposit on a place of their own, and it seems so eager were they to leave Maurice's parents that they moved in without much more than a bed, a kitchen table and chairs. They set about making it as homely as possible before I was born.

One of the most moving items I found among Esmé's papers, after she died in 2019, was a letter she wrote from hospital after giving birth to me. She had been disappointed not to be able to give birth at home, as she considered that to be the most natural place to be, but without support from her mother-in-law, and with her own mother so far away, she had little choice. At that time, fathers were not allowed to be present at their children's births. It seems that she was left alone for several hours during labour. But this is not what she focuses on in the letter. Written in pencil to her mother-in-law, it described me, the new baby, but also expressed concern for Maurice. They clearly had a loving marriage. It was January and very cold outside. Esmé feels guilty because she is enjoying the warmth of the hospital but she is worried that the house is cold, as the coal delivery had not arrived as expected. She is concerned that Hetty ensures that Maurice is well looked after, and does not catch cold, for if he does, he will not be able to visit her. Given that she, like other new mothers, had to spend around ten days in hospital after the birth, this is an understandable concern, for he was likely to be her only visitor. As ever, Esmé aimed to document key moments in her life, and she asked Hetty to save the letter for her, for when she came out. Esmé was shocked by what she saw as neglect in hospital during childbirth. She made sure that when my brother was born, two years later, she had a home delivery.

Esmé's ambition was to become a teacher but despite having the education and qualifications to enter teacher training, it was difficult to prove this, since her examination records had been lost during the war. For a few years, before we children were born, she served as a Sunday school teacher, while working as a shorthand typist. When my brother and I were aged seven and nine, she explored the option of teacher training, and I recall her looking at college brochures and toying with this idea, but instead she chose to return to work and save enough money to take the whole family on holiday to Singapore to see her parents.

Everyday racism and politics

By the 1970s, public and private attitudes to so-called mixed marriages had shifted from those of the mid-century. Yet my grandmother, while she outwardly accepted my mother as one of the family and helped to look after us, her two grandchildren, held on to some of her original views. When I was in my late teens, she went so far as to express her disapproval of the Black boyfriend of one of her great-nieces on the grounds of skin colour. When I challenged her, she made the inevitable reference to the problems of 'half-caste' children. She was suffering from rheumatoid arthritis and was by this stage housebound, but I was so upset that I walked out on her.

Not wishing to bring my parents into it, I went round to her brother's house, sharing much of what had happened with her brother and sister-in-law, but making sure that I didn't mention their granddaughter, the girl with the Black boyfriend. The couple exchanged knowing looks and the brother went straight round to see Hetty. I think he warned her that if she persisted in voicing such views, she would lose contact with her grandchildren. She never did so again.

I did not, of course, see all the challenges my parents had to face. I suspect they protected us from the knowledge of the overt expressions of racism they encountered, just as we, in turn, generally protected them from stories of the everyday racial harassment and slurs we suffered at school and university. But I do remember certain things that my mother did, which I think were acts of self-preservation and protection.

When I was about nine years old my parents bought their first car. I say car, but it was in reality a small Austin A35 van. The four of us, my parents, brother and me, would go on holiday, travelling to Dorset, Devon and Cornwall, to Wales and to Scotland, touring from place to place and making hot drinks along the journey on a small Primus stove. The van had no backseat windows, so we children, positioned behind our parents, had to peer though the windscreen between their heads for a limited view of the wonderful scenery we encountered, sometimes only viewing the most beautiful places through a torrent of rain, with windscreen wipers swishing back and forth. In the late afternoon, on arriving in a new town or seaside resort, we would look for a bed-and-breakfast place, never on the seafront or in a prime location, but set back where it was a little cheaper. The price of a room was often listed outside along with the 'vacancies' or 'no vacancies' sign. Maurice would drive and, when we arrived, he would get out to see if a bed-and-breakfast would take the four of us. My mother, brother and I would remain in the car. Sometimes Maurice would tell Esmé she should go and ask, but she always refused. I thought at the time that it was strange she was quite so adamant. I now realise that she probably did not to want to risk the humiliation, as a woman of colour, of being told that there were no vacancies, and that the B&B owners had simply forgotten to remove the 'vacancies' sign. My father wouldn't take us in with him either, but this didn't seem strange to us.

My brother was fairer-skinned than me back then, but I don't recall either of us encountering any awkward behaviour from the people we lodged with. People remembered our family everywhere we went, so we were aware that in their eyes we looked unusual. Invariably, they commented on my curly hair and which parent each of us looked like (in my case, always my mother). I assumed that all children experienced this. Generally, in the company of our parents, we were treated well.

Back then, in the 1960s and early 1970s, there were few laws to protect people from overt discrimination. The 1965 Race Relations Act banned racial discrimination in public places and made promoting racial hatred a crime, and the 1968 Race Relations Act made it illegal to refuse housing, employment or public services to a person on the grounds of colour, race, ethnic or national origins but those laws were primarily concerned with eradicating discrimination in housing and employment. It was not until 1976 that a further Race Relations Act addressed discrimination in education and in a range of services, such as hotels and boarding houses. And even then, it did not cover B&B accommodation if the service was offered in a person's place of residence. The humiliation and discrimination my mother feared was not unlawful at that time.

From the 1970s onwards, both Esmé and Maurice were active in local anti-racist and multicultural associations in Hertfordshire. My parents, particularly my mother, had a gift for making friends, and no doubt this won over many people who otherwise might have treated her with suspicion or hostility. Esmé was always ready to engage in struggles for a more just society, such as providing accommodation for homeless people, since seeing homelessness or poverty caused her distress. She always asked questions and looked to the causes of social injustice, although oddly perhaps she was sometimes reluctant to label such activity as political, and avoided joining a political party. Maurice, by contrast, was more overtly political. He was a lifelong member of a trade union, and ready to write letters to his MP, or even the prime minister, if he felt strongly about injustice. He invariably would ask Esmé to help him draft any such letter.

Throughout my teenage years, we would frequently have lively debates about national and international events at the dinner table, arguing a point and, if necessary, interrupting each other. There was an etiquette relating to respect for one's elders, especially outside the house, but disagreeing with my mother and father, who had normally opened the topic under discussion, was considered okay at our table. I was shocked as a young adult to find that at the houses of some of my friends' parents, it was considered bad mannered to interrupt other family members and to talk passionately about any issue.

Perhaps Esmé was also protected by living in a small town as it was not until the 1990s that she ever personally encountered racist slurs in the street. It was at the time of increased antagonism and hostility to people of colour – which coincided with the arrival of Bosnian refugees in the UK. It seems ironic that this should have happened to her almost five decades after her arrival in the UK, when Britain was offering an official welcome to refugees from another part of Europe. We encounter a similar irony today, as a number of British people show willingness to welcome white Ukrainian refugees into their homes, while those fleeing Afghanistan or conflict in Syria struggle to get recognition of their refugee status, and when they do may be forced to live in cramped hotel accommodation, often with young children, for well over a year. Official attitudes to migrants and refugees, whereby asylum claims are seen as dubious or even bogus, undermine the rights of all people of colour, including UK citizens. Dehumanising language and dehumanising processes encourage hate speech and intolerant behaviour across a section of the wider population. Simply put, hate breeds hate.

Those who enter into cross-cultural and interracial relationships sometimes also encounter direct expressions of racism and intolerance within the intimate spaces of family and friends. In these spaces, in my experience, it's not crude language or physical violence that causes hurt; rather, it is the breaking of assumed bonds of trust and solidarity that causes a different kind of violence.

In the mid-1980s, I went with my parents to visit two of my father's oldest friends, who had been present at my parents' wedding. This couple had known Maurice since their late teens when they attended the same youth club; the two men had worked together; and the two couples had holidayed together, along with us children. From nowhere, or so it seemed, this person, whom I will call Paul, blundered into what I can only describe as a racist tirade about mixed marriage. His wife and daughter looked embarrassed; my parents were unusually quiet. Schooled by my parents since early childhood to respect my elders, I hesitated at first. Then, as Paul was getting into his stride, calmly, but deliberately, I challenged him.

'Why did you attend their wedding if you disapproved so much?'

His reply revolved around the children of such marriages, and the confusion they would experience.

'But you are talking about me! How can you speak about me, on behalf of me, without listening to me? What you are saying is plainly nonsense.'

Paul did not retract, but he must have seen he had walked into a blind alley. The conversation reverted to lighter topics and before long we set off home.

Although an adult woman, I was quite expecting my parents to reprimand me for showing disrespect. But they had been equally shocked by Paul's words, and praised me for putting him right.

Throughout the 1980s, careless exchanges of this nature were commonplace, but were infrequently acknowledged by the vast majority of white people as racist. It was not that I had never encountered such antipathy before – quite the contrary. What was shocking was that this was someone whom I had always liked and trusted, and was a family friend.

Marriage, citizenship and rights

The challenges faced by couples entering romantic relationships across boundaries – racial, cultural, religious and
national – in the mid-twentieth century were influenced by
the politics of the day and by both world wars. During the
inter-war period, the number of interracial relationships
appears to have been on the increase.[11] Many men from British
colonies served as soldiers, including over a million Indian
soldiers, of whom 12,000 saw action on the Western Front.[12]
They were not treated equally to their white counterparts,
and many were angry at both their mistreatment and the lack
of recognition or commemoration of their sacrifice. Those
demobbed in Britain, along with others who had worked in
key war roles such as in munitions factories, now expected
equal citizenship rights.

If these men were expressing a new sense of confidence
in this period, so were white British women. They too had
played key roles during the First World War, and achieved a
sense of social, economic and political independence.

As historians of the mid-twentieth century have observed,
couples crossing cultural, religious and national barriers found
their stories were being played out 'against the backdrop of a
transforming world order, the emergence of a universalist human rights discourse, along with the persistence and
strengthening of older imperial notions of citizenship'.[13] This
was the era of the formation of the United Nations and of the
Universal Declaration of Human Rights (UDHR), proclaim-
ing on 10 December 1948 that: 'recognition of the inherent
dignity and of the equal and inalienable rights of all members
of the human family is the foundation of freedom, justice and

peace in the world'.[14] The UDHR asserted freedom, equality and dignity as a standard for all people. It was subsequently utilised by colonised peoples in their struggles for independence and rights. My parents' marriage was part of the growing number of interracial, inter-religious and binational marriages that took place during or subsequent to the Second World War, in the metropole, across the British Empire and beyond, as individuals found themselves as displaced persons, refugees or soldiers stationed in a new country.

In Britain, 1948 also saw the passing of the British Nationality Act, which strengthened and codified older imperial notions of British nationality. It defined it by creating a single status, that of 'Citizen of the United Kingdom and Colonies' (CUKC), which applied across the United Kingdom and all of its colonies. The passport on which my mother travelled to Britain in 1949, confirms this CUKC status. Its cover, although in other respects identical to a passport issued in the UK, nevertheless made it clear that this was a passport issued from Singapore and inside it also has the additional 'Colony of Singapore' as its place of issue. The rights of British nationals, including rights of residence in the UK, were equal for all British subjects across the empire. Esmé and her brothers, born in Miri, British North Borneo, had lived their whole lives as British subjects. Their parents were also British subjects, born in India. Esmé's parents and brothers remained British subjects until 1963, when Singapore became a state of Malaysia. Theoretically, they could have all travelled with her in 1949 and remained in the UK. But they would have needed the fare and, of course, jobs to support them when they arrived.

These two sets of rights, those of the UDHR and those of colonised peoples, were both used in the campaign in support of Seretse and Ruth Khama, after the couple found they were exiled from Seretse's homeland by the British authorities, following their marriage. It would seem that the two sets of rights were not seen at the time as contradictory or in tension. In the eyes of campaigners, universal rights and British nationality rights seemingly complemented each other.

Perhaps not surprisingly, nationality laws were strengthened across the British Empire, at the very time that empire was coming to an end. India achieved independence in 1947. After two world wars, the British Empire, and the empires of other European powers, had lost their importance, so many colonial peoples no longer needed to fight to achieve their goal of freedom. Former British-ruled islands in the Caribbean achieved independence between 1962 (Jamaica; Trinidad and Tobago) and 1983 (St Kitts and Nevis). In other colonised territories, such as Kenya, bloody struggles and brutal repression continued through the 1950s, with the country achieving independence in 1963.

It may seem strange that there was such concern in official quarters in Britain about interracial marriage in the immediate aftermath of the Second World War, Those, like my parents, who had crossed national, religious, ethnic or cultural barriers were defying establishment norms on which a sense of national unity was based. They were also, in their personal lives, crossing the boundary between the coloniser and the colonised. Couples engaged in boundary crossing of this type were the living embodiment of a more complex and much messier reality. Mixedness was then, and remains today, the norm, as many people discover when they look closely into their personal histories, so anyone who claims it is a late twentieth-century or early twenty-first-century phenomenon is either ill-informed or deliberately seeking to mislead. It is only when we unpeel the complex layers of our personal identities that it becomes clear that these boundaries, apparently fixed, immutable, have been constructed and imposed on people by nation-states, keen to create an exclusive, and often over-simplistic, loyalty. I am proud to think that my parents crossed so many lines.

Esmé with her mother-in-law, Hetty, 1949/50 in Kings Langley

3

Growing up mixed: From the mid-1950s to mid-1970s

Audrey on holiday with grandparents, Charlie and Hetty Osler, *c.*1958

'You are not half this or half that. You are one hundred per cent British – like your father and me,' my mother always asserted. Her concept of Britishness was not dependent on colour or creed; however, her view often stood in sharp contrast to my everyday experiences.

As a child of a 'mixed marriage' growing up in the 1950s and 1960s, I found my mother was both generous and caring, and did all she could to protect her children from ignorant and wilfully intolerant behaviour; my father, likewise, did his best. But there are limits to what even the most caring parents can do to protect their children from the wider political climate of intolerance and bigotry.

It seems improbable that my mother or her family in Singapore could have fully anticipated the social climate in the UK when she took the decision to board the ship that brought her to England. Likewise, the extent of everyday racism in society was probably not so well understood by my father, a young white man who had grown up in wartime Britain, in a small and largely homogeneous semi-rural community.

My mother encouraged me to believe that I could achieve any dream: 'Stand up for what you think is right and have high ideals. But celebrate small everyday successes'; and 'Of course you should apply for a university place, take no notice of her. What does she know?' when a domestic science teacher told me I should forget the idea and I'd be lucky to get a place at a teacher training college. Yet even before I started school, there were questions from other children, challenging my identity and sense of belonging.

Since we were taught at home that we were not half anything, it followed that we should also reject the widely used term 'half caste', one that continued to be used until the 1980s.

I remember as I prepared to leave home in the early 1970s, moving to Yorkshire to attend university, a family friend invited me out for a drink. He was also the child of a white British father and a Singaporean mother, although in his case I believe his mother's family was originally from Sri Lanka. This dark-skinned but blue-eyed boy, just a year older than me, had already spent a year at Loughborough University and had attracted rather too much unwanted attention. He warned me to have a ready answer, preferably false, when people asked me *what* I was, as he claimed they would inevitably do.

Arriving on campus, the vague feeling that I'd had that my family life was somewhat different from that of many of my peers was soon reinforced. What I had taken to be an ordinary upbringing turned out to be at variance from that of most of the other students I met.

Growing up mixed

In many respects, my childhood was typical of any child growing up in smalltown 1950s and 1960s Britain, in a family that was neither rich nor poor but where the income had to be carefully managed. There was a strong make-things-last culture, no doubt typical of the era. Although my mother quickly found work as a shorthand typist on her arrival in Britain in 1949, in the mid-fifties it went unquestioned that she would give up paid work to raise her family. Many women had been forced to give up their jobs because of returning servicemen, who were seen as more deserving. But women's equality at work was certainly not uppermost in my consciousness as I navigated my way through the everyday challenges of childhood.

My early recollections are generally rose-tinted, particularly those relating to outdoor games and activities. We played in the woods and fields at the end of our road. At infant school, we would go on nature walks in the lane behind the school, making bark rubbings and dragging into the classroom armfuls of greenery: leaves, sticky buds, flowers and even abandoned birds' nests from the hedgerows. Teachers would remark that we were lucky to have bright modern classrooms overlooking fields, and compare us to London children who, we were told, attended school in old Victorian buildings where the windows were placed too high to see out, and whose outside space was a small yard.

In the school holidays, during cold or wet weather, we amused ourselves by organising painting exhibitions among neighbourhood children or making models out of plaster of Paris and painting them in garish colours. Another activity was decorating potato-heads with plastic features: eyes, noses, moustaches and hats. And my personal favourite, from about the age of seven, was writing stories.

Once the weather got warmer, we would walk to the woods just a few minutes away and sit on a grassy bank to eat our chocolate Easter eggs. In the early summer, we built camps out of abandoned milk crates, threaded through with branches and camouflaged with greenery. When the harvest was gathered in, we would garner the spare scraps of hay to make cosy private spaces where we could hide away, chatter and read in the final days of the summer holidays.

I may be painting a picture of a rural idyll, but this is only part of the story. I attended school in Hemel Hempstead, a fast-growing new town, built in the 1950s and 1960s to accommodate Londoners in the post-war period. The quiet, traffic-free, narrow lane where, as infants, we went on nature walks with our teacher was, by the time I started secondary school, a busy road bordered by new detached houses. The area was undergoing rapid change, but it had probably never been, certainly not for the previous 200 years, a quiet backwater.

The back garden of our family's 1950s two-bedroom bungalow backed on to a railway embankment, built in the 1830s and forming part of the line that linked London to Birmingham, Manchester and Glasgow. The construction of this embankment required a significant influx of migrant workers into the area, both English and Irish. The railway embankment separated us somewhat from the village on the far side. I lived there with my mother, father and my younger brother Charlie, born when I was two years old. The line was not electrified until the mid-1960s, and I recall standing in the garden waving to the steam trains as a small child. The guard on a slow goods train would invariably wave back. Gradually, faster diesels replaced steam engines, but these were still sometimes slow enough for crew members to spot a child and return a greeting.

In front of our house, a few lorries trundled back and forth to a poultry farm run by a Lithuanian family. As children, we were sometimes sent to buy eggs. The children on the farm would occasionally offer to show us the chickens and the few pigs they kept. I did my best to avoid entering the smelly, noisy, overcrowded chicken sheds.

My paternal grandfather worked in one of the local paper mills built in the early nineteenth century adjacent to the

Grand Union Canal, which ran parallel to the railway, a job he had taken up on leaving school in the early 1920s and where he continued until retirement. His only break came in the Second World War when he was unlucky enough, having reached his early thirties, to be conscripted into the army to serve in Egypt. Every Saturday lunchtime, at the end of his five-and-a-half-day working week, he would call by on his bike with a small box of sweets for each of us children, fruit gums for my brother and fruit pastilles for me. My grandparents enjoyed sweets and readily indulged us. They had been denied them for a decade, as sugar rationing was introduced early in the Second World War and continued until 1953. My grandmother did a lot of baking and sewing, making dresses for me and my dolls.

As a small child, I accompanied my grandparents on a couple of occasions on seaside holidays, to Weymouth and Kent. On a few occasions my grandparents were asked by other holidaymakers whether they had adopted me. Clearly, strangers found it difficult to conceive that grandparents and grandchildren could look so dissimilar or that an olive-skinned child with dark curly hair could be a blood relation of a fair-skinned blue-eyed couple. Complete strangers assumed the right not only to stare but to ask questions they themselves would have no doubt found impertinent. The word 'miscegenation', still sometimes formally used to describe sexual relations or marriage between people of so-called different races, continues to carry negative undertones today. From the first time I heard it, in the 1970s, I have found it both pejorative and offensive. But as a child, when I heard these questions put to my grandparents, I thought those asking were rather foolish. It was a generational issue: how could these people possibly mistake my grandparents, who although only in their forties seemed to me rather old, for my parents?

In many respects my early childhood was unremarkable. Most of the things that mattered to me took place within five or six miles of home. My father worked very long hours as a telephone engineer, and so it was my mother who took primary responsibility for parenting. In many ways, I had a protected early start. Yet we were, in the white neighbourhood where we lived, worked, played and went to school and church, highly visible. With a father who could trace his family back in the immediate neighbourhood though several generations, but with a brown-skinned Anglo-Indian mother who had been brought up in Singapore, nearly 7,000 miles away, we were, to many people, a curiosity.

In the neighbourhood, there was no chance of anonymity. Everyone knew us. When we were old enough to travel by bus without an adult, the bus driver would ask: 'How's your mother?' As a small child, I didn't think of my family as unusual. But it was in everyday encounters, as I grew up, that I began to uncover clues concerning the depth of racism in society.

Our home was modest, but it was always open to international visitors. These visitors were not just extended family, or family friends, but also people my parents did not know, for example, friends of friends who were visiting the UK for an extended period, who might be studying, for example, at a London university. When nurses from Singapore and Malaysia started working at our local hospital from the mid-1960s, my parents would welcome them, my mother no doubt understanding that these young women were likely to be homesick and struggling to cope in a new environment.

One of our most frequent visitors was Kitty, a Chinese woman from Singapore, and long-time friend of my mother. Kitty was a continuing presence, coming alone, occasionally bringing her boyfriend, 'Uncle Mac', and later her husband, Peter. We sometimes went on picnics, carrying our supplies along a quiet lane, climbing over a style, and enjoying our meal on a rug laid out on the grass. Occasionally, we went on an outing by Green Line bus to what felt like far-flung places, such as Kew Gardens or Whipsnade Zoo. Most embarrassing for me was any visit to a Chinese restaurant, either locally or in London. Kitty would invariably glance at the menu and then go on to order dishes that were not on offer. But the real action occurred when Kitty took over the kitchen at home, bustling around, introducing new recipes, creating noise, laughter, interesting aromas, delicious flavours and minor chaos.

Our home, built immediately after the war with a decent-sized living room, two bedrooms, a bathroom/toilet and a small kitchen, gained slightly more space when the kitchen was extended in the early 1960s by knocking through to what had been a coal shed. This meant there was just enough space to seat four around the kitchen table for meals. When we had guests, we ate at a dining table in the living room and if the guests were staying overnight, they slept on a sofa-bed. At this time, my parents also swapped their slightly bigger bedroom for the one I shared with my brother. Theirs was then partitioned to make two tiny single rooms with sliding doors for us children. My brother's room was corridor-like with a built-in cupboard and a table either side of a chimney breast. Mine was square and just big enough to squeeze in my bed, wardrobe, chest of drawers and a tiny fold-away table for homework. It was a tight fit, so I generally completed my homework at the kitchen table where there was space to lay out my books.

Our 'normal' life was in reality very different from that of my young friends in the neighbourhood, at school or at our local church, and I was later to realise what a privileged upbringing I had. My parents' guests, friends and strangers, opened a door to varied people, cultures and languages, exposing me to a much wider world than most of my peers. I had a far richer range of experiences than most, and this was true even among children from families who were more comfortably off, where the parents had enjoyed access to better educational opportunities than mine.

In the early 1960s, my mother went back to work part-time outside the home. A trip to Singapore was in her sights.

Learning injustice

When the time came for me to start school, academic considerations were no doubt discussed, but I don't recall this. The nearest school was about a mile away. My mother was very much against me going there as it was an old, draughty building with outside toilets. The primary school my father had gone to involved crossing the canal and he was very much against this. I later found out that he had fallen in as a child, and he feared the attractions of playing by the water might led us to undergo a similar fate. So, I was enrolled at Chambersbury Junior and Mixed Infants, about two-and-a-half miles from home, and not on a direct bus route. For a five-year-old, starting school in the cold of January, it involved what at first felt like a long walk, twice daily.

My school was a new-build, part of a post-war initiative to invest in education. It is said that between 1950 and 1970 there was a new school completed in Britain every day. Hertfordshire exemplified this in its innovative school-building programme. The architecture and furnishings were experimental, with the interiors resembling some of the most attractive classrooms designed today in the early twenty-first century. Classrooms were spacious, consisting of two adjoining squares, one equipped with hexagonal tables where children sat in groups, and the other furnished with toys, dressing-up clothes, a classroom library and, for the youngest children, a sandbox. Our infant teachers were energetic young women, probably straight from college. It turned out that my parents had made the best choice available. Chambersbury was on a large campus, which included another primary school, a secondary modern school and a grammar school, which I was later to attend.

Soon after starting school I was admitted to hospital for what was, at the time, a ubiquitous surgical procedure: having my tonsils removed. I had suffered from tonsillitis for some time, and I was assured that this operation would put a stop to it. I went confidently and was placed on a ward with other children who were to undergo the same procedure, two younger boys. I would be in hospital for a week and my father had promised to visit me. It was while in the hospital that I first became aware of unkindness and of what I interpreted as prejudice towards girls.

On the ward, there was a West Indian nurse who wore glasses and proved to be rather strict. After the operation, instead of getting better, like the boys, I began to feel more and more unwell, refusing the food that was offered. When I complained of a sore throat, the scary nurse told me off, comparing my behaviour with the exemplary conduct of the boys. My most serious crime was to refuse ice cream; she insisted that all children liked it and wouldn't believe that I was finding it extremely painful to swallow. She told me I was such a bad girl that my parents would not visit. To reinforce this, she produced a bottle of Lucozade and offered it to the boys, telling me one of their fathers had brought it in, and telling them that I wasn't allowed any.

On the day I was due to be discharged, my father came to collect me. There was another nurse on duty, and I was still complaining of a sore throat. When she looked, it transpired that the doctors had left a swab in my throat and I had developed an infection. As we left the hospital, I asked my father why he hadn't visited as promised. He explained he had come with a gift of Lucozade but was advised he should not see me. Didn't I remember getting it? My fear of hospitals persisted for over four decades.

At school, one of the daily rituals was walking in pairs into morning assembly. The girls would line up together, then the boys would line up alongside us, and children would then walk hand-in-hand. I was the only child of colour in the class. One morning, a boy named Michael refused to walk with me saying I had dirty brown hands. I thought this was very unfair but wasn't keen to walk with this boy anyway as he happened to be one of the grubbiest and smelliest children in the class. After that, several boys would do their best to avoid walking with me. Never did the teacher intervene. I endured this indignity for some weeks or months, not believing I had the right to speak out.

Learning to speak truth to power

I don't believe that, as a child, I ever heard the phrase 'speaking truth to power', but I really wish I had, as the concept would have been empowering in my teens. In 1966, the headteacher at my secondary school made a special announcement in one of the rather formal morning assemblies. He told the five hundred or so students and teachers gathered there that two 'coloured' students would shortly be joining us, a boy in the year above me and his younger sister in a class below. He told us that these children were exceptional, and they were very unlikely to be followed by any other coloured students since we were a selective grammar school. We were encouraged to 'reassure' our parents that these new students were not part of a new trend.

I already knew who these two new students were as I had met them briefly during the school holidays. They and their mother, who was Scottish, stayed in our street with a friend of hers for a short time, before finding a more permanent home. They had recently arrived in the UK following a military coup in Ghana. Their father, a former government minister, had been arrested and imprisoned (this was the first time I understood the concept of a political prisoner) and they were forced to flee.

As I listened to our headteacher's announcement, I figured there were few differences between me and these children. All of us had one parent who was white and one who was not. In their case, it was their mother who was white. All day, I contemplated going to see the headteacher to ask him why he had made the announcement and why he thought we needed to reassure our parents. In the end, I decided against it. I worked out that it might have consequences I was not ready to handle. I think I realised I might hear things I wouldn't want to hear. But I also knew better than to repeat his comments at home, fearing this would bring one or both of my parents quickly into school. Largely, I wanted to protect them, but I also knew this was bigger than I could face. It was an official message from school that the new students were in some sense interlopers. It was also a message to me, that I did not really belong. The new students were Paul and Rosie Boateng. Paul, like both his parents, was passionate about politics. He became a Member of Parliament in 1987, and later a government minister.

This was an age when race was discussed, but in very different terms from later decades. Clearly, I had learned, in some indirect way, not to draw too much attention to myself. I recall writing, at the age of twelve or thirteen, a story in my English class about the impact on a child of mixed race of the South African apartheid state's legal prohibition of mixed marriage. I received a good grade but was relieved not to have to read it out or discuss the issues in class. This was a time when seemingly liberal-minded teachers would propose the discussion of such a topic as: 'How would you feel if your daughter or sister decided to marry a coloured man?' On one occasion, a boy, who lived very close to my grandparents, threw stones at me and used racist words. My father went around to his house, and the episode was resolved by the boy receiving a spanking from his father. This made me wary, as for many weeks, if not months, I feared his revenge, but in fact he never bothered me again. At this time, it was possible, on a day-by-day level, to avoid being overwhelmed or consumed by this prejudice and hatred. All this was to change in 1968.

Feeling like a stranger at home?

In April 1968, Conservative MP Enoch Powell gave his widely reported 'Rivers of Blood' speech in which he claimed that continued immigration, and the very presence of people of colour in Britain, would lead to catastrophe. His rhetoric highlighted the threat of evil and a future time 'when the black man will have the whip hand over the white man'. He told various anecdotes to warn of the threat posed by allowing Commonwealth immigrants to settle in Britain, immigrants who would have children who would compete with white people for resources and jobs. In his concluding remarks he gave the warning: 'As I look ahead, I am filled with foreboding; like the Roman, I seem to see the River Tiber foaming with much blood.' This 'Rivers of Blood' speech predicted widespread violence and bloodshed in the UK. I had no idea that Powell had been responsible as minister for health in 1960–3 for the recruitment to the NHS of many Black migrants to the UK, many of whom came, pre-independence, as British subjects.

For me, the constant repetition and discussion of Enoch Powell's words on radio and TV, together with their subsequent repetition and discussion in the community, proved to be one of the most difficult experiences of my early teenage years. Powell's speech confirmed the indirect message of my headteacher's announcement two years earlier, that I did not belong. What was previously implicit was suddenly made explicit. Powell claimed that white people 'found themselves made strangers in their own country' but the reality was that many young people of colour, including me, were made to feel like unwanted strangers in our own country. Discussion of policies that would encourage recent migrants to return to their countries of origin caused me to fear for the future of friends and family.

Expressions of racism became normalised and widespread. I learned there were at least three categories of citizens: first, those who were white and who were born in Britain; secondly, those who were born in Britain but were not white; and finally those who were 'immigrants', not born here and not white, and who should be given incentives to leave. Both in the 1960s and today, a xenophobic atmosphere has blighted the lives of migrants and has had a long-term, damaging impact on the social and political climate, both for people of colour and, indirectly, for all.

In the early 1970s, I went to university and, perhaps naively, expected my teachers and professors to have more enlightened attitudes. Realising after a couple of months that I was studying a degree that did not suit me, and wishing to transfer to history, the university careers service arranged an interview with a professor in the School of History. I attended and put my case forward. The professor, a Stuart historian whose work I knew and respected, opened the interview by noting the good reference I brought with me from the professor of social anthropology with whom I had been studying, going on to undermine me, and the reference, by observing that this professor was easily swayed 'by a pretty face'. He asked me a few questions and then told me: 'Unfortunately, our quota of places for international students is full.' 'But I am British,' I replied. 'You don't look it,' was his riposte. I knew then that I needed to find another department in another university.

For growing numbers of British citizens of colour, not just in London and other big cities, but in small towns and rural communities, we were the visible reminders of Britain's impe-rial aspirations. Like other young people of my generation, I knew little of empire and learned next to nothing about it at school, yet we all were influenced by it, even as the era of empire was drawing to a close, and former colonial territories were achieving freedom and independence. I was both hyper-visible and frequently invisible.

Back to the future?

While the experiences of children of colour growing up in Britain today have changed, the social context has not improved consistently, nor has racism gone away. Just as Enoch Powell promulgated a racist climate that impacted on my childhood in the 1960s, so some contemporary politicians use language and policies that impact negatively on people of colour today.

When in the post-Brexit era, political leaders talk about 'global Britain' they frequently seem to be using a code for 'imperial Britain'. Some politicians, born long after the Second World War and the mid-century independence struggles of colonised peoples, seem to be caught up in an imperial fantasy, which they promote and propagate under the banner of 'leaving the European Union'. Global Britain is part of a foreign policy designed to serve the interests of big business and financial institutions. Fair trade, global cooper-ation and even human rights are likely to be put to one side. Aid is less about reducing global inequality and more about reproducing asymmetrical power relations, as existed in imperial times.

Government policies with racist outcomes do not happen by chance. The most vivid recent example is the 2018 Windrush scandal, whereby many migrants from colonies or former colonies, who settled in Britain, found themselves in later life, and frequently in retirement, denied healthcare and other rights. A number were wrongly detained and threatened with deportation. Families were separated, and in eighty-three cases individuals were unlawfully deported to countries they left as children or young people. This was part of a long-term strategy to make the UK as uncomfortable as possible for migrants and asylum seekers. In 2012, the UK Home Office, under the leadership of then Home Secretary Theresa May, introduced a 'hostile environment' policy. The policy had a direct impact on many who migrated to Britain in the 1950s and 1960s from former or then existent British colonies, generally as workers or as children of migrants. Those who arrived before 1973 were neither required to hold nor given documents on entry. They were given automatic right to remain and had in many cases attended school and worked for more than four decades in the UK before the government started demanding documentation of them. Then were then targeted and subjected to racist treatment. They became victims of a policy designed to discourage immigration.

The Windrush scandal is a stark reminder that twenty-first-century British governments have enacted policies with explicitly racist outcomes. Racist harassment is not reserved for the most vulnerable but may be endured by any person of colour. The African-American Meghan Markle was first heralded as a symbolic step in the modernisation of the British monarchy when her engagement to Prince Harry was announced but the modern fairy-tale love story fast degenerated into racist attacks.

The work of expert historians of Britain's imperial past, taken on board by organisations such as the National Trust to present a more accurate history of some of the properties they run and explain how their associated wealth was acquired, is rejected by organisations and politicians with a political agenda. Such politicians urge schools to teach about the glory of empire. Academic historian Alan Lester argues that the distancing, denial and disavowal policy practiced by groups such as Restore Trust, who want to avoid any re-examination of history, is part of a deliberate strategy to refute the claims of Black and brown Britons who want recognition. He concludes: 'Acknowledging a divided past of White supremacy is the first step towards a shared, multi-racial future. Disavowing the racial divisions of the past is a recipe for division in the future'.[1]

Society does not simply grow out of the racism of the past. We do not necessarily see improvements in levels of tolerance and justice. For things to change for the better, injustices cannot be left for people of colour to endure or challenge. Twentieth-century struggles for greater racial justice, led primarily by migrants and the children of migrants from former British colonies, have not guaranteed a just future for later generations. This is, in part, because all struggles for justice are ongoing and incomplete and therefore need to be renewed, but also because the current national and international political climate is marked by renewed authoritarianism, intolerance and disregard for the most vulnerable. Racism expresses itself in different forms and needs to be challenged anew in each generation.

I know how much racist words and actions, directly or indirectly, invariably continue to hurt children.

Esmé with Audrey and baby Charles, 1955

4

When British meant white: Singapore 1934–45

Hilda and Walter Roberts, Singapore, 1939

The tick-tock man announced his arrival each evening by playing a distinct rhythm on two pieces of bamboo; we would hear him before we saw him under the streetlights. He was selling delicious hot Chinese food, such as Hainanese chicken rice, Hokkien prawn mee (rice noodles), nasi lemak (rice cooked in coconut milk), each wrapped in banana leaves. It was 1965, I was twelve years old and on my first visit to Singapore island, before it evolved to become the shiny city-state it is today, making it easier for me to imagine how Singapore might have looked, sounded and smelled three decades earlier, when my mother first set foot there as a seven-year-old, along with her mother Hilda and her two brothers, Dudley and Ralph. Singapore had largely recovered from the destruction and economic shock of the Second World War bombing and occupation, and was confidently asserting its independent identity.

My own childhood memories remain vivid, no doubt because this was the first time I had travelled outside the UK. We'd made the thirty-six-hour journey by plane so Esmé could return to visit her parents for the first time after sixteen years of separation, and we were staying with family friends, Tiny and Roland, in the suburban neighbourhood of Serangoon Gardens.

I soon appreciated how much of Singapore social life centred on sharing food with friends. Culinary skills were never a prerequisite for joining in, since there were infinite varieties of Indian, Chinese or Malay fare for sale, easily and cheaply available from the tick-tock man and various other hawkers who plied their trade on the streets or set up stalls at the outdoor food centres. Eating curry puffs in a lively café after a Sunday morning church service felt so much more fun than returning home in England to a roast lunch.

The Serangoon Gardens neighbourhood was well named; bungalows were set in lush green gardens, and ceiling fans whirred, somewhat ineffectively, to cool the hot, humid, cloying August air. At night we slept under mosquito nets, which I quickly learned to tuck in carefully around the edges. Deep, open concrete monsoon drains marked the sides of the roads. The local shops included a European-style café where I was allowed to go alone and, if my pocket money permitted, treat myself to a coke with an ice-cream float.

I found myself with more freedom to explore than I normally would have been given for, sadly, my grandfather died two weeks after our arrival, and the adults were all suddenly busy and preoccupied. One of the things I did was to try out my language skills. At home we had a book, *Teach Yourself Malay*, in which I had shown an interest from the age of about seven. Having established that no one among my peers knew any Malay, I had practised it as a secret code. Now, in Singapore, I was able to turn this code into a means of communication.

I was surprised one evening to spot our host Roland on TV, just before he was due home from work, discussing politics and Singapore's breakaway from the Malaysian Federation – its effective beginning as an independent nation.[1] In fact, it turned out to be Roland's brother, a minister in the Singapore government. This was one of many examples that made me realise that Singapore was, in many respects, a small, everyone-knows-everyone country, and perhaps still is. I met adults from a much wider range of walks of life than I had ever encountered in the UK. Networks of people who had grown up and gone to school together continued to keep in touch and support each other, whether they were part of the country's elite, in professional roles such as law and teaching, or among those whose childhood traumas from the war years had left them vulnerable and on society's outer edges, without regular employment or secure homes.

In the evenings, we sometimes visited a brightly lit *pasar malam*, a night market that seemed to sell anything and everything, including varieties of fruit I had either never come across in 1960s England or only ever tasted from cans. Lychees, for example, turned out to have beautiful, rough, bumpy, rose-pink outer skins and to be much creamier than the tinned version with which I was familiar. Rambutans were much sweeter and had deeper pink-coloured outer skins that looked as if they might be spiky, but turned out just to be hairy. We were in Singapore at the height of the durian season, and its pungent cheese-like aroma permeated the air, but I refused to taste this fruit, since I was convinced smell and taste went together. I would linger over the dizzying collections of trinkets on display including plastic bangles, embroidered silk purses, small Buddhas and carved wooden buffalos. A visit to the *pasar malam* inevitably included a stop at one of the ubiquitous food stalls with their seductive aromas.

For me, who from early childhood was addicted to any live performance of theatre or dance, and who had once, still dreaming, walked into a lamp-post on the way home from school after watching a dress rehearsal of *A Midsummer Night's Dream*, the best part of any evening, apart from staying up late, was the open-air Chinese *wayang*, or street opera. The word *wayang* means puppet in Malay, but street opera features human performers. In truth, I could barely distinguish the human actors, high up on their stage, from puppets, with their long, elaborate, colourful costumes, garish masks, and white and red painted faces. There were incessant, yet ever-startling, cymbals and gongs, and melodic string instruments. Each performer delivered their lines loudly, either singing or speaking in a high-pitched voice, performing in exaggerated ways, and with make-up and costumes that made it easy to distinguish the goodies from the baddies. The ability to understand the language, Teochew, was not essential to enjoyment of the show, and it attracted a multilingual audience. The whole spectacle allowed everyone to follow something of the story, whether it was one of tragic love, heroic tests of physical strength, loyalty to family clan, or perhaps some mixture of all three.

Most of these aspects of Singaporean life I first experienced in the 1960s, such as the tick-tock man, the Chinese *wayang* and the *pasar malam*, would have certainly been around in the 1930s when my mother arrived in Singapore. Today, Singapore citizens still enjoy the *pasar malams*, located across the city, and were reportedly rushing back to them in 2022 after a two-year closure due to COVID-19 restrictions. They remain crowded and lively, yet they look somewhat different – no longer a string of trestle tables set out along the side of the road, but more like giant marketplaces with semi-permanent stalls. By the beginning of the twenty-first century only a few elderly people were showing up to watch the *wayang*, and the Teochew language or dialect, originally from the Chinese Eastern Guangdong province, is today spoken and understood by few people outside of China. Nevertheless, during the pandemic, some *wayang* performances went online. While it is difficult to claim that Chinese *wayang* is making a comeback, the now elderly players are finding new global audiences on YouTube. Sadly, the tick-tock man is no more. This tradition was probably fading out even as I encountered it.

Singapore, as it was in the 1930s and even the 1960s, is barely recognisable as the same place as today's city-state with its luxury shopping, high-rise geometric architecture, vertical gardens and public housing programmes. Back then, on the island of Singapore, there was something of a divide between the city, its suburbs and the luxuriant green countryside, some of it still covered by forest and mangroves. Perhaps the common thread through the decades is the famous food culture. Yet in 1934, when my grandparents set up home with their three children, Singapore was by no means a frontier town. The multiple new smells, flavours, sounds, dress styles and colours that Esmé and her brothers encountered must have made as deep an impression on the three children arriving from India as they did on me, arriving from England, three decades later.

They came from Madras, and were simply moving from one part of the British Empire to another. I was travelling from London, the former imperial metropolis, to what had been a far-flung but extremely important colonial possession, a key seaport enabling Britain's wealth, trade and standing in the world. For me, the trip was exciting because I was visiting the country with which my mother identified and where she had grown up, and meeting my grandparents for the first time. I knew relatively little about Singapore's history, or its importance to Britain over the previous 200 or so years.

A prized seaport and colonial territory

Singapore did not develop gradually, like most other great seaports. Before the nineteenth century, none of the European colonial powers seemed particularly interested in the island, although they had each sought to extend their influence and economic power across the region, including the Malay peninsula and wider archipelago, encompassing the islands of modern-day Indonesia. The Portuguese were the first Europeans to arrive in the region, eventually capturing Malacca (Melaka) in 1511 from Mahmud Shah, and destroying a settlement in Singapore, around 150 miles to the south. Portuguese traders and colonists were followed by the Dutch and British.

The presence of the Portuguese, Dutch and British in the region is aptly illustrated by a visit to Malacca, today a three-hour journey from Singapore by road, and the town's colonial-era church buildings. Tourists will find the ruins of the sixteenth-century Portuguese grey-stone church, St Paul's, at the top of the hill, and the mid-eighteenth-century Dutch, red-painted lower church at sea level. These two churches together tell the European colonial story in brief. St Paul's and the accompanying Portuguese fortress are the remains of the first European Christian trading base in South-East Asia, which was surrounded by numerous Malay Muslim sultanates. The Dutch conquered the city in 1641, ousting the Portuguese, banning Catholic worship and reconsecrating the Portuguese church for their own Protestant worship. The upper church, or *Bovenkerk* as it became known by the Dutch, was used by them for well over a century. They then built the lower Dutch Reformed Church, deconsecrated the old church, and incorporated it into the town's fortifications, and continued their worship for a further seventy years at the bottom of the hill. The lower church stands today alongside other public buildings they built in the old town square.

In 1824, following the signing of the Anglo-Dutch Treaty, Malacca came under the control of the British East India Company, and some years later the lower church was in turn reconsecrated as an Anglican place of worship and renamed Christ Church. It seems a hallmark of the colonising authorities that they each, in turn and across the centuries, stamped everything with a new name and asserted their religion as superior to all others. The new colonial power seemed impelled to proclaim its authority in this way. The upper Portuguese church was used by the British as a powder magazine and allowed to fall further into disrepair. Today's visitors might be forgiven for assuming that the distinctive red colour of Malacca's Dutch colonial buildings reflects the appearance of the town while under Dutch control. In fact, they were originally painted white, and it was not until long after the Dutch had given up control of the town that the church and neighbouring *Stadthuys* or town hall were painted red. It is the same red as many houses and barns across Scandinavia, a colour relatively cheap to produce in the early twentieth century and no doubt easy to maintain.

It was only in 1819, more than three centuries after the Portuguese had established themselves in the region, when any colonial power appeared to see potential in Singapore island, situated at the tip of Malaya. It was then that Sir Thomas Stamford Raffles negotiated with the sultanate of Johor to permit the British to establish a trading port on the island. In 1867, the British established Singapore as a crown colony, opening the way for the future development of Singapore as an important seaport within the British Empire. Within a few decades, Singapore had become an international port whose fortunes were dependent, to a considerable extent, on the global economic climate.

The 1929 Wall Street crash, and the subsequent loss of important United States trade in tin and rubber – key materials in the manufacture of cars and tyres – no doubt left their mark, for few people could afford the luxury of a new car. Yet by 1934, Singapore seemed to have bounced back and its future looked positive. Despite the global depression, it remained a lively and resilient city, and a port of considerable economic and strategic importance. It was a magnet for migrants either fleeing conflict in China or pulled in from other parts of Asia slower to recover from recession.

1930s Singapore

In the 1930s, newcomers to Singapore city centre would have been struck by the distinctive British colonial architecture and handsome, probably unmatched, Botanical Gardens, where those with leisure might relax in the shade, enjoy a concert from the bandstand or even have a picnic, if they were willing to run the risk of sharing it with monkeys. These gardens, created in 1859 close to Orchard Road, the upmarket shopping district of the day, with its fancy department stores, were certainly an oasis in bustling, early twentieth-century Singapore.

Residents and visitors alike might stroll along wide avenues and observe the imposing white Palladian or neo-classical-style government buildings set in acres of green lawns, all designed to impress. Generally speaking, those with money in their pockets, and particularly Europeans, would not choose to stroll anywhere during daylight hours on account of the powerful sun, sweltering heat and humidity. This heat persists through the night and, without the aircon which modern Singaporeans take for granted, the only relief came under the huge electric ceiling fans which graced public buildings, restaurants and coffee shops, and of course, the extensive airy houses and bungalows of the more affluent, comfortable suburbs.

Away from the administrative centre, people were packed more closely together, frequently living in overcrowded and unsanitary conditions. Among the cramped housing were small temples, and the smell of incense mingled with that of the throng of the clammy, sweaty inhabitants forced to live cheek-by-jowl.

People seemed to follow their own religious practices without unnecessary pretentions or questioning of each other's traditions, as part of everyday life. In the area known as Little India, on Serangoon Road, close to where my grandparents would make their home, was the dazzling Sri Veeramakaliamman Temple, built in the Dravidian style of southern India, with an elaborate collection of colourful statues. Small mosques were scattered across the island, in rural *kampong* or villages, while the impressive Masjid Sultan, built in 1824, with its massive golden domes, stood proudly in the central district known as Kampong Gelam. St Andrew's Cathedral, constructed in the 1850s in Gothic revival style, using Indian convict labour, stood equally proudly overlooking the open space of the Padang, across from Singapore Cricket Club.

In the economic slump of the 1930s, the streets were busy with people working as street hawkers, selling food, and as rickshaw pullers. With many people underemployed and no government social security, large numbers of people relied on the informal economy. Families and friends, coming from the same place, would support new migrants to the city, providing housing and work opportunities.[2] The British authorities in Singapore offered no social security safety net such as existed in the UK during these difficult years.

For those who were not members of the elite that enjoyed the use of a motor car, the best way to move about the city, travel to work, go shopping or visit the entertainment districts was to hail a rickshaw. A Chinese rickshaw puller stood between two shafts at the front of a small carriage just big enough for one or two adults. Dressed in a loose shirt and baggy trousers often cut off below the knee or mid-calf, and wearing a wide conical hat of woven bamboo or cane to protect him from the sun or torrential rain, the puller would run from place to place delivering his passengers. Rickshaw pullers did not own their vehicles but worked for a Chinese owner. The other main source of transport in the city centre, and the most commonly used one to travel out to the various suburbs, was the electric trolley buses that operated alongside the rickshaws, bicycles and a few motor cars.

Singapore's status as a trading city was illustrated by the godowns, giant warehouses that lined the busy river, where goods were loaded and unloaded, and men shouted instructions to and from the boats. The river made itself known long before it came into view by its overwhelming stench. It not only carried colourfully painted Chinese junks but much of the settlement's sewage, and was not cleaned up until the late 1970s. Today, the few remaining Chinese junks are not working boats, but tourist gloss. The godowns, full of spices, rubber and tin, have now made way for smart restaurants or been repurposed as luxury hotels or upmarket emporia.

In twenty-first-century Singapore, it's sometimes difficult to imagine the city of the past, since so much has simply disappeared. The once ubiquitous, brightly painted, sometimes peeling and frequently highly decorated shophouses, with their Chinese lettering, that lined the streets are now few and far between. These two- or three-storey terraced buildings, graced by five-foot walkways – narrow arcades along the ground-floor shop frontage, protecting pedestrians from the sun – were largely torn down in the 1970s. Those that remain no longer sell useful, everyday goods, spilling from the shop on to the pavement, and have also been repurposed. They are now described as heritage sites, their arcades decorated with potted plants, selling tourist tat or expensive handcrafts, or used as boutique hotels.

Today, the simplest way of uncovering Singapore's past is through a visit to the National Museum. In this hi-tech facility not only the streets but the smells of the past have been recreated, although the worst of these are thoughtfully contained. Singapore's complex history is retold there, but in this retelling some of its complexity and its contradictions have, I fear, been lost, and some of its people and their stories made invisible.

Singapore was built not as one city, but many. The British laid out their plans with specific areas designed for the various ethnic groups: Chinese, Malays, Indians, and Eurasians and Europeans. Street names, such as Arab Street, offer insights into the origins of former traders. Malays frequently lived in *kampong* or rural villages, a way of life that continued into the early 1970s, when most *kampong* were bulldozed and their inhabitants moved to the extensive public housing projects for which the modern city of Singapore is well known.

A rural *kampong* was made up of traditional Malay houses with walls of hardwood. They were often constructed on stilts to protect against flood and vermin, with verandas and thatched attap or zinc roofs. In these rural settings, the residents would grow much of their own food and keep chickens. But during the economic slump of the 1930s, it was not just Malays who were into market gardening or small-scale farming. Anyone fortunate enough to have a small plot of land cultivated vegetables and kept livestock to help make ends meet.

Back then, some suburban housing was still edged by forest or mangrove, and any such home left unattended for more than a year in the hot, humid climate would quickly begin to be swallowed up by creeping vegetation. In 1967, then prime minister Lee Kuan Yew envisioned Singapore as a garden city and attempted to weave greenery into the urban planning for the city-state. By the 1980s, urban planners were planting 'instant trees' along the highways. Today, they are reimagining the garden city of Singapore and building vegetative buildings or vertical gardens.

Singapore is densely populated, with around 5.7 million people on a land mass of 719.9 square kilometres (278 square miles). That means more than 7,800 people per square kilometre. Visitors or residents in search of a green space need to head for a public park or a reserve like Bukit Batok Nature Park. There are no longer swathes of forest separating the city from some of its suburbs, and the original rural areas of the early twentieth century have long since disappeared. The protected wetlands and mangrove forests, while important, are only small pockets of green.

Yet the vision of veteran architect and urban planner Cheong Koon Hean, CEO of the Housing and Development Board in 2010–20, has enabled the garden city concept to come into its own in the twenty-first century.[3] There are some amazing trails, such as the 10-kilometre Southern Ridges recreational trail that links five parks. Visionary planning has enabled Singapore residents to enjoy a much greener lifestyle than, say, the residents of Hong Kong, an island city with a landmass roughly one and a half times that of Singapore, less densely populated overall, yet one that has struggled to address similar urban planning challenges. Extensive land reclamation projects mean that many of the original beautiful beaches have simply disappeared, and Beach Road as well as the colonial-era Raffles Hotel, which once overlooked the sea, now lie somewhat inland. Its sea views have been replaced by those of bustling shopping malls. In Singapore, nature is not always what it seems, but has been recreated. The best Singapore beaches may well be the artificially constructed ones off Sentosa Island.

Migrants from India

In 1934, my grandmother, Hilda Roberts, made the ten-day journey from Madras to Singapore by steamship with her three children, to re-join her husband, Walter, who had found work there. Hilda and the children almost certainly travelled on one of the two British India Steam Navigation Company sister ships plying this route, the *Rhona* or the *Rajula*, docking in Rangoon, in Burma (Yangon, Myanmar) and Penang before arriving in Singapore. Travelling with three young children, Hilda may well have shared a berth with another family. Nevertheless, a cabin, even for shared use, represented upmarket travel. The ships crossing the waters between India and the Malacca Strait commonly carried a large number of deck passengers – travellers who had secured cheap passage and each night rolled out their mats to sleep on deck. Most of those coming from India, like the Roberts family, were migrants seeking work in Malaya or Singapore. All were, of course, travelling from one part of the British Empire to another.

The couple had spent eighteen months apart while Walter looked for work in Singapore, where his brother Alfred was employed on the naval base. In this respect, Walter was following a common pattern of migration to the city, whether from India or China, with new migrants looking to family members already settled in the city to assist them in finding work. Hilda and the children had been staying at her father's home in Madras, until Walter was once more in a position to provide a home for his family. Singapore had, of course, experienced the impact of the global economic depression, but by 1934 things appeared to be looking up, and once Walter found a job and a suitable home for the family, they were reunited.

Unlike most migrants, Walter was not only literate, but also city-educated and a high school graduate, so probably had high hopes of a good job. In fact, the first stable employment he could find was working for the British and Foreign Bible Society, a missionary organisation that paid very modest wages and relied on the commitment of its workers, and so the family had to manage with very little money. This work came to an end with the outbreak of war, and it was only in the post-war period that Walter finally found a job with better pay and conditions, working as an immigration officer for the Singapore Harbour Board.

The world was an unstable place in 1934, but Walter could not have anticipated the turmoil into which his family would shortly be plunged in the Second World War. Japan had been militarising rapidly from the 1920s. In 1931, it had invaded Manchuria, in north-east China, taking control of the area rich in natural resources, and set about establishing a puppet state. In 1934 it renamed the province Manchukuo. That year also saw the Great Fire of Hakodate in Hokkaido, with an official death toll of 2,166, nearly 10,000 people injured and over 145,000 people made homeless. One of the worst city fires in Japan, it wasn't caused by an earthquake but spread from a house fire that quickly destroyed not only neighbouring wooden dwellings, common in Japanese cities of that era, but two-thirds of the city, including school and hospital buildings, a courthouse and a department store. Later in 1934, a typhoon in Osaka killed over 1,600 people and ruined the rice harvest. To the superstitious, such events must have felt like portents of a dark future.

Perhaps the European colonial powers, concerned first with the threat of fascism and then war in Europe, were too distracted by developments at home to pay much attention to their colonies in the East. As in Japan, nationalist and authoritarian movements were strengthening their grip on many European countries. In February 1934, there was an attempted far-right coup d'état in France; Adolf Hitler was consolidating the power of the Nazi Party in Germany; and in June 1934 he met the Italian Fascist leader Benito Mussolini for the first time. June and July 1934 saw a string of political assassinations by the Nazis, marked by the Night of the Long Knives in Germany and followed by the assassination of the Austrian chancellor a few weeks later. In Britain, the influence of the British Union of Fascists declined as British hostility to Nazi Germany grew, yet the party continued to exploit anti-semitic feelings in London and elsewhere.

The rise of fascism and the threat of war were clearly not the preoccupations of the three young children, adjusting to their new life and new schools in Singapore. This was the year that Disney's Donald Duck make his first film appearance, albeit in a supporting role, in *The Wise Little Hen*. And the *Daily Mail*'s publication of a photo of the Loch Ness Monster in April that year provided a welcome distraction for all ages. The story was picked up by newspapers across the globe including Singapore's the *Straits Times*.

It is perhaps only with hindsight that we might judge Singapore in the mid-1930s as a poor choice of location to build a new life and bring up a family. In 1934, most people living in India, Burma or Malaya who studied a map of the region would probably have concluded that Singapore, with its substantial naval base and military presence, was incredibly safe. The British authorities were, at that stage, firmly of that opinion, as it was one of the most heavily defended places in the empire.

The house in Sophia Road

Walter could not afford private accommodation for the family. Instead, the couple and their three children lived on the ground floor of a large, sprawling old house in Sophia Road. Above them were a middle-class Chinese couple and their daughter,

Stella. Situated in a spacious compound, there was plenty of room both indoors and out for the three children: Dudley, aged nine, his sister Esmé, who was seven, and the baby of the family, five-year-old Ralph. There was a large, grassed area, where the Roberts children and Stella set up improvised tennis and volleyball games. The family could no longer afford live-in servants as in Madras, but Hilda, used to such support, had part-time help for cooking and childcare. Ralph was frequently in the care of a Chinese amah (the East Asian name for an ayah or maid), and became a fluent Mandarin speaker.

Their upstairs neighbour, Mr Thé, set up a shorthand and typing class. Underemployment meant that middle-class, as well as working-class, Singapore residents had to be creative to earn sufficient money to support their families. The Chinese couple on the upper floor were no exception. During the daytime, they set aside part of their living accommodation for Mr Thé to teach his private classes. The students were dubbed the Pitmanites, after the Pitman shorthand system they studied.

The children's home life was totally transformed from what they had known in India. In Madras, they had lived as part of a large extended family, in the comfort of Hilda's parental home, with Grannie Lydia and Grandpa William Weston. Removed from their grandparents, aunts and uncles, and from the cousins they had grown up with, they had to make a considerable adjustment. Esmé was later to look back on those carefree childhood days in Madras with fondness.

The house in Sophia Road was not far from the city centre, and could be easily reached by trolley bus or rickshaw. It was on a hillside, with Little India to one side, and not far from Government House, the mansion built on a former nutmeg plantation and completed in 1867 in the style of an eighteenth-century neo-Palladian colonial Indian mansion. This mansion had been designed for Singapore's first colonial governor, after the British crown took control from the East India Company. Today, it's the Istana, the official residence of the president of Singapore and the working office of the prime minister. Esmé recalled the considerable diversity of the city in which she found herself, with 'a mixed population of other Eurasians, Chinese, Indians, Malays, and Japanese, as well as a Dutch and English community'. She also remembered Japanese migrants from that pre-war era, running small businesses, generally cheap ten-cent stores.

As in India, the family attended church each Sunday morning and the children returned in the afternoon for Sunday school. Their Christian worship was not confined to going to church. Each morning, Walter would lead the family in singing the hymn, 'Holy, Holy Holy! Lord God Almighty' while they ended the day with the lullaby hymn: 'Day is Done But Love Unfailing'. Writing this in Wales, I like to imagine them singing it to the Welsh tune, 'Ar Hyd Y Nos' (All Through the Night). While in Madras, Hilda had come into contact with the Christian Brethren and so it was at their church in Bras Basah Road that the family worshipped.[4] The church was situated in one of the older central areas of town, which includes the National Museum and the National Archive and now makes up part of the cultural and arts district. Each Sunday afternoon, the same rickshaw puller would be waiting for the children outside the compound to take them to Sunday school, and the children would return home by trolley bus. Although the Singapore of this era had a reputation for its underworld, drugs and crime, it seems that it was considered quite safe for the children to travel independently to and from school and Sunday school.

New routines were quickly established. As in Madras, all three children were sent to Anglican schools. Esmé attended St Margaret's, the oldest girls' school in the city and a short walk from her home, while her brothers, Dudley and Ralph, travelled three miles out of town to another Anglican school. All three children were still of primary-school age, but both schools had primary and secondary departments, and the plan was for them to complete their schooling at one institution. Their parents must have been glad to offer them some stability after uprooting them from Miri in Borneo, where they were born, and then again from Madras.

War time

The global threat of war grew through the 1930s, though no doubt those not yet affected, across both Europe and Asia, assumed in a spirit of trust that it would not touch them directly. By 1937, Japan controlled large swathes of China and that year Major General William Dobbie, the British officer who oversaw the Malaya Command (1933–9), commissioned an inquiry to assess the risks of a Japanese attack on the Malay peninsula, and ways of forestalling any such attack. The inquiry concluded that Singapore could no longer be viewed as a self-contained naval base, asserting that more forces were urgently needed on the peninsula to prevent the conquest of the island.[5] Dobbie raised these concerns again in 1938:

> It is an attack from the northward that I regard as the greatest potential danger to the fortress [of Singapore]. Such an attack could be carried out during the period of the

north-east monsoon [October–March]. The jungle is not in most places impassable for infantry.[6]

Dobbie's recommendations were shelved. By 1939, war had broken out in Europe. It seems that the British authorities were focused on Europe. In an attitude that mixed arrogance with complacency, Britain remained confident that its military could withstand a Japanese attack on Malaya and Singapore. Along with most Singapore residents, the Roberts family placed their faith in the authorities' preparations and their judgement that they would be safe.

By late 1941, tensions were rising and, at school, the Roberts children were drilled in what to do in the event of an air-raid. They were issued with ID tags, so they could be identified in the supposedly unlikely event of an attack. Yet the official view was still that Singapore was safe, and that people's lives were set to continue more-or-less uninterrupted. Both Singapore and Malaya had received additional regiments of soldiers to support their defence, with fresh troops arriving from India, Australia and New Zealand. Most of these young men had never fought in a war.

December marked the end of the school year and the long school holidays began. Esmé was fourteen years old, and had just completed her Junior Cambridge examinations.[7] She was considered a bright student and had been put a year ahead of her age group. She was expected to do well and go on to study for college entry, and her ambition was to be a teacher. The exam papers were due to be mailed to the UK but it is not clear whether they were sent or, if so, whether they ever arrived.

On 8 December, well before daybreak, the first air-raid on Singapore began. Although the air-raid sirens sounded, there was no blackout, making it all too easy for the enemy to hit their targets. This was the terrifying first indication to the Singapore population that war had broken out in South-East Asia. That day, Walter enrolled as a member of the Singapore Local Defence Corps, a civilian volunteer force assembled to repel the Japanese military.

In a series of synchronised attacks, on 8 December, units of the Japanese Imperial Army landed in a number of places along the east coast of the Malay peninsula and in the southern part of Thailand. It seems that the British only started to suspect that an attack was imminent a couple weeks before it happened. Across the Pacific, thousands of miles away, the Japanese carried out a simultaneous attack on the US naval base at Pearl Harbor on 7 December (the different date simply reflecting the date line across the Pacific). Amphibious landings were supported by bombing the air bases at Alor Setar, Sungai Petani and Butterworth, in the north-west of the Malay Peninsula, effectively wiping out the Allied air defence while the aircraft were on the ground.

In northern Malaya there was an exodus south, with Chinese and Europeans managing rubber plantations, or working as mining engineers or in local government, heading with their families towards Penang, hoping to flee by boat to India or to Singapore. The roads were busy with traffic as people hurriedly grabbed what few possessions they could and fled. Arriving in Penang, it quickly became clear that only Europeans would be evacuated, although plainly they were not the only ones fleeing to safety. Many people feared the *Kempeitai*, the Japanese secret police, would have information about them. Certainly, the Japanese invasion was aided by a string of spies. Meanwhile, the north–south highway to

Singapore was clogging up with traffic. Refugees and soldiers who had become separated from their units in early battles with the Japanese were also fleeing south.

This focus on the evacuation of British and European citizens seems disturbingly similar to what happened in Afghanistan in August 2021, when a large-scale evacuation of foreign residents occurred but many vulnerable Afghans, such as those who had worked as interpreters for the military, were left behind when US and NATO troops departed, following the fall of Kabul to the Taliban. Britain's imperial project in Malaya and Singapore, and the wealth it generated, depended on a large number of non-European inhabitants, mostly Chinese and Eurasian, who served in key roles in the government, police and judiciary, and as managers of key enterprises, such as mines and rubber estates. Yet when it came to saving human lives, the British authorities and military focused on white British and fellow European citizens, such as the Dutch. Others, of non-European or mixed European heritage, a number of whom saw themselves as British and indeed had been educated to see themselves as such, and had acted loyally to Britain and British enterprise, were simply discarded.

The Japanese quickly established naval supremacy, and on 10 December sank the battleship HMS *Prince of Wales* and other ships that had only just arrived in the area. On land, the Japanese soldiers quickly made their way south. Several decades later, Esmé recalled that the Japanese soldiers 'rode bicycles through the Malay peninsula, occupying the whole country.' It seems these bicycles were not brought with them, as that would have complicated the beach landings, but were systematically confiscated from civilians and retailers as soon as the troops landed. The bicycles allowed the Japanese forces to move at speed and attack the retreating Allied forces. By cycling along backways and plantation roads, the Japanese soldiers were also able to surprise forces guarding bridges and other strategic positions on main roads, attacking them from the rear. Although bicycles had been used in wartime before, this was probably the first time that they were used so effectively by infantry.

The Japanese did not take prisoners, which would certainly have slowed them down; it seems they were instructed to kill any enemy soldiers they captured. By 11 January 1942, a month after their arrival on the Malay peninsula, the Japanese military occupied Kuala Lumpur and were less than 200 miles from Singapore.

Fleeing refugees and soldiers separated from their units swarmed into Singapore. The military personnel and civilian volunteers like Walter who had joined the defence force were resisting attack and dealing with regular air raids, including daytime raids from 12 January, after the capture of Kuala Lumpur. Esmé recalled how the family were forced to seek shelter in the monsoon drains in the garden.

Throughout the campaign, the Allies had greater numbers of ground troops, starting with 140,000, twice the number of Japanese military personnel in Malaya. But on 31 January 1942, the Allied forces retreated to Singapore, destroying the causeway that linked the island to Johore Bahru on the tip of the peninsula, overestimating, it seems, the numbers of enemy forces. Fortress Singapore's defences were designed to repel an attack from the sea, and the guns facing out to the water couldn't stop a land attack. The Japanese were soon crossing the narrow strait between Johore and Singapore in inflatable boats. The combined forces of between 85,000 to 90,000 Australian, British, Canadian, Indian and New Zealand military personnel on Singapore island alone seemed powerless in the face of the smaller Japanese force.

As in Penang, the British arranged for the evacuation only of European civilians, starting with women and children, and this mission was largely accomplished. The Japanese soldiers arrived on the island on 8 February. Most of the population of around a million was crammed into a small area of the town by this stage. Esmé experienced many of the hardships of occupation, but the thing she most resented was having her education cut short:

> Singapore held out for several weeks. My father was in the civil defence. There were Australians and New Zealanders in Singapore helping us. The Japanese were dropping bombs on us. The British were evacuated to India. On February 15 Singapore surrendered. The Japanese remained for three and a half years. We never went back to school again.

As in Penang, no serious attempt was made to evacuate anyone other than Europeans. As the ships started to depart, Walter tried to persuade Hilda to take the three children to Madras, but she refused: Walter, as a member of the civil defence force, could not join her and she didn't want to leave her husband behind. In any case, there was no guarantee that they would have been allocated places. The authorities made a clear distinction between the white British and other Europeans, like the Dutch, and those like my grandparents, my mother and uncles. Although all had been born in parts of the British Empire, either in Madras or, in the case of the children, in Miri, Sarawak, at this critical moment their Indian heritage and skin colour, however light, determined their second-class status. The decision not to protect those most vulnerable to the Japanese assault, including children and those who worked for the government, even those who held significant positions such as magistrates, was a moral failure, visible to the whole world, and the inference was clearly not wasted on the local population. Malaya and Singapore were British territories, but as far as the British colonial authorities were concerned, the British were white.

Living under occupation

We all had to register in so-called national groups: Chinese, Indians, Malays and Eurasians. The occupying forces interned a lot of people. Any British that remained were put in Outram Road prison in Changi.

This is how Esmé recalled treatment of different ethnic groups during the occupation. At one point, the soldiers tried to take Hilda away. She was quite fair-skinned and the Japanese soldiers took her to be a white woman. It was only when Walter showed her ID, which confirmed she was born in India, that they relented and let her go.

As ever in wartime, civilians suffered, but women were especially vulnerable:

To begin with everything was chaotic. Once things settled down, the town was fine but things gradually got worse. The island's food supplies were raided by the occupying army and we heard rumours that the food was being shipped to Japan to feed the Japanese people. Rice and other foods were rationed. The Japanese soldiers did not really bother us, but my cousin was taken away. They said she was raped. She was taken to live with this Japanese man. She had a baby, but she lost it. She was malnourished and got tuberculosis.

The family were forced to leave the house in Sophia Road and live in the countryside:

They took our home, which was in town, and comman- deered it for their own use. We had nowhere to go. My father had a friend in some sort of local government and he created a job for him. We moved into some unfinished bungalows in Yiochukang, on Serangoon Road. We had no running water and had to use a well, but there was electricity.

Despite the fact that Hilda, Walter and the children were physically unharmed by the Japanese military, all, including the children, were exposed to some of the worst atrocities of the occupation:

The Japanese didn't trust the Chinese and each hated the other. They took some of the young Chinese men – and some older men – and they shot them. It was said at the time that the Indians did not pose a problem to the Japanese since all they were thinking of was Independence. Many people lost their lives. On one occasion we heard how men had been beheaded and the heads displayed in town. My elder brother Dudley went to see for himself.

Following the British surrender on 15 February 1942, over a fifteen-day period there was a systematic purge, known as the Sook Ching massacre. Ethnic Chinese were targeted. Mass graves were discovered in 1962 and, in 1963, Singapore inaugurated a civilian war memorial for all those who had died, including those who were victims of the Sook Ching massacre. It is estimated that between 50,000 and 70,000 men and boys lost their lives at various mass execution sites across the island.[8]

It seems that Walter's efforts as a member of the Local Defence Corps extended beyond the initial attempts to repel the invasion. He was given a certificate of service from 8 December 1941 to 5 September 1945, but never talked to his family about any resistance activities in which he was involved. Esmé recounted:

I remember one night that some Chinese men came to our house. They wanted help from my father to enable some British men – some runaways – to escape. I'm not sure if he did this on more than one occasion. But we children did not really know what was going on – it was dangerous and it was important that we knew very little.

There was an acute shortage of food, and the family were in poor health:

We were all undernourished. My father got beriberi. My mother and I both had malaria, because they weren't able to keep the place clean. In Yiochukang we had a garden and we grew some vegetables, sweet potatoes and tapioca, because the rice ration for a month only lasted for two weeks. The bread produced was like rubber. By the end of the war my mother had lost a lot of weight and we just had two dresses between us which we shared.

As the occupation progressed, Walter was able to build some kind of working relationship with one or two Japanese officers. An officer would sit in the back of the church services, presumably charged with ensuring that nothing untoward was going on, and grew interested in the Brethren's religious beliefs.

Schools did not reopen for some time, and the children needed to find work to help support the family. Esmé found herself a job with the utility company, and recalled small acts of kindness from one particular officer, Kakamoto, towards the family:

> A Japanese officer who lived on his own nearby would sometimes come and sit with my father in the evening and talk. My younger brother Ralph had found work at the local telephone company and I found a clerical job. The trolley buses were very unreliable and the transport system was breaking down. This officer, Kakamoto, got us transport into town to work. I would carry vegetables from local suppliers with me into town to share with family and friends. Sometimes I had to walk the four miles or so back home after work, and I was sick for much of this time with malaria.

During the occupation, Esmé learnt to speak Japanese, and later in life she took this up again. Not realising the risks, she and her young fellow workers were invited to perform songs they had learned at the military camp and accepted the invitation:

In our lunch break we were offered Japanese lessons. In return we received a ration of rice. So, this was very attractive. We learnt some Japanese children's songs. We were asked to go to the military camp and sing them. My father was not at all happy about this but there was little we could do, once we had agreed. It worked out all right, but I never went again.

During the occupation, civilians often showed acts of kindness towards each other. This happened to the Roberts family, when they were forced to move a second time from their accommodation to make way for the Japanese military. This time, the family had to split up and Esmé's elder brother Dudley had to find somewhere else to live. Yet at a time of crisis, a further act of kindness came from an unexpected quarter:

After a short while we were forced to move out from our place in Yiochukang. The Japanese took the bungalow. We lost our garden and the food. But when my father was admitted to hospital with beriberi, Kakamoto came and visited him and placed some money under his pillow. One of our other neighbours, a Malaya-born Chinese woman – a *nonya* – was living with her partner, her son and her servant. Her partner volunteered to work on the railway; what became known as the Siam Death Railway. When the Japanese took the bungalow she invited us, my mother, father, and younger brother to stay in one room. This woman had only two bedrooms and a kitchen and toilet.

The occupation continued for three and a half years, and with the constant challenges and frequent dangers of everyday life, together with difficulties in getting independent news, and the disinformation and rumours this engendered, it must have seemed interminable. Esmé recalled how they learned that the war was coming to an end:

> You weren't supposed to listen to the radio broadcasts, but some people did. We knew something about the atomic bomb when it was dropped on Hiroshima in August 1945. We knew the Japanese were losing the war. When the bomb was dropped, Kakamoto broke down and cried.

A postscript

The post-war period saw continuing tensions and violence in the city. Esmé's older brother Dudley, who had more or less completed his schooling, found work as a draughtsman, but Ralph, the younger one, could not settle at school after the disruption of the occupation and left after some months, eventually finding employment on a rubber estate in Johore, just across the strait, in Malaya.

In June 1948, the British colonial authorities announced a state of emergency in Malaya, followed by a declaration of emergency some days later in Singapore itself, on 24 June.[9] Having acted as a resistance movement during the Japanese occupation, the Malayan Communist Party (MCP) first turned its attention to trade union activism, labour unrest and strikes, and, from 1948, to armed insurgency and a struggle for independence from the British. The Malayan

National Liberation Army, the armed wing of the MCP, began attacking rubber plantations, mines and police stations, and derailing trains.[10]

In response, British General Sir Harold Briggs, director of operations in Malaya in 1950–1 and a former officer in the Indian Army, devised a military plan that involved the destruction of people's homes and forced resettlement of more than 400,000 Chinese peasant farmers and indigenous people from their lands in Malaya and into new settlements.[11] The goal was to prevent civilians from supporting the communist guerrilla forces, or supplying them with food, information and possible recruits. Briggs's strategy echoes that of British commander Frederick Sleigh Roberts in the colonial Second Boer War (1899–1902) in southern Africa, who built concentration camps to corral civilians and prevent them from providing provisions to fighting men. In 1949, the mass displacement also saw the deportation of 10,000 ethnic Chinese from the Malay peninsula to the People's Republic of China.[12] In following the Briggs plan, the British authorities not only broke the newly agreed Geneva Convention relating to the treatment of civilians, but antagonised the local population.

With the rise in violence, Ralph left the rubber estate and returned to Singapore where, through his mother's contacts, he found a job in the police force. In the early 1950s, the MCP targeted British interests in Singapore with the aim of causing disruption and drawing the resources of the colonial power away from the armed struggle in Malaya. The communists carried out a string of violent acts, including sabotage and arson, murders and assassinations. There was a real risk of law and order breaking down in Singapore. Both Dudley and Ralph volunteered to help keep order in what were exceptionally tough times. Although Dudley was able to put his experiences during the occupation and the post-war conflict behind him, and went on from his work producing technical drawings to study as an architect in Australia, Ralph struggled. He drifted for many years, suffering from bouts of alcoholism, and never fully recovered until the 1980s, after both his parents had died.

Looking back across the decades it is difficult to imagine some of the harrowing experiences to which many civilians, including children, were exposed both during the Japanese wartime occupation and from 1948 onwards. This remains one of the unexplored and largely undiscussed consequences of empire. It seems that not just in Britain, but also in Singapore, the period 1948–60 on the Malay peninsula is barely discussed in accounts of the twentieth century. Certainly, this is the view of several local reviewers of *State of Emergency*, Jeremy Tiang's historical novel, largely set in the Singapore of this period.[13]

War and the subsequent anti-colonial struggle disrupted people's education, dreams and hopes, and although many, perhaps the majority, of those who survived went on to live fulfilling lives, others suffered for decades.

Maurice Osler, Singapore, 1947/48

5

An ambivalent belonging

Lydia Ann and William Weston, my great-grandfather. Madras, c.1920

It was the mid-1960s when I first met my maternal grandparents in Singapore. I recall them at the then tiny Changi airport, both dressed head-to-foot in white, with Hilda wearing a fitted dress and heeled shoes and stockings, despite the intense, cloying heat. By then Walter had turned seventy and

Hilda was in her late sixties. I didn't get to know either of them as a small child and so everything I have pieced together about their lives in India comes from stories my mother told me, from researching public archives and family documents, and from recent conversations with one of my mother's cousins who grew up in Madras in the 1950s.

Walter was a warm but serious character, ready to talk to the twelve-year-old me without the patronising manner that so many adults seemed to adopt back then. He was conscious of the standards of behaviour he should set for his grandchildren, and he first checked with my mother before he allowed himself to smoke a single cigarette each evening. Since we regularly saw our English grandfather smoking, it was not a problem. Hilda, by contrast, was quite playful, doing what seemed to me funny, curious things, like reading palms and telling fortunes, always in a light-hearted manner. They seemed a little old-fashioned, but this might have been because they were a decade or so older than our English grandparents. It might equally have been because they held on to some of the values of the Victorian era in which they were born; they had come of age before the First World War in a society of which I knew little, and Singapore was more socially conservative than my English neighbourhood.

The Westons

Hilda was born in 1897 and grew up in a comfortable home in the residential area of Pudupet, Madras. Her father, William Robert Weston, worked first as a foreman in a government printing office, later as a clerk and then as a prison officer, modest but secure jobs in government service that guaranteed a pension. In 1893, William married the eighteen-year-old Susan Amelia Sherman.

Sadly, Hilda, the couple's second child, never knew her mother, who died a few months after her birth. Her father remarried when she was less than three years old, and Hilda and her sister Mabel were brought up by their stepmother, Lydia Ann. Lydia Ann and William went on to have eight children. The youngest child was born after both Mabel and Hilda had left home to be married. One of the children, Beryl, recalled that on payday William would buy treats for the children, give Lydia sufficient money for housekeeping, and then spend the rest on drink.

Lydia Ann is not one of my direct ancestors, but she was an important family member. She was twenty-three when she married the widower William Weston, and cared deeply for her two stepdaughters and was well-loved by her many grandchildren. Esmé spoke very warmly of the woman she knew as Grannie. Born in Madras in 1878 to an Anglo-Indian mother and a rather feckless British soldier father, she was therefore, from the perspective of the colonial authorities, at risk of inheriting the very worst characteristics of both the Victorian working class and the 'natives'.

Her father, Joseph Walmsley, was a Lancashire weaver who became a soldier and married a girl from his hometown. When, in 1867, his regiment was sent to India just fifteen months after he had wed, he was obliged to leave his wife behind: a soldier did not get accommodation in barracks for his dependents or an extra living allowance.

The 1857 Indian Uprising had threatened the stability and prosperity of the British Empire and so Joseph's regiment, the 4th Queen's Own Hussars, were sent to enforce the authority of the Crown and ensure the British were not caught out again. Joseph was soon promoted to the rank of corporal and at some point, he either heard about the death of his English wife, or he assumed it, and he married Elizabeth Smith, an Anglo-Indian woman, and they had a child, Selie Blanche. By the 1870s when they wed, the colonial authorities were discouraging such mixed-race marriages. Doctrines of white racial superiority, promulgated by the colonial authorities in the second half of the nineteenth century, meant that it became unusual for British army officers to marry or live with Indian and Anglo-Indian women, as they had done previously. These wives and partners were excluded from social occasions and did not mix with European spouses, but officers had often acknowledged and provided for their children.

Working-class enlisted men, however, generally took little notice and Joseph's marriage was an 'off the strength' marriage, that is, one without permission from his superiors but nevertheless legally recognised. To complicate things, he then took a third wife, Margaret McGrath, an 'on the strength' marriage this time, shortly after which Elizabeth, still his second wife, gave birth to a second daughter, Lydia Ann. The first child died just two weeks later. Joseph's regiment left India in 1876, the year Lydia Ann was born, and Elizabeth was left to bring up her daughter alone. Joseph eventually returned to India around 1881 after his discharge from the army, and Elizabeth went on to have another two children and then died in childbirth. Joseph married yet again to a fourth wife and Lydia Ann was brought up by her from the age of six.

Then Joseph died and poor Lydia, aged twelve, was seemingly placed in an Anglican-run orphanage. Lydia was more fortunate than many Anglo-Indian children placed in these institutions, even when their parents were alive and well, for she was old enough to know something of her parents. From the late eighteenth century, the Bengal Military Orphan Society 'assisted' enlisted men and non-commissioned officers who had Anglo-Indian children by paying them a government subsidy of three rupees per month for each child. When a child reached the age of three, the soldier had to pay back the money at a rate that used up much of his weekly wage, or else he had to give the child over to the orphanage.[1] Anglo-Indian mothers were stereotyped as immoral and therefore unsuitable parents. Although the arrangements were theoretically voluntary, this loan system became a means of separating mixed-heritage children from their parents, and ensuring they were brought up as Christians and as useful, if second-class, members of society. This eighteenth century 'voluntary' separation of Anglo-Indian children from their mothers might be understood as an experiment by the colonial authorities, since it was a forerunner of mass forced removal of mixed-descent children – the Stolen Generations – from Aboriginal and Torres Strait Islander mothers into state and mission-run institutions in Australia from the late nineteenth century onwards.

Young people released from orphanages in India found it difficult, if not impossible, to trace their parents since records were poorly kept and sometimes did not even include their mothers' names. British rule in India was reliant on large numbers of working-class soldiers like Joseph serving for lengthy periods, yet the army and the colonial administration discouraged them from creating a family life. Effectively, the system broke up many Anglo-Indian families. Lydia's younger sister Lucy would have been totally dependent on her for any sense of who she really was.

Lydia would have been taught reading and writing, and received instruction in religion and morals, but other than training in domestic skills, she would have had few life choices. Marriage to the widower William – even if he was much older than her – would have been a relief for her. Her parents – and therefore Lydia Ann herself – were judged by the authorities to be shameful because by this stage of colonisation such uncondoned marriages and relationships accounted for the existence of a substantial Anglo-Indian community in late nineteenth- and early twentieth-century Madras. Thankfully, she found happiness and sense of purpose in creating a family life for Hilda and the other nine children, but what a deeply scarred childhood she had, thanks to her British soldier father and British colonial practices.

Hilda was of a generation of Anglo-Indian women who were neither educated for employment nor expected to work outside the home, but instead were being prepared to be good wives and mothers. She attended a school supported by the Anglican Christ Church, situated in the church compound. This was where her family worshipped, not far from their home. The school had both primary and secondary sections, and it is likely that Hilda would have completed her primary grades and remained at school until the age of thirteen or fourteen. She no doubt assisted her stepmother Lydia with the younger children, though Lydia also had an ayah to help her. Hilda was not trained for any specific work, but much later she did some voluntary teaching.

Her brothers and younger sisters, by contrast, did take up careers. Her younger brother Noel studied to be a pharmacist, eventually travelling to England to complete his studies, while his wife, Cynthia, worked as a nurse in India and later in England. I knew my great-uncle Noel quite well, but unearthing more about Hilda's family took quite some research.

In 2018, on my way to work on a peace and reconciliation project in Sri Lanka, I stopped off in Chennai (as Madras has been called officially since 1996) for a long weekend, hoping to find out more about my grandparents' early lives. On the Saturday morning, knowing the Weston family to have been Anglicans but not knowing where in the city they had lived, I took myself to the city's oldest Anglican church, St Mary's – actually India's first Anglican church, the original garrison church at Fort St George – thinking it would be a good starting point. I shared my quest with the caretaker who confirmed that the church held some records and encouraged me to return the next day, after the morning service, to meet the pastor. I had a flight to catch on Sunday afternoon, but I went back. Pastor Ruth Kiruba Lily Elizabeth invited me into her office in the vestry and asked me to tell my story again. I could tell I was an unusual visitor, a woman of Anglo-Indian heritage, looking for information about grandparents who had left the city around a hundred years ago.

Pastor Ruth would not be hurried, although I was all too aware I had a plane to catch. She asked many questions about my grandparents, about their move to Sarawak and then Singapore, my mother and her move to England, and wondered aloud on how these family stories had been passed through the generations, despite the various geographical dislocations. Then she opened the bottom drawer of her desk and pulled out a huge and somewhat dilapidated book, over 140 years old: a record of marriages. We read the handwritten entries, slowly turning the pages looking for the names Weston and Roberts, scanning the years between 1915 and 1925. I was ready to stop as I was certain my grandparents had left Madras by then, but Pastor Ruth persisted. We found

one relevant entry, the marriage in February 1927 of my great
uncle Harry Weston (Hilda's younger brother) aged twenty-
four, to the seventeen-year-old Thelma Nagle Joyce. Harry is
described as a 'cable operator' (a telephone operator who man-
ually connected callers by placing a plug into a switchboard).
In front of me was the signature of William Robert Weston,
my great-grandfather, acting as witness to his son's marriage.

I made it to the airport on time and a few days later I shared
my experiences in Chennai with my Sri Lankan university
colleagues. They were unsurprised by Pastor Ruth's interest
and so, on reflection, am I. I believe my family's storytelling,
and my curiosity about my grandparents' lives in Madras a
hundred years earlier, touched a chord with Pastor Ruth. My
colleagues, stressing how important it is, culturally, to know
who you are, suggested that, as a Christian and therefore a
member of a minority religion, the pastor would without
doubt be interested in an Anglo-Indian family who were twice
a minority, by religion and by ethnicity.

Although Hilda and her older sister Mabel did not work outside the home, their younger sisters took paid work, both before
and after marriage. Society changed after the First World War
and so did women's educational and training opportunities.
The younger sisters, who left school in the 1920s and 1930s,
entered the workplace at a moment when they and other
Anglo-Indian women had a wider range of options.

An Anglo-Indian lifestyle, like that of Europeans in India,
included Western-style meals, Western-style clothes and fashions, and, for most, household servants. These things were
relatively costly, and women's incomes were essential to accommodate this way of life. Ivy, whose husband Tom, a merchant
seaman from Britain, was constantly travelling, continued to

live in the family home and go out to work after her marriage. Her sister Beryl was a skilled stenographer and had a career in business administration, working for a multinational company, and so Lydia, after she was widowed, eventually came to live with Beryl and her husband Sam, and helped bring up her two daughters. The youngest sister, Lucy, took up nursing, a popular career among young Anglo-Indian women of her generation. Lucy married a man who worked on the railways, and so the couple lived in a railway colony, a purpose-built community that came with its own church, community buildings, shops, schools and other facilities that were designed to promote a sober European lifestyle among its European and Anglo-Indian residents, and discourage them from mixing socially with Indians.

Hilda's childhood home was a colonial-style villa with two floors, almost certainly rented rather than owned – since the family would have lacked sufficient resources to buy such a house – with a terracotta-tiled roof and high ceilings. Photos from the 1930s, when Hilda returned to India with her three children – my mother and her siblings – to stay with her parents while her husband looked for work in Singapore, show it was situated in a good-sized compound. Hilda would have shared a room with her children. There was a garden for Esmé and her brothers Dudley and Ralph to play in, and the rooms were likely built around one or two courtyards with louvred shutters and a wide veranda to allow a good flow of air. The courtyard would have a kitchen on one side, which may have linked it to a second courtyard. There would have been enough room to accommodate the three generations of the family – perhaps twelve or so people – living there during the early 1930s. The Weston children, particularly the girls, were known for their playfulness, and one of my mother's aunts, Ivy, was often the ringleader, teasing and playing jokes on her siblings, nephews and nieces, as my mother recalled. This was something that remained with them through to adulthood, for I recall how decades later when these sisters – by then in their forties and fifties, and living in England – got together, how much fun and laughter there would be.

The Roberts

My grandfather, Walter Roberts, grew up in the neighbour-hood of Vepery, not far from where the Westons lived. His family were originally Unitarians and were, according to my mother, said to own the Madras Christian Unitarian Church (more of which later in this story). In this respect, the family were distinctive within the wider Anglo-Indian community, for this was one of only two Unitarian churches across India. Although Walter's father, Samuel Turnbull Roberts, was orig-inally brought up in this tradition, it seems the Roberts family turned to Anglicanism towards the end of the nineteenth cen-tury. The India Office records show Walter's older brother and sisters being baptised into the Anglican church around 1889, both as adults and as children of around four to six years old. Presumably, they had previously been baptised in the Unitarian church, and these baptisms marked their new Anglican alle-giance. Before that, the records of the family are sparse, as the Unitarian church did not pass on its record of baptisms, mar-riages and burials to the colonial authorities, as was the custom in Anglican and some non-conformist churches. Walter was born in 1893 and baptised and brought up in the Anglican faith.

Walter's father, Samuel Turnbull Roberts, worked as a clerk

in the Public Works Secretariat in Madras. *Thacker's Indian Directory* records him as being on furlough in 1891 and therefore probably travelling to England. This implies he held a relatively senior position, unusual for an Anglo-Indian, but possible if his employers recorded him as European. This in turn suggests, first, that Samuel was relatively fair-skinned; and second, that his parents were able to give him a relatively good education, possibly alongside European boys, for example, the children of army officers. In the middle of the nineteenth century, attitudes to race had not hardened in the way they had by its end. Prior to the opening of the Suez Canal in 1867, which made travel to and from India easier, there may have been a shortage of relatively well-educated European men to fill civil service posts. This may have meant that no one asked too many questions about Samuel's parentage when he secured his post.

He was a widower with five children when he married for the second time. I was not able to discover the identity of Samuel's second wife, Walter's mother and my great-grandmother. My mother believed Walter's mother to be Portuguese, but 'Portuguese' was a term frequently applied to those in the Eurasian community who were of Indo-Portuguese rather than Indo-British heritage, and whose communities dated back to the sixteenth century. They frequently had Portuguese surnames and were often Catholics.

Indian nationalism and the beginning of the end of British rule

Samuel probably saw the public celebrations in Queen Victoria's golden jubilee in 1887, celebrations that took place across India as well as in Britain. In 1858, the British crown had taken direct control of India from the corrupt British East India Company, which had ruled much of the country for some 200 years. The queen's golden jubilee was not only seen as an opportunity to strengthen the power of the British in India but also to promote empire at home, and so a number of rulers of Indian princely states[2] were invited by Victoria to join the celebrations in London, alongside European royalty.

The occasion of the queen's jubilee was ineffective in shoring up an inefficient colonial administration and it could not mask growing antipathy to British rule. The authorities consciously and deliberately divided the population by class and ethnicity, and assumed that the mixed heritage Eurasian community of which my grandparents were a part would be loyal, and so they did not need to worry about winning their support. Yet Eurasians found themselves in an unsettled and unsettling position, between the British ruling class and the rest of the Indian population. The employment opportunities open to them were restricted, and shrinking. Few were wealthy or highly educated, and while some, like the Westons and the Roberts, were much better off than the mass of the Indian population, others were very poor.

Those engaged in the struggle for independence could look across to Canada for inspiration, where in 1867 four colonies had established a self-governing democratic state within the British Empire.[3] And in India there was growing political mobilisation in the second half of the nineteenth century. The founding of the Indian National Congress in 1885, although initially supported by urban elites, many of them educated in the universities of Madras, Calcutta and Bombay, marked an important stage in the growth of nationalist feeling. They were making demands on the colonial authorities, particularly in terms of civil rights and access to government positions. They held Britain responsible for draining India of its wealth. The economies of India and Britain were closely intertwined, with raw materials, notably cotton, being exported to Britain and finished textiles sent back to India to be sold in the burgeoning Indian markets. The British textile manufacturers grew rich at India's expense.

Those challenging British rule saw a direct link between the rulers' lack of accountability to the people and the poor living conditions and suffering they observed.

In 1911, when Walter and Hilda were still teenagers, they had been reclassified by the colonial authorities as Anglo-Indians. This term, which had previously been used to describe both Eurasians and Europeans born in India (sometimes referred to as domiciled Europeans), was applied to all of mixed heritage who could trace British descent through the male line. From the mid-nineteenth century onwards, people of mixed Indian and European decent had been variously classified for different official purposes, sometimes in contradictory ways. The administration attempted to defuse political opposition with a policy of 'Indianisation', which involved making concessions to Indians, opening up employment in the civil service and other sectors from which they had been excluded. This did little, of course, to address concerns about hunger or unfair trade. The official approach suggests that the colonial authorities saw nationalism and political opposition as an expression of discontent rather than a challenge to their legitimacy. Not only did they fail to secure loyalty from their Indian subjects by opening up jobs to some of them, but their policies left my grandparents, and others from the Anglo-Indian community, with an uncertain future.

The early twentieth century saw the further growth of Indian nationalism. At the turn of the century, a more radical faction of the nationalist movement challenged colonial education and its devaluing of Indian culture and values. Others were calling for religious freedom. Despite this, during the First World War, Indians made a significant contribution to the war effort in support of the British, with 1.3 million Indian soldiers and labourers serving in Europe, Africa and the Middle East. Indian princes contributed to the war effort with supplies of food, money and ammunition. The popular revolt the British feared did not occur.

But the 1915 Defence of India Act seemingly undermined, rather than strengthened, British authority in India, giving the British powers to use extreme force and intimidatory tactics to ensure Indians' submission to their will, including wide powers of preventive detention, internment without trial, and restrictions on writing, speech and on freedom of movement. Unlike parallel measures in the UK, there were no legal requirements to demonstrate that those targeted were, in fact, hostile to the authorities. The outcome, not surprisingly, was the generation of resentment and hostility at what were seen as restrictions on legitimate political activity. There were a number of failed conspiracies across the country and anti-colonial activity in Bengal and the Punjab, but the popular uprising the British feared still did not happen.

Some posts to which Anglo-Indians might have aspired, and for which they were appropriately skilled, remained closed and reserved for Europeans. Then, as we shall see, the authorities attempted to defuse political opposition by buying off one set of people at the expense of another, to the detriment of Anglo-Indians. Their race-based policies were emphasising and cementing differences between various sectors of the population.

As India edged its way towards independence, the Anglo-Indian community in early twentieth-century Madras found themselves in an uneasy position between the British and the rest of the Indian population. Their assumed loyalty to the British crown and their partial European heritage meant that they were often distrusted by their fellow Indians yet taken for granted by those in power. Official policy left many feeling neglected and misused, while the British colonial authorities' sense of inherent white superiority, strengthened by nineteenth-century Darwinian theory and early twentieth-century eugenics, judged anyone of mixed heritage inferior.

I do not know what either of my grandparents thought of the developing anti-colonial movement in India in the early twentieth century. What I can be confident of is that, along with members of Anglo-Indian communities across the country, they experienced the direct and detrimental impact of steps taken by the British authorities to maintain power and defuse and dispel the force of the growing Indian nationalist movement.

Employment opportunities

It is not clear what Walter did when he first left school. In the early twentieth century, Walter and other Anglo-Indian men living in Madras, categorised for employment purposes as statutory natives, found themselves excluded from many of the benefits of being European. Anglo-Indians have been described as being in a liminal position in colonial India and nowhere was this more the case than in employment.[4]

In the late nineteenth and early twentieth centuries, in both employment and social life, Anglo-Indians encountered race-based policies, prejudice, judgemental attitudes and exclusion. The ways in which the British authorities used Anglo-Indian personnel, both at times of civil unrest and in the vast government bureaucracy, meant that they were likely to be distrusted by and alienated from other Indian communities. Ironically, Anglo-Indians, increasingly treated with disdain by the European community, were, to those Indians challenging British authority, the very face of the British state.

While in the early nineteenth century Anglo-Indians were frequently characterised as *crannies* or clerks, and then later also as 'railway people', it is clear that at the beginning of the twentieth they spanned a wide range of employment sectors. So, for example, while officially Anglo-Indians were excluded from combat roles in the military, those with fair skins and the right connections might well be employed, just as Sikhs were, in the British Army. Anglo-Indians were long used, not just in non-combat roles such as buglers and medical orderlies, but to defend the empire, as and when it was expedient.

In 1917, some ten years after Walter completed his schooling, with the First World War still raging and with many Indians volunteering to serve Britain in the army, Walter was working as a guard on the Madras and Southern Mahratta Railway.

A proposal of marriage

On 8 August 1917, from his family home in Vepery, Madras, the twenty-four-year-old Walter Roberts wrote to his future father-in-law, William Weston:

Dear Mr Weston

    *Having come to the conclusion that the happiness of your
daughter and mine in life depends on us being united in
Wedlock, I shall be thankful if you will kindly give me your consent to our union.*

    Believe me

    I remain

    Yours sincerely

    Walter Roberts

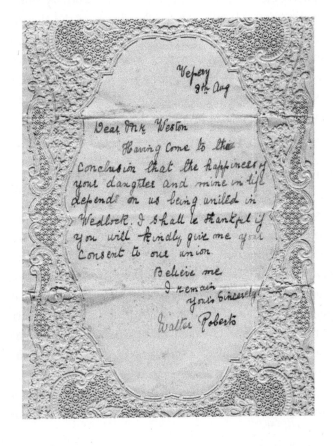

This letter, written on beautiful paper with a cut-out design around its edges, was kept by Hilda throughout her life, after which it passed to her daughter, Esmé, and then to me. Their marriage was in fact arranged by their families, in all likelihood by Walter's mother and Hilda's stepmother, Lydia. Once the couple had met and agreed the match, and William Weston had given his formal consent, the nineteen-year-old Hilda became engaged to be married, and the couple had a few months to get to know each other.

They were married six months later, in February 1918, at Christ Church Madras, the family church of the Westons, which served a predominately Anglo-Indian congregation. I think that Walter was a rather serious young man, and it seems likely that Hilda's younger sisters may have found their new brother-in-law less fun than their brothers, who were far more used to their teasing and games.

Railway people

It seems likely that Hilda and Walter began married life in one of Madras's railway colonies where they would have been allocated a bungalow with a garden. Hilda joined the railway people, as they were known. Posts on the Indian railways offered a degree of security, a pension, housing and also, frequently, schooling for children in railway schools. In terms of pay and prospects, Walter would expect to reach the maximum pay as a guard after three years, and would hope to be promoted to station master.[5]

The colonies were built by the railway companies to house European and Anglo-Indian employees. Rents were modest and set at around one tenth of an individual's salary.[6] While railway employment continued, the tied housing was an attractive perk, but change was afoot when soldiers were demobbed at the end of the First World War. As Indian and British soldiers who had volunteered or been conscripted into the war effort were absorbed back into the workforce, there was increased competition for railway posts. This, together with policies of Indianisation that enabled the railway companies to employ Indians at lower rates of pay, threatened Walter's job security and that of other Anglo-Indian employees.

Policies of Indianisation, increasing the numbers of Indians employed in specific occupations and introduced to defuse nationalist feeling, brought benefits to the railway company. In the 1880s, around 80 per cent of train drivers in the largest railway company, the East Indian Railway, were Europeans, mostly recruited from England. The rest were Eurasians, generally paid on slightly lower rates, since Indians were not considered responsible enough for the roles. By the 1890s, Indian drivers were being taken on, but their rate of pay was 10 per cent of that of their European and Anglo-Indian colleagues. Evidence suggests that Europeans employed on the railways earned twice as much as Anglo-Indians, partially because of the type of jobs they took up.[7] The Anglo-Indian community leader and activist, Frank Anthony, writing in the mid-twentieth century and looking back on developments from the 1880s, observed how in the last years of the nineteenth century and the first half of the twentieth century prior to independence, British policies of Indianisation frequently meant de-Anglo-Indianisation.[8]

It seems that Walter had little choice but to accept this

racially stratified and divisive system of pay when first he took up the post. But after marriage, the increasingly precarious system of employment threatened the young couple's security. If he were to lose his job in one of the frequent restructuring exercises, they would not only be without an income but also without a home. Eviction would not have been the disaster it might have been if they were living in an exclusively railway town, along the line, for they would have had the option of moving into Hilda or Walter's parental home. But as newlyweds who had just established their own home, it would have meant losing their newfound independence.

Whether Walter did, in fact, lose his position or whether it was the threat of losing it that led him to apply for a job in Miri, British North Borneo, the pressure to find alternative employment was significant. His chances of finding an alternative job in another sector were restricted by his categorisation as a statutory native, debarring him from various opportunities in Madras.

Manufacturing Britishness

Both Walter and Hilda were educated in Anglican schools, supported by the church. Through their schooling, they were encouraged to think of themselves as British citizens. From the last quarter of the nineteenth century, in the government-funded primary schools of the railway colonies and elsewhere, there was an explicit requirement to reinforce Britishness.[9]

In a similar fashion, railway colonies were designed to promote British values and a British way of life among

Anglo-Indian and European workers. Families living in the colonies had little privacy since these communities existed to protect 'European morality' and respectability and to prevent such 'crimes' as adultery. In fact, they had the opposite effect: the tight controls bred resentment among their residents and their racial exclusiveness became a source of outrage and discontent. The colonies effectively *created* national, cultural and racial differences, positioning Indian tradition and European modernity as incompatible. Not only were children to learn Britishness at school, but adults were encouraged to follow British habits through the Railway Institutes. These social clubs complemented the churches in promoting idealised middle-class European lifestyles. Since Indians were thought to be a threat to this way of life, they were excluded from the colonies and prevented from accessing more senior posts within the railway structure. The British authorities judged Indians to be far beyond the saving grace of British efforts to impose respectability. They were required to secure accommodation outside of the colonies, reinforcing a boundary and, no doubt, a sense of injustice.

Anglo-Indians, on the other hand, although mocked and treated with disdain by these same British authorities, were believed to have the potential, by dint of their European blood, to develop British respectability, if appropriately supervised and managed.

A fresh start

Sometime between 1920 and 1924, Walter and Hilda choose to leave Madras. I like to imagine that they had tired of the deeply patronising attitudes of the colonial authorities. As they followed political developments, they may well have wondered what their place might be, if and when India achieved independence. They were young, and may have also shared a general youthful longing for new experiences and adventures away from home.

A personal tragedy also may have propelled them on their way: the painful loss of their first child, born prematurely, preceded their choice to make a fresh start in a place where they were completely unknown. Walter responded to an advertisement for the post of shopkeeper in the small town of Miri, in Sarawak, in the British colony of North Borneo.

They were moving from a city that had a nearly 300-year history of British rule to what was a very new British colonial enterprise. Miri was, at the turn of the century, a fishing village surrounded by rainforest. Then Shell identified a potential oilfield and in 1910 set up a drilling operation. Oil was struck at 130 metres; a rig was built and the boom began. An oil refinery and submarine pipeline quickly followed, and before long Miri was the new seat of the British Resident, and a key administrative centre.

The young couple, arriving from the city of Madras, with its sophisticated infrastructure and communications, must have found their new life a huge contrast. When they arrived, the first proper roads had recently been built, including one linking Miri to Lutong, just five miles north along the coast, and the first bicycles and motorcycles were being imported. These developments were followed by the establishment of two schools, a Chinese and an English one, for employees' children.

Walter's new job came with a comfortable bungalow built

on stilts, like the traditional longhouses of the region, but equipped with running water and the facilities they would have expected back home in Madras. Walter almost certainly cycled back and forth to his job in town. It was here that Hilda gave birth to her three children: Dudley, born in 1925, my mother Esmé, born in 1927, and Ralph, born in 1929. The children were free to play at the edge of the forest. There could not have been a greater contrast to life in a highly regulated 1920s Madras railway colony.

The oil boom continued throughout the 1920s, rotary drilling was introduced, and by 1929 production reached a peak of around 15,200 barrels a day. Water supplies were improved, forests were cleared and more roads built. But by the early 1930s the boom was over, and the migrant labour that had flocked to the town was leaving. The young couple needed to act fast to avoid catastrophe. Singapore, they decided, was to be their next destination. They packed up their belongings, and Walter left for Singapore to find work, while Hilda travelled on, taking their three small children back to Madras for an extended stay in the Weston family home. It was agreed they would stay there until Walter found a job and could send for his family.

Although this must have been a period of huge uncertainty for the parents, for the three young children their stay of a year or two in Madras was a delight. Esmé, who was by then five or six years old, recalled carefree days, living in a large house as members of an extended family, along with her mothers' sisters and brothers, aunts and an uncle, who were either studying or out at work. Hilda was not the only married daughter who had brought her children to live with their grandparents. Hilda's younger sister Ivy, married to an English officer in the merchant navy, who was often at sea serving on an ocean liner, was also living back home with her parents. Dudley, Esmé and Ralph had their young cousins, Audrey (whom I am named after) and Eric, as playmates.

Esmé and her brothers went to the local St Matthias High School, where their father had been a student. Esmé kept her primary-school transfer certificate, given when she graduated at the age of seven from the infants' department, which states that she is qualified to continue her education in a 'European' school and work towards a UK school leaving certificate. This was apparently an era of transferable qualifications across the British Empire. Family members attended church regularly.

Every Saturday Hilda would take the children to visit their paternal grandmother Roberts, who lived with her eldest son and his family. This was a real treat for the children with the highlight being the chauffeured limousine that their grandmother sent to pick them up and return them in a grand style. She had been a widow for some forty years, and the pension from her husband Samuel's employment in the Madras Public Works Department, as well as her son's and perhaps her daughter-in-law's employment, allowed this branch of the Roberts family to live more comfortably than the Westons.

Meanwhile, in Singapore, Walter had linked up with his older brother Alfred, who was working as a health inspector at the naval base. After eighteen months living in Madras, Hilda received the call to join him: he had found a job and accommodation for his young family. Esmé recalled how the children found it a wrench to leave family members even as another new life was beckoning.

This was 1934, and as this family left Madras, no one could have predicted that the Second World War was going to unravel their lives.

The long view

For the British colonial authorities in India, the nineteenth century ended very differently from how it began. At the beginning of the century, travel to and from India and across the country was slow. The East India Company had managed vast tracts of land in the form of three presidencies, or administrative units, but by the latter half of the century the British had instituted a system of indirect rule through the Indian royal courts while the presidencies were divided into smaller and more manageable administrative sectors, known as provinces. An enhanced telegraph and postal service, and an extensive railway network that criss-crossed the country, made the administration and economic exploitation of such a vast territory feasible. Anglo-Indians played a key role in the development of these communication services. Colonial policies, both political and ideological, had shaped the lives of Hilda and Walter and other Anglo-Indians in Madras for more than a century before they were born.

Eurasian communities

Until the early nineteenth century, mixed heritage Eurasians were free to different degrees to draw on both Indian and European cultural influences in the lifestyles they adopted. Those living and working in areas ruled by Indian princes, interacting with Indian employers and trading with Indians, would more readily adopt local cultural customs, and a number embraced Islam. Some used both Indian and European names and had flexible identities, moving across cultural and linguistic boundaries, and no doubt switching according to the situation and company in which they found themselves.

Throughout the nineteenth century, Anglo-Indians living in a presidency city, such as Madras, would have experienced life differently from those working in areas ruled by Indian princes. Pre-colonial Indian cities had long been diverse, with traders engaged in long-distance commerce across the sub-continent and beyond.

When I visited Chennai and looked at late seventeenth- and early eighteenth-century maps on the walls of the Fort St George Museum, I was shocked to find the city divided into two clear zones: White Town, around Fort St George, and Black Town beyond, where the varied non-Europeans – Indians, Armenians, Arabs and Jews – resided and had their various places of worship, including a synagogue, mosque and orthodox church. The new colonial presidency cities became physically zoned by race and structured in complex ways by relationships of power and economic interdependence between the British and local populations.

Growing British dominance across India led to new power dynamics and placed increased pressures on Eurasians to follow European cultural norms. At the time of the 1857 Indian Uprising, they were required to visibly demonstrate their loyalty to the authorities. In nineteenth-century Madras, Bombay and Calcutta, each with sizable local Eurasian pop-ulations, Eurasian children were more likely to be brought up in the Christian faith, with many benefitting, particu-larly from the mid-century, from social networks centred on churches and schools. As the nineteenth century progressed, a growing network of churches and schools in the colonial cities supported a specific Anglo-Indian culture, which in language, faith and styles of dress followed European mores. It was economically and politically expedient for most Eurasians to be absorbed into this developing culture.

As the nineteenth century wore on, with the political strengthening of the British presence across the country and improved communications, came the tighter defining of racial and cultural boundaries, and a move from official encouragement to discouragement by the authorities of intimate interracial relationships. Since colonial rule in India was premised on a myth of European superiority and, increasingly in the later nineteenth century, on rhetoric that stressed racial purity, the very existence of a growing Anglo-Indian community presented an ideological challenge to the British rulers.

Earlier in the century, the wills of army officers and senior East India Company administrators frequently indicated that these men were ready to acknowledge and support their Eurasian children. Some of them were sent to Britain by their fathers for education. By the end of the century, policies which had either promoted or condoned intimate relationships between British men and Indian or Anglo-Indian women were reversed. Late nineteenth-century science promoted eugenicist theories and sought to justify notions of 'racial purity', claiming that those born of interracial unions were degenerate, and were inevitably physically and morally weak individuals. Indian mothers of Eurasian children, many of whom had married the father of their children, either according to local custom or in Christian ceremonies, were generally referred to by later generations at best as concubines, but also by epithets designed not only to downgrade their status but to highlight their assumed loose sexual morals.

By the late Victorian era, the British elite were less willing to acknowledge their Anglo-Indian half-brothers and sisters, cousins, uncles and aunts, even when these individuals were clearly successful and accomplished individuals. Fathers from the elite classes might continue to provide for such children in their wills, but whereas in earlier times they had been acknowledged as their children, later on any reference to a blood relationship was dropped. The very existence of a Anglo-Indian community might be a source of discomfort and embarrassment to some. For example, Robert Jenkinson, Earl of Liverpool and prime minister of the United Kingdom in 1812–27, had a Eurasian or Indian great-grandmother, Isabella Beizor.[10] If his great-grandmother's background was recognised during his lifetime, it was certainly something that was conveniently forgotten later in the century.

Such attitudes persist into the present. Today, some online sources proclaim Lord Liverpool's Indian heritage, but others stress it is barely worth mentioning, suggesting he was unlikely to have been, for example, more than one-sixteenth Indian. One source goes so far as to suggest that since Isabella Beizor was formally married to Lord Liverpool's great-grandfather, she must certainly have been Portuguese, rather than mixed race. Some sources are effectively apologising for Lord Liverpool's apparently 'tainted blood', revealing the authors' modern-day sensibilities, which sadly echo those of late Victorian elites. If the writers were referring to someone's royal or aristocratic ancestry, albeit one sixteenth or less, this would be presented as a source of pride, not something to be minimised.

Despite the hardening of racial boundaries and official restrictions on people of mixed heritage, Eurasians were not helpless victims. Many repeatedly petitioned the British authorities for justice. One of the most well-known, the 'Petition of the East Indians to the House of Commons', was put before the Westminster parliament in 1830. The petition had been delivered by John Ricketts, a Eurasian political campaigner from Calcutta, who made the month-long journey to London to request that the designation as 'statutory natives' be lifted and that members of his community be freed from restrictions on their employment opportunities and ambitions.[11] Ricketts had the support of fellow Eurasians in Madras and he doggedly campaigned from the 1790s onwards, continuing for a number of years after his petition had proved unsuccessful at Westminster.

Managing the Anglo-Indian threat

Over the course of the nineteenth century, the opportunities available to Anglo-Indians in both employment and education were influenced, to a very large degree, by the economic needs of the colonisers. Mixed-heritage communities also discovered that their chances were frequently shaped by political expediency. They were alternatively valued and preferred or thwarted and undermined in their ambitions according to official policies, first those of the East India Company and later the British crown. Arguments were put forward in parliament that Eurasians, as Anglo-Indians were designated, might directly challenge British authority, or that their presence could indirectly undermine it, and thereby encourage Indians to rebel. The growing number of fair-skinned people, both European and Eurasian, living in poverty in the bazaars of Indian cities threatened to subvert the myth of European superiority. The failure of the colonial authorities to address the problem of European/Eurasian poverty and destitution not only served to highlight for the Indian population an obvious European weakness, but it also exposed the British as careless, even callous, towards their own people.

On the other hand, if usefully and appropriately educated in Christian morals, the British saw in the Anglo-Indian population a valuable pool of trusted employees. From the perspective of Viscount Canning, governor-general of India from 1856 and subsequently viceroy from 1858, such education might reduce any potential threat and equip both them and poor Europeans with practical vocational skills. He acknowledged an official responsibility towards the group of people of partial European descent, seeing them as effective workers, but expressed concern about their identity:

> They are a class which, whilst it draws little or no support from its connection with England, is without that deep root in and hold of the soil of India from which our Native public servants, through their families and relatives, derive advantage.[12]

Canning put forward proposals for the mass education of Eurasian children that would fulfil two goals: it would turn them into useful employees and it would enable them to identify first and foremost as British. He recognised his proposals would be costly, and so expected the costs to be shared three ways: by the Anglo-Indian community, individual benefactors and the government. While he recognised the importance of Christian teaching within such an education, he expected the new schools to be nondenominational and open to Catholics and Presbyterians, as well as to those who were members of the Established Church. He was no doubt aware that this was also an expressed preference of the Eurasian community.

Canning based his policy on proposals first articulated by George Cotton, bishop of Calcutta, for building schools in the hill stations, where the cooler climate was thought to be good for both the moral and physical health of the children in question. Recognising the fees for such schools would be beyond the means of most families, both men recommended that additional, more affordable schools should be built on the plains, nearer to the children's families. Certainly, though, part of Cotton's plan was to take such children away from what he saw as the problematic influence of their families and educate them in boarding schools.

Cotton was particularly concerned about the religious and moral upbringing of children who were nominally Christian but who, unlike the Indian population, could not access education and Christian teaching from missionaries. He was concerned that their 'ignorance and evil habits' would have a disastrous impact on the Hindus and Muslims among whom they resided, and was concerned in no small part about what he judged to be their 'great moral and spiritual danger'.[13] It should be noted that Cotton's fears for Eurasian children, expressed shortly after his arrival in India in 1858, were not the result of any official inquiry or research. He did not provide concrete evidence of the widespread degenerate behaviour he clearly feared or anticipated. It seems that, for Cotton, the very existence of a mixed-race population provoked anxiety and confirmed the existence of degenerate behaviour.

Today, some of the schools founded at this time to serve

disadvantaged and middle-class Eurasians and Europeans still bear Cotton's name. Ironically, these schools now educate the Indian elite, and seemingly derive their status and prestige in modern India in part from their long tradition and association with the era of British rule.[14] It is said that the expression 'bless their cotton socks' comes from Cotton's insistence that the children in the schools he established were provided with socks, no doubt a welcome item in the chill morning air, which the bishop may well have blessed before distributing to the students in question.

The colonial authorities wanted to ensure that Eurasians were trained and educated to be useful and compliant citizens, and this required them to pursue a delicately balanced approach. For the majority of Eurasian men, this meant being educated to a level that would enable them to fill lower grade posts in the colonial service and other jobs that supported the colonial infrastructure, while ensuring that they were also taught their place in society. As Valerie Anderson expresses it, from the perspective of the rulers: 'Eurasians had to be prepared to live and work in a manner considered to be appropriate to those of European descent and yet remain excluded from the power and status of the European elite.'[15]

The emphasis was primarily on the education and training of boys and young men. Relatively little consideration seems to have been given to the education of girls. While girls from elite families might be sent to England for a period, there was limited provision in India for the education of other European or Eurasian girls and young women in schools or vocational colleges, even in cities like Madras. The official expectation was that Anglo-Indian girls would be trained to be good Christian wives and mothers. Like Hilda.

Hilda Weston with her younger sister, Marjorie, and
brothers Jimmy (seated) and Harry, c.1912

6

Empire and Enlightenment

My great aunt Mabel (neé Weston), Hilda's older sister, as a young mother c.1917

I had wondered where my maternal family name, Roberts, came from – though I knew it was an Anglo-Indian name. That question and those around the myth that my family owned a Unitarian church were solved by my exciting discovery of a letter dated December 1817 from my great-great-great-grandfather. All was about to fall into place.

But first, I should travel back further, when my ancestor's name was not Roberts but Thiruvenkatam Mudali.

In 1784, the fortified town of Madras was released from lock-down and, forty miles away, sixteen-year-old Thiruvenkatam Mudali set out from his village, Mahkarai, near Chingleput town (Chengalpattu, Tamil Nadu), to walk through the war-ravaged landscape to Madras in search of work.

The lockdown had been imposed by the Madras authori-ties, the British East India Company, which was trying to stem the flow of desperate and displaced famine-stricken villagers who were flocking to the town from across the surrounding Carnatic region (modern day Tamil Nadu) looking for food and work. Madras, an important military base, seaport and commercial centre, was, in good times, a magnet for workers as they could command better pay than in the rural areas, but warfare had destroyed land and livelihoods.[1]

War and devastation

The war that had just come to an end when Thiruvenkatam set out for Madras was the Second Mysore War (1780–84) between the East India Company and Hyder Ali, the sultan of Mysore, and later his son Tipu Ali. The sultans of Mysore, who owed nominal allegiance to the Moghul emperor, were the de facto rulers of southern India and the principal opponents of the British East India Company in the region, after the defeat of the French in 1763.

Landowners and land labourers alike suffered in the prolonged conflicts, a power struggle for territory and wealth. Thiruvenkatam's father, Lakshmanan Mudali, was a local landowner and member of the elite agriculturalist Vellalar caste.[2] The war had left them in 'very indigent circumstances', and then both parents died in the war.[3]

The East India Company records portray the enemy as a ruthless military strategist intent on hindering its efforts to bring prosperity to the region; these records continued to shape the narratives of some British historians more than two centuries later. One Western historian, using the Company's partial account, records how Hyder Ali sent his horsemen from behind an imaginary line, stretching west of the Company base at Fort St George, and extending inland for between thirty to fifty-five miles to burn and destroy whole towns and villages, devastating livelihoods, food supplies and infrastructure in this strategic coastal region.[4]

However, while Hyder Ali was undoubtedly a clever military and political strategist who used his skills to become the effective ruler of the Mysore Kingdom, the East India Company was equally ruthless. As the Company gained control, it turned over vast tracts of land previously set aside for food crops to its own cash crops, cotton and rice. It seems that combatants on both sides practised a scorched earth policy of devastation to prevent the enemy from utilising the land and its resources.

The war brought ruin to an area of some two thousand villages and as many as a quarter of a million people.[5] Those who were not killed outright suffered famine and sickness. A severe drought in the early 1780s compounded the suffering, with contemporary accounts suggesting that many villages within the Madras presidency, the area governed by the Company, became totally depopulated.[6] Some former agricultural labourers may have taken up work loading the Company ships; those who had appropriate skills may have attached themselves to traders in the town, while others were driven through hunger to contract themselves to work as lascars on these same ships transporting the Company's goods to Europe and China.

Thiruvenkatam's parents had ensured that he had some education, and he could read and write in Tamil, his mother tongue. The family's status meant they would have almost certainly engaged others to work their land. Thiruvenkatam was the second of five children, but if any of his sisters or brothers survived, the war and subsequent events meant he was never to see them again. With both his parents dead, it must have seemed to Thiruvenkatam that he had little to lose. As he left his home area, venturing beyond Chingleput towards Madras, he may have hoped for the good fortune of a ride on a bullock cart to ease his way on this unfamiliar and uncertain journey.

A change of luck?

To a newcomer like Thiruvenkatam, arriving in Madras from the stricken countryside, the city, with its white-washed buildings, would have looked prosperous and flourishing, and unlike any town he had previously seen.

It reflected a mix of influences: local and colonial, trading and military.

The original colonial settlement of Madras was divided into Fort St George, with its surrounding White Town for the European settlers, and Black Town and its suburbs for the Indian residents. The early British colonisers made a clear and crude distinction between themselves (and presumably other Europeans living among them) and the Indian population living as their neighbours. What had been a simple trading outpost, operating alongside a fishing village and a collection of agrarian communities, was already an important military, transport and trading hub, which would soon serve the development of the British Empire in South and East Asia and beyond.

Thiruvenkatam must have felt his luck had changed. He was taken in by someone he describes as 'a Mahometan Moorman', an Arab trader residing in Black Town.[7] This trader offered the young Thiruvenkatam board and lodging in his family home.

It seemed a world away from the insecurity of war and resultant famine that had blighted his childhood and led to the death of his parents.

The young boy's sense of security was tragically short-lived. Within six months, he was trafficked by the Arab trader to another Muslim man, a sailor on board an East India Company ship, the *Hastings*. Then he was sold on to an English officer on the same ship.

I stumbled across the details of Thiruvenkatam's story more or less by chance. I had planned a return to Chennai to discover more about my family's history, tying my visit to further work in Sri Lanka, but the Easter 2019 terror attacks in Colombo and concerns about security put the trip on hold. In 2020, the COVID-19 pandemic brought an end to further travel. I was then reliant on online investigations.

I came across an unpublished essay by Raja Mylvaganam on William Roberts and the early years of the Madras Unitarian church,[7] discovering that William Roberts and Thiruvenkatam were one and the same person and that Roberts had written to Unitarians in London. By tracking down Raja and phoning him in Copenhagen, I was able to link William and his sons to my immediate ancestors.

Fully expecting to wait until the COVID-19 lockdown was lifted before I could search for William's correspondence in Unitarian archives, I came across his first letter while surfing the internet. When in 1817, William reached out to strangers in London, he knew he would likely wait a year or so for any reply. Since communications were not only slow but uncertain, he took care to copy his letter and send this copy separately, to increase his chances of reaching the intended recipients. He could never have imagined that more than two hundred years later a direct descendent would read his words, while isolated in England during a global pandemic.

Both copies reached Unitarian Rev Thomas Belsham, who was so moved by William's story that he published the letter. This published version was eventually placed in the British Museum and subsequently digitalised by Google.[8] This is how I came to read it on my laptop.

The letter recounted, in a matter-of-fact way, what had happened to Thiruvenkatam, aka William Roberts, as a boy in 1784:

This man [the Arab trader who gave him lodgings] had

afterward artfully sold me as a slave on board a country ship called *Hasting* to another Mahometan Tindal named Dauhood or David. Dauhood shortly entered me in the service of an English European officer in the same ship for his own benefit.

Thiruvenkatam was to remain enslaved, working aboard the *Hastings* for that officer, for a number of years.

At the time Thiruvenkatam was abducted and enslaved, the East India Company had been involved in the slave trade for around a hundred years, transporting enslaved people across the Indian and Atlantic Oceans. The Company had made vast profits for its shareholders and had extended its operations to China, trading in a variety of commodities, including cotton, silk, tea, spices and opium. Trade, colonisation and military force were interrelated, with the Company engaged in fierce competition with other European colonial powers across Asia.

Thiruvenkatam's story is not an anomaly. Slavery and slave labour were a distinct feature of British colonial activity in India and the Indian Ocean. Of course, this history has largely been eclipsed by that of the transatlantic slave trade and the horrendous and brutal mass transportation of enslaved Africans to the plantations of the Americas and the Caribbean, in which much of Europe was implicated.

In Britain there was a long struggle between anti-slavery campaigners and influential pro-slavery interests in the late eighteenth century. Anti-slavery activity, together with the Saint-Domingue slave uprising (1791) and the emergence of Haiti (1804) as an independent Black republic, led parliamentarians to take action in an attempt to avoid similar uprisings on British Caribbean plantations. What followed was the

1807 Act for the Abolition of the Slave Trade and subsequent 1833 Slavery Abolition Act.[9] Eighteenth- and early nineteenth-century British campaigning focused on the Caribbean; in India, Company administrators were generally careful to avoid the word 'slave' in written communications and to admonish colleagues who did so.

After the 1830s, an indenture system operated. It guaranteed the British authorities in India with an ongoing supply of forced labour from impoverished and destitute British colonial subjects made to work for an agreed period in return for subsistence. Possibly as a result of this, the story of slavery in India seems to have been quietly forgotten in Britain, with the colonial practice of enslaving Indians never an explicit part of our history nor the school curriculum.

The *Hastings*, the ship Thiruvenkatam was trafficked to, was named after Warren Hastings, the British colonial administrator who became the first governor-general of Bengal, overseeing the three British Indian presidencies of Calcutta, Bombay and Madras, from 1772 to 1785. Hastings, together with Robert Clive, is generally credited with the founding of the British Empire in India.

The East India Company ensured that when Queen Victoria came to the throne in 1837, although she did not yet style herself 'Empress of India', she could ostensibly already claim the title. Following Clive's victory at the 1757 Battle of Plassey over the nawab of Bengal and his French allies, the Company consolidated its strength across the subcontinent to become the leading colonial power in the region, pushing out its rivals, the Dutch and French East India companies. Warfare, plunder and corruption made Robert Clive and other military leaders and administrative officials immensely rich. Company shareholders were guaranteed huge profits. Significantly, the taxes on the local population brought more annual revenue into the British treasury than taxes raised at home, leaving a lasting impact on the Indian economy.[10]

Thiruvenkatam's enslavement in the service of empire was also the age of the European Enlightenment. His subsequent life reveals the tensions and contradictions of an era in which the ideals of rationality and freedom were promoted at the same time as slavery and the subjugation of peoples outside Europe continued unabated. The Enlightenment ideals represented an aspiration for humankind. But who was recognised as fully human?

Learning the ropes

When Thiruvenkatam was brought on board, the crew of the *Hastings* were loading provisions and cargo in preparation for trading between ports along the Bengal coast. It was Dauhood, the ship's tindal, responsible for the supervision and disciplining of deck crew and deck maintenance, sails, rigging and ropes, who purchased the boy. Seizing a chance to make a profit, he sold Thiruvenkatam on to one of the European officers on board, a man by the name of Robison.

The ship's crew was a diverse group of men, in skills, experience and backgrounds. The *Hastings*' officers, as on all Company ships, were Europeans, but the sailors' backgrounds were varied. Indian seaman, known as lascars, would have made up the larger part of the crew and were generally Muslims, since Hindu rituals and beliefs generally served as a prohibition to seafaring.[11] Other seamen were no doubt recruited from England and South-East Asia. Thiruvenkatam almost certainly worked as a cabin boy, serving Robison and other ship's officers as needed. He might well have helped as a deckhand when required. The lascars and Chinese seamen were cheap labour, paid between one-sixth and one-seventh of the European rates of pay, but the work of the trafficked and enslaved young Thiruvenkatam cost nothing.[12]

Thiruvenkatam lived, ate and slept alongside this assorted company of men, many of whom had travelled the world. He was exposed to new ideas, cultures, languages, beliefs and reasoning. His first language was Tamil, but onboard ship he started learning some English, as a result of the demands of Robison and other officers. It is possible Robison or one of the others nicknamed him William. No doubt some of these Europeans found the name Thiruvenkatam something of a tongue-twister.

Thiruvenkatam needed the lower ranking seamen to guide him in the art of survival at sea, metaphorically and literally 'learning the ropes'. He was learning European manners and how to serve an English officer, and discovering how to live among the ship's community.

The risks in seafaring were high. Not only was there the danger of piracy, but also illness. On board, conditions were unsanitary, and seamen frequently fell victim to 'the flux' (dysentery) and scurvy, because of the restricted diet. On shore, too, there was the threat of sickness. Seafarers from Europe generally had little immunity to tropical illnesses, such as malaria. Cholera and typhoid were a danger to men of all ranks.

The ship made a number of journeys up and down the west coast of India and, while in port in Bombay (Mumbai),

Robison, Thiruvenkatam's master, fell sick. As he lay on his deathbed he asked the ship's captain, Alexander Jamieson, to arrange for Thiruvenkatam's release from slavery. Jamieson had observed the boy and was clearly impressed by his work. Not only did he pay him for the years that he had served Robison, in keeping with the dying man's wishes, but having secured his loyalty with this gesture, the ship's captain then chose to employ him. It is interesting to note that, writing nearly two decades later, Thiruvenkatam refers to Robison as his 'benefactor'.[13] This seems a generous assessment but he knew that the alternative would have been to be sold on as part of Robison's estate.

A change of religion and trade with China

The *Hastings'* next voyage, and Thiruvenkatam's first as a free man, was from Bombay to China. It was on his return from this first Chinese voyage, and after spending more than three years living and working among Muslims who, according to Thiruvenkatam, were confident of the superiority of their faith over Hinduism, that he began to question the value of his own beliefs. His comment suggests that he almost certainly experienced a degree of mockery from his unschooled fellow seamen, perhaps reflecting wider tensions between the two ancient Indian religious traditions. Eventually he opted to convert to the faith of his fellow seafarers:

> Continually [from Muslim seamen] hearing the unhappiness of the heathen religion of stock worship, and the superiority and superior privileges of the Mahometan

religion, I became a convert to their religion and was circumcised.[14]

Explaining this decision some thirty years after the event, he described his conversion to Islam as 'nominal': 'I call it nominal, because I was not even instructed in the first article of the Koran, which is the doctrine of One God'.[15] This was to be the first of three changes of religion, each made as he found himself in new circumstances and exposed to new ideas.

France and England 1788–90

Alexander Jamieson had already hired a 'Portuguese' servant (probably a person of mixed Portuguese and Indian descent) to accompany him on the voyage back to Europe but, having grown attached to Thiruvenkatam and recognising his usefulness, suggested he accompany him to Europe. The young man, perhaps understandably, was at first hesitant, but was finally persuaded.

Jamieson and Thiruvenkatam set sail in January 1788 on the East Indiaman *Bessborough* under the captainship of Alexander Montgomery.[16] The *Bessborough* had left Europe in April 1786, and this return journey to Europe turned out to be its last ocean voyage, after which it was judged unseaworthy and hulked.[17] Jamieson, as a passenger freed from the responsibilities of captaining a ship, had the chance to get to know Thiruvenkatam better and see him in a new light. He soon recognised that the young man could be trusted to serve in his household when he next went to sea.

Thiruvenkatam worked for the Jamieson family in

Dunkirk and Boulogne in 1788–9, while Captain Jamieson returned to sea. It was here that he began to learn to read in English and was instructed in Christianity by his fellow servants. He almost certainly took the name William for himself at this point, if he had not already done so at sea. Among the few books available was the Bible, and he set about reading it.

In 1789, Mrs Jamieson and her children travelled to London and the newly named William accompanied her. While in London he made his second change of religion. On 3 August 1789 he was baptised into the Anglican church, formally taking the name William Roberts. Where Roberts came from we don't know – perhaps from his sponsor. The simple ceremony took place at St James's Church, Piccadilly, with a friend, Butler, an African, acting as his sponsor and godfather.[18] Butler's friendship was later literally to be a life-saver. William marked his baptism by purchasing a Common Prayer Book of the Church of England and a New Testament. Unfortunately, the service caused him to be somewhat late in getting back to Mrs Jamieson's London lodgings. It was to cost him dearly.

After returning with William to Boulogne, Mrs Jamieson dismissed him from his position for lateness and disobedience. It's also possible that she was uneasy at his adoption of Christianity, believing she might have to accept him as the equal of her European servants and so grant him additional rights, such as equal pay. Unfortunately, Captain Jamieson, for whom he had worked for some four years, and who had brought him to Europe, was not there to intercede on his behalf. William managed to negotiate his return fare to London and letters of recommendation to friends of Mrs Jamieson, whom she asked to arrange his return passage to

India. The expectation was that he would work his passage by serving English travellers on board ship.

It was common practice during the eighteenth and nineteenth centuries for families travelling to and from England to India to employ Indian women and men on the journey. Many of these servants were likely be long-serving household members. Once in England, an Indian servant might become a status symbol for a European family and a nostalgic reminder of a splendid colonial lifestyle. Some child servants were even dressed up and treated as family pets. However, many servants, having fulfilled their purpose on board ship, caring for individual Company employees or families and children, were regarded as mere chattels and disposed of once the ship had docked in England.

This meant that there was a ready supply of Indian labour in London and other port cities, men and women who were looking to work their passage home, and no doubt hoping to find longer-term employment in a European household on arrival. Many Europeans there judged Indian servants as more reliable than Europeans, who might find it difficult to cope with the change in climate and conditions. It seems that Indians were considered less likely to abscond than European servants, either to marry or set up a business.[19] Generally speaking, Indians were also cheaper to employ and their understanding of local conditions and culture made them particularly useful. During the late eighteenth century, around the time William was looking for work, many advertisements could be found from Indians searching for such posts. For example, one 'East Indian' advertised in the pages of the *Daily Advertiser* for a place with 'a single gentleman, or as a footman in a small family'. He appeared both skilled and versatile and could:

Shave and dress hair, read, write and understand common
accounts, clean plate and furniture well, and do anything in
that capacity as he [had] been brought up to do it all his life,
would look after a saddle horse or two.[20]

Quite clearly, as William recognised, competition for
employment was stiff and the letters of recommendation
he carried were of some importance in securing a passage
home. On arrival in Britain, he took the trouble to deliver
them as instructed. However, on the journey from Dover to
London he met a Frenchman, a Monsieur Mouron, who made
William an attractive job offer. William agreed a salary and
a livery with his new employer, subject to one month's trial,
and set out for Bath with Mouron.

Unfortunately, this was not a good move. It was 1789
and there were numerous minor French aristocrats seeking
refuge from the French Revolution in England. Mouron was,
as likely as not, one such refugee. After two months in Bath,
and no sign of the promised livery, William decided to quit.
It seems that Mouron had spotted a rather naive young man
whom he could exploit. In his account, William chose not
to dwell on the problems he encountered in Bath while in
Mouron's employ, simply noting: 'The best thing I did here
was the purchase of a Bible.'[21] What is clear from this account
is that William was developing a love of books, and a growing
interest in philosophical questions.

William returned to London and called on Mrs Jamieson's
friends, only to discover he had missed his chance of a working passage to India. Stranded in London, he was homeless and
destitute: 'Here I found myself in great distress; no friends –
no home – nor any support except my godfather the above

mentioned African; he truly proved a steady friend.' The cold and damp of the autumn and winter of 1789–90 on the streets of London was especially difficult. Butler, his friend, was likely employed as a butler and living in his employer's household. He could provide William with a little food and perhaps, occasionally, a few hours' warmth in a servants' kitchen, but little more. To have allowed William more would have risked his position.

William was not exceptional in finding himself in such a vulnerable position in London. In a letter published in the *Public Advertiser* in December 1786, a reader using the pseudonym Truth appealed to the directors of the East India Company to provide immediate free passage to Indian women servants stranded in London on ships about to depart:

> When a family return from India, they generally bring over with them one or more female blacks to take care of the children, under a promise to send them back to their native country free of expense – Many no doubt have the honesty or humanity enough to keep their word; but the number of those poor wretches who are daily begging for a passage back, proves [the majority are abandoned by their employers]. Many of them, I am informed have been in England two or three years; and some must for ever remain here, unless the Company will generously give them a passage.[22]

Responding to Truth's letter, a gentleman going by the name Orientalis, serving as an apologist for the Company and its employees, asserted that all servants arriving in recent years had been returned 'greatly to the honour of their masters' and that Truth 'perhaps mistakes West Indian for East Indian Blacks'.[23]

Not only did all such foreigners apparently look alike, but the social problem of West Indian women destitute on the streets of London was, according to Orientalis, one with which neither the East India Company nor its employees need trouble themselves. The stark reality that the Company was part of Britain's global trade network, and implicated in supporting slavery in the West Indies and the eventual arrival in London of formerly enslaved people of African descent, was not something Orientalis was willing to concede. The plight of people who had been forcibly transported to the Caribbean colonies and had worked on Caribbean sugar plantations, so as to enrich Britain and benefit people in the British Isles and beyond, could be ignored, and complicity in their circumstances overlooked. There was, in reality, little honour, honesty or humanity shown to either East or West Indians.

Employment in Madras

It was after a long, distressing winter that William finally found an opportunity to work his passage to India as servant to George Hoar on the *Queen*, sailing from the Downs off the Kent coast on 5 April 1790, docking in Madeira fifteen days later, and after a long sea voyage arriving in Madras on 5 September of that year. William must have served Hoar well over these five months at sea, as Hoar offered him employment in Madras, later promoting him to the status of butler:

On our arrival at Madras Mr Hoar agreed to keep me as his dressing servant at five pagodas per month, and in a few months made me his butler at six pagodas. This turn of fortune was very seasonable and [I was] very grateful after the bad fortune I had experienced in England.[24]

Fifteen years after his first arrival in Madras as a boy fleeing from destitution and the devastation of war, William was back in the city, with a new name and a secure job but he appears to have been quite isolated, spending most of his time working, with limited opportunities to make friends. In his little leisure time, he focused on improving his reading of English:

Now, from the first, my chief motive for endeavouring to learn to read English was to read the Bible to my own satisfaction. I had no other books but the Bible and the Common Prayer Book of the Church of England; these were my friends, and the writers of them my instructors. As at that time I had no friends or acquaintance, being quite a stranger at Madras, I was at all times in my master's house. Whenever I had leisure the Bible was in my hands.[25]

He identified what he took to be discrepancies between the teachings of the Book of Common Prayer and the Bible concerning the nature of the Trinity, but he was frustrated in his study due to his insufficient command of the English language. His isolation from other Christians was such that he was unaware that the Bible had already been translated into Tamil and printed back in 1714 by missionaries at the Danish colony in Tranquebar (Tarangambadi), some 200 miles south of Madras.[26]

Enlightenment

In 1793, aged thirty-one, William accompanied Mr Hoar to London, where he stayed for around seven months. He came into contact with some of the radical ideas of the time, which were being read and debated among the servant classes.

William further indulged his passion for books. By this stage, his enthusiasm for Bible study was waning a little, as he was unable to reconcile the inconsistencies he had identified in Christian teaching. It was an encounter with a fellow servant, newly employed in the Hoar household in London, that was to lead to his third and final change of religion, and set him determinedly on his future path:

> Mrs Hoar's new maid-servant, a young woman by name Miss Raw, one evening having a small Tract in her hand, made me sit down by her work table in the servants' room, and read several pages to me, and then left the book on the table and took to her needle. I took that book in my hand, and was turning page after page: in the end I came to a catalogue of Dr. Priestley's and the Rev. T. Lindsey's publications [Lindsey's *A list of false readings and mistranslations of scripture*] . . . I think I had no sleep almost all night. The next morning after my breakfast I went and bought this List from Johnson's.[27]

Johnson's was an important London bookstore, run by the influential bookseller and publisher Joseph Johnson. He was best known for publishing writers such as Mary Wollstonecraft, William Godwin, Thomas Malthus and the feminist economist Priscilla Wakefield, works on medicine and children's literature, as well as the writings of a range of religious dissenters such as Anna Laetitia Barbauld, Joseph Priestley and Theophilus Lindsey. In 1799, Johnson was found guilty of seditious libel for publishing one of Unitarian Gilbert Wakefield's pamphlets and served six months in prison. The bookstore was to prove a valuable resource for William, both in acquainting himself with some of the leading radical Enlightenment thinkers publishing in English, and as a place where he might link up with some of those thinkers and activists.

Radical pamphlets or tracts, published by Johnson and others, were being avidly read by working women and men such as Miss Raw and her brother John. They were drawn to the teachings of Unitarianism, a form of Christian teaching that argues for the oneness of God, as opposed to the Trinity; the moral teachings of Jesus are understood as inspired by God, but Jesus himself is not considered to be God. The Unitarian movement was gaining popularity in the wake of the French Revolution and the spread of Enlightenment ideals. Followers placed emphasis on freedom of conscience and expression, and, in a new religious ethic, reason replaced mysticism. Individuals were encouraged to apply reason not only to the interpretation of scripture but to the politics and pressing concerns of the day, rather than rely on church hierarchies or political authorities to guide them. It is not hard to see why such ideas were seen as threatening by those with vested interests, or why they might lead to accusations of sedition. It was an action-orientated approach to life that fitted well with William Roberts's own commitment to study, beliefs and conscience. As literacy and self-education flourished among working women and men such as the Raws, so the Unitarians' radical approach to religion, belief and political activity was gaining more followers.[28]

The pamphlets and arguments he encountered made a deep impression on William:

> When I came to consider the contents [of Lindsey's list], I was astonished to see that my doubts were not without foundation; and that the doctrine of the Trinity, at which I stumbled, was not the doctrine of the Bible. The ardour of my Bible study returned with redoubled vigour.[29]

He returned to Madras with several new books, some of which he had purchased and others that were gifts from John Raw.

Shortly after his arrival in Madras in 1794, William left George Hoar's household and began working for the family of William Harrington for an increased wage of eight pagodas a month. He was now in a position to support a family.[30] William found a period of stability with his new employer and remained working in Harrington's household for twenty-seven years.[31] He records:

> After I came into the service of Mr Harington and got [a] little settled, I sent to Tranquebar and purchased the Bible in my own language. This Tamul [Tamil] Bible, with the English one, became a great help, and explained many difficulties.[32]

In his correspondence with the Unitarians in London – the key source from which I have been able to reconstruct his life story – William makes relatively few references to his family.

It seems that he married around 1794, and that his first child, a daughter, was born shortly after. We know he had three daughters and three sons: the eldest, Theophilus, was born in 1807; the second, Joseph, was born in 1816; and the third and youngest was William, born around 1820.[33] He doesn't give his wife's name, nor that of his daughters. It is possible she was employed in the Harrington or another European household. If, like Miss Raw, she was attracted to Unitarian ideals, she may possibly have been white, but it seems more likely she was Indian or of mixed Indian and European heritage, and probably a convert to Unitarianism from another Christian tradition.

Founding a mission in Madras

William's new Unitarian faith placed considerable emphasis on education. By 1795, he was instructing others in Madras in the Unitarian Christian faith and beginning to provide schooling for local children, while continuing in his work as butler to the Harrington family. In 1797, William ordered from England further studies by Priestley and Lindsey, Sales's *Koran* and Brandt's *History of the Reformation*.[34] The titles suggest he wished to engage with both Christian missionaries and Muslims about their beliefs. He also established a working relationship with the Reverend Marmaduke Thomson, the Madras agent for the Calcutta Auxiliary Bible Society, who helped him secure further copies of the New Testament, and he managed to get hold of additional copies of both the Old and New Testaments from various sources.[35] He reports how he engaged in debate with British Army officers and India-born Europeans.

These were difficult years in Madras: in the wider region of the presidency controlled by the East India Company there were famines in 1804–7, 1811–12, 1824 and 1833–4, and while tens of thousands died each year, many others made their way to Madras from the countryside, as William and an earlier generation had done back in the 1780s.[36] Cholera hit Madras in 1818 and seems to have been endemic in the city until the late 1830s. The authorities did little to address it and, while the disease was initially badly understood, concern focused on the European colonists and little was done to help the poor and marginalised in the city.[37] These conditions combined to make the new Unitarians' challenge of serving the needs of the poor in Madras increasingly challenging.

In 1806, William made his third trip to London, this time accompanying Mrs Harrington and her children for a short visit, lasting just forty days. Not surprisingly, as soon as he was able, he made his way back to Johnson's bookshop to augment his growing personal library, purchasing among other items Joseph Priestley's *Church History* and works on comparative religion. While in the bookshop he met a young man named Hunter who helpfully provided him with a written introduction to the Reverend Jeremiah Joyce, who was the secretary of the Unitarian Society for Promoting Christian Knowledge and the Practice of Virtue by the Distribution of Books. Somewhat unusually, Joyce had begun his working life as a glass painter and it was only as a more mature man that he trained for the Unitarian ministry. Joyce, just five years older than William, was a radical thinker who in 1794 had been accused of high treason. Although the charges against him were subsequently dropped, Joyce spent twenty-three weeks in prison.[38] The two men met, seemed to get on well and had a rewarding conversation on religion. Joyce suggested they might meet again and presented William with more than a dozen Unitarian Society tracts. William returned to Hunter to see how a second meeting might be arranged. William recalled:

> Mr Hunter, two days before my leaving London, told me that I may go to him any time at his house in Glocester Place, Camden Town. The very next day I went, but to my great sorrow he was not at home; I waited till evening, and came away. The day following I left London for India.[39]

His huge disappointment must have been compounded by the fact that Joyce was the only English Unitarian that he got the chance to meet in person, for this turned out to be his last visit to London.

William's search for knowledge was not merely for knowledge's sake. Although he tried, often without support, to resolve big philosophical questions in his own mind, he was eager to share his ideas and to argue with others, including those who were theologically trained or had the formal education he lacked. The books he read and conversations he engaged in fed his efforts to educate and support others, efforts that focused on the poorest and most vulnerable sectors of Madras society. He not only dedicated himself to this task but expected his family members to share in it with him, to the best of their ability. His oldest son Theophilus Roberts worked as an assistant to his father at the Purasaiwakkam church in the Madras area, and to Abraham Chinniah at Secunderabad, until his death in 1838–9. As a self-educated person, William reflected after twenty years of work in this endeavour:

Though my poverty and mean situation in life, and also my disqualification and incapability to teach, be two great impediments; yet as far as lay in my power I always made a point of answering, and instructing, and giving all the information I was master of to all those of my countrymen who would [listen].[40]

Building a chapel, 1813

On returning to Madras from London in 1806, William Roberts began the work of sharing his Unitarian faith with others. By the end of 1813, the small congregation William brought together opened their own chapel in Purasaiwakkam. He was combining his role as minister/teacher to this congregation with his ongoing work as a butler in the Harrington household. He recorded:

We have a burying-ground of our own, and a small place of worship opened on the 19th December 1813. Those of us that can conveniently go, meet there for divine worship; and if I am there present, which happens about once in two or three Sundays, I read the Prayers and some portions of Scripture, and sometimes after prayer explain some parts of Scripture ... Here we baptise, administer the Lord's supper, give marriage, and bury our dead.[41]

By 1816, he noted:

Among those who have been my hearers, about ten families and some individuals have embraced the Unitarian faith; seven out of the ten families are original converts from heathenism. All of them are poor, their situation in life is much meaner than my own.[42]

The congregation did not yet have support from the Unitarians in London, either for their chapel or their school. Although his income as a butler was modest, William was not as poor as the members of his congregation, who had little beyond their daily needs. It seems likely that the plot of land and the materials needed to build the church were provided largely from William's own resources. So, I see that the family myth and my mother's belief, that the Roberts family *owned* the Unitarian chapel, makes sense.

By the second half of the twentieth century it seems that no one in the family was a member of the Madras Christian Unitarian Church. However, it was not until the 1970s that the Roberts family still living in Madras finally relinquished any claim they might have on the chapel, accepting it now belonged to the congregation. The chapel was built in what was, effectively, a village on the edge of the city. Today, Purasaiwakkam is a busy residential and shopping area of Chennai close to Chennai Central and Chennai Egmore rail stations.

Introducing my great-great grandfather, William's son

Proposing his son to be his successor in the church, William Roberts wrote to the British and Foreign Unitarian Association (BFUA):

My second son Joseph Roberts will be fourteen years next
month: he has learned to read Tamul in our school: he is
now learning to read and write English in the Veprey free-
school. I pay a rupee a month for his schooling. Joseph,
if placed under English Unitarian masters, may easily be
trained up for [a] Native Unitarian Teacher.[43]

The BFUA committee responded positively and by the end
of 1830 Joseph had arrived in Manchester, England, to begin
this training in the care of Revd R. Beard 'with a view to his
future usefulness as the Agent of this Association, and successor to his father in Madras and its neighborhood'.[44]

After less than three years in Britain, the nineteen-year-
old Joseph was invited to London and formally introduced to
the BFUA at their AGM at the Chapel in Finsbury, London,
on 29 May 1833. He made a very favourable impression on
his sponsors:

During his stay in London . . . your Committee and several
of their friends enjoyed the opportunity by personal inter-
course, and by hearing him on two occasions in pulpits of
the metropolis, of witnessing the results of his education,
and they most favourably impressed with his mental attain-
ments, his amiable dispositions, his moral habits, and his
truly Christian temper.[45]

Unfortunately, by 1834, when he was in York attending the
Unitarian College, Joseph was in poor health. So much so that,
despite the clear benefits he was getting from the college's specialist leadership training, it was decided to send him back to
Madras before the end of winter.

Joseph left for India in February 1835, his education cut short, but his hopes of employment as a teacher still intact. Unfortunately, things did not go well. Joseph subsequently wrote from Madras expressing his frustration at the discrimination he experienced:

I am quite unable to procure a situation here to support myself. I thought after the education I have received in England I might be able to keep a good school at Madras, but I am a Unitarian, and in this country that is enough to blast anyone's prospects, let it them be ever so good.[46]

William, too, expressed his concern a few months later:

Joseph is still unemployed and I think is likely to remain so till he hears of something from your very respectable Committee. He had some thoughts of opening a school, but he has been advised not to do so as he would be the loser by it after he had made the necessary arrangements; for a Unitarian in India will meet with little or no support.[47]

It seems that the BFUA committee was unwilling to support both William and Joseph, and instead sent Joseph a grant of £20 to cover clothing and other necessities, so he would not be entirely dependent on his father.[48] They had trained Joseph for a leadership position but had also fostered his taste for English culture. William's work was tolerated, as it was directed at the very poor, but Joseph had ambitions to teach the children of more well-to-do people, and it was the combination of his education and his beliefs that were so alarming to those in power. The London committee noted:

Educated in this country, but without the means of subsistence in his own, your Committee could not but sympathize
in the difficulties and singularity of his position, as that of a
youth who had partaken of English tastes and English culture, returned to find his living as a native, yet a Unitarian
Christian, in the neighbourhood of Madras. But he was
brought to this country to be fitted for assisting and ulti-
mately succeeding his aged father; and neither the state of
our funds, nor any prospects of adequate beneficial result,
admitted of our giving him a regular salary as an additional
missionary in India.[49]

It is not clear whether the English Unitarians had doubts
about Joseph's character or whether they believed he might be
developing alternative plans for his future, not directly related
to the Madras mission, but they deliberated at a meeting in
June 1838 to ask his father:

Supposing . . . we are willing to make some annual allowance to Joseph for his special support, is he thoroughly
determined and disposed to devote himself to missionary services in our cause at Madras? Are his present
feelings, intentions, and abilities such that we can look
to him with confidence for the fulfilment of the objects
of his education as a cordial assistant to his father now,
and a powerful and efficient labourer in the same field
after him?[50]

Unfortunately, the BFUA was not to get a reply as William
died on 8 April 1838. It was Joseph who informed the BFUA:

With feelings of extreme pain and sorrow I take up my pen
to communicate to you the melancholy tidings of the loss
of my poor and much-beloved father. He is no more; he
breathed his last on Sunday, the 8th of April, at a quarter
past four o'clock in the afternoon, aged sixty-nine years, six
months and eight days ... He was taken ill on Sunday the
4th of March; his chronic disease terminated in consump-
tion, and after more than a month's severe and lingering
illness ... he was released from his suffering, and was
interred at the Unitarian burial-ground on Monday the 9th,
at eight in the morning. I had to perform the melancholy
duty of reading the service over him, and you can better
imagine than I can express my feelings on that occasion.[51]

There was ongoing correspondence between Joseph and
the BFUA until around 1840, when the BFUA terminated its
support for Joseph.

Joseph seemingly went on to marry a Miss Turnbull,
and his marriage and the baptism of his children probably
took place in the Unitarian chapel. One of his sons, Samuel
Turnbull Roberts, was my great-grandfather.

Samuel eventually found a senior enough post in the colonial administration to enable him to travel to England on
secondment, which suggests he was recorded as a European
and was light-skinned. This leads me to believe that his
mother, Miss Turnbull, was a white woman or a light-skinned
woman of mixed descent. I think his choice of life partner
may have had something to do with the committee's view of
Joseph's suitability to serve as a Unitarian minister in Madras.
It would seem that this, in the early nineteenth-century, was
the beginning of the European mix of our mixed-descent

Roberts family. The European–Indian mix of the Westons, the family of my maternal grandmother, Hilda, can be traced back to the previous century.

Madras Christian Unitarian Church has, despite BFUA's reservations back then, continued in existence to the present day. It was William's third son, William, who took over its leadership and continued as pastor until his death in 1899.

Border crossings

William Roberts was unafraid to cross cultural borders in his everyday work and life in Madras. He reached out to a relatively wide spectrum of contemporary society and he didn't seem to distinguish people either by caste or ethnic origin. Not only did he engage in debate with Catholics at St Thomas Mount (the oldest Catholic community in India), but he also attracted the interest of people referred to as 'country-born gentlemen' and 'respected natives', and the European Regiment at Secunderabad. He similarly took time to debate with Hindu theologians. Through his travels he had encountered many ways of life and different cultures. The 'country-born gentlemen' with whom he conversed were men of European descent, born in India. Many of them traced their heritage exclusively from Europe, whereas others may have had Indian mothers or grandmothers, since in the eighteenth century many military men of all ranks and Company officials established formal or informal marriages with Indian women. Among the Catholics of St Mary's Mount, there were no doubt many of mixed Indian–Portuguese descent.

Neither education, class nor caste seem to have compromised

his desire to interact with others. Although he had worked as a servant in European households and was entirely self-educated, he corresponded with some of Britain's leading intellectuals. Quite late in life, when he saw the Madras authorities restricting the rights of the dissenting Christians of his congregation, he challenged their discrimination on moral and legal grounds. His own formal caste position as a Vellalar did not prevent him from working and worshipping with poor and excluded Indians.

In matters of religion, William also crossed boundaries: born a Hindu, he had converted to Islam, then to Anglicanism, before discovering Christian Unitarianism. It might be questioned as to whether his early changes of religion were expedient, but they don't appear to have brought him personal benefit. He remained on board the *Hastings* for some years as a Hindu before adopting Islam, the religion of his fellow sea-farers, and continued as a Hindu while he remained a slave. It was only later, on regaining his freedom, that he adopted Islam. Likewise, in London, when he had recently converted to Anglicanism from Islam and found himself homeless, he might have found support in the local London community of Muslim seafarers had he reverted, but he chose to remain with his newly adopted religion.

Effectively, through the Unitarian tradition he was interpreting Enlightenment values in the social and cultural context of the urban poor in Madras. He worked in a very practical way with people who, like himself, found themselves in a colonial city, often displaced, dispossessed and disadvantaged by the wars between the Indian leaders of the region and the East India Company. William Roberts's life story is inspiring. I feel considerable pride in my great-great-great-grandfather.

Maurice, Audrey, Esmé and Charles Osler, *c.*1960

7

The fantasy of empire

Esmé as a local celebrity, Kings Langley, c.1950

There remained the nagging memory of the story that my family supposedly have a relative buried in St Paul's Cathedral.

Not all relatives prove to be a pleasure in the discovery . . .

Inconvenient truths

The risk of uncovering uncomfortable truths about family members is something for which anyone researching their history needs to prepare themselves. It might seem perverse to look for a connection with someone who invented the concentration camp, and who today would likely be judged a war criminal, but I was determined to solve what increasingly looked like an unsolvable puzzle.

Where are we *really* from? Answering this question requires us to look critically, not just at the evidence, but at the assumptions behind the narratives we read. Once we look beyond the usual, dominant narrative and look closely at the true story of our nations, we are able examine power relations and see how power intersects with questions of class, gender and race. Family stories enable us to do this. Effectively:

> Family stories and belief systems, while very personal and private, also reflect public ideologies within shifting class formations . . . Clearly, class and the economic structure are not the only systemic context of people's lives, nor the only structure of power. Race/ethnicity and gender relationships are intimately intertwined with class as well as with each other.[1]

So, family stories offer fresh insights into how racism plays out and how it intersects with class and gender. Racism is both a simple concept and one that operates in complex and changing ways. It is an everyday process, but not something that is inevitable or cannot be challenged.

A young woman of colour visiting St Paul's in the 1950s, and asking to be shown an ancestor's final resting place, was always going to have been misjudged, whether she anticipated it or not. Whether Esmé was yet fully aware of how she might be perceived at the august London cathedral seems unlikely, but she was given short shrift when she got there. It was inconceivable to the guardians of St Paul's that she might locate a family member in the hallowed cathedral, alongside the remains of the great eighteenth-century artist Joshua Reynolds, Alexander Fleming, the physician who discovered penicillin and transformed modern medicine, and Christopher Wren, the building's great architect. Neither was it plausible that she would find a family memorial, standing alongside those of Florence Nightingale or William Blake.

But Esmé was not deterred, and never questioned the accuracy of her father Walter's claim. It took three visits to St Paul's, over the course of several decades, before she was taken seriously. It was not until 1999, fifty years after she first arrived in the country, that Esmé, by then in her seventies, was led by a helpful guide down into the crypt and shown the tomb of Frederick Sleigh Roberts. Could he really be connected to my Roberts family?

A national hero

In his day, Frederick Sleigh Roberts (1832–1914), 1st Earl Roberts of Kandahar, Pretoria and Waterford, was regarded as a highly successful military leader and recognised as a national hero. A public statue of Frederick Roberts was erected in the Maidan in Calcutta (Kolkata) in 1898, but removed after independence and later placed in an artillery centre in Nashik, Maharashtra. Along with the memorialisation at St Paul's are equestrian statues of him at Kelvingrove Park, Glasgow, erected in 1918, and on Horse Guards Parade, London, unveiled just a few years later. His name is listed on numerous honours and memorial boards; and there are even pubs named after him in Nottingham and Liverpool.

On his death, Roberts lay in state at Westminster Hall and was given a state funeral, something normally reserved for monarchs, details of which would have been reported across the empire, particularly in India, where he spent more than forty years of his long career. At the time of the funeral, my grandfather Walter would have been a young man of around twenty, and no doubt the event was discussed within the family and the wider Madras community.

Frederick Sleigh Roberts is not so easily recalled today in Britain, or as well-known as his protégé, Lord Kitchener, who succeeded him as commander-in-chief of the British Army in the Second Boer War (1899–1902). That said, his name may be better known in Waterford, Ireland, where the Roberts family were established and where he met his future wife. Kitchener, with his distinctive heavy moustache, is remembered in the famous and frequently reproduced First World War recruitment poster, designed by Alfred Leete, pointing directly at the viewer, with the rallying cry: 'Britons, Lord Kitchener wants you. Join your country's army!' Another 1914 recruitment poster showed Lord Roberts, with the slogan: 'He did his duty. Will YOU do YOURS?' available in both English and Welsh.

If not an architect of the British Empire, Frederick Sleigh Roberts was a key force in ensuring its preservation in the second half of the nineteenth century, as his career indicates. Rudyard Kipling, colonialist sympathiser, author of *Jungle Book* and 1907 Nobel Prize winner for Literature, also born in India, was a great admirer. He wrote two poems about Roberts, the first confirming the nickname given to him by his soldiers: Bobs. Kipling is now widely recognised as a controversial figure, and Roberts is easily his match, responsible as he was for the violent enforcement of British colonial rule across various territories.

An unsavoury family connection?

Was it possible that somehow I might be related to this icon of the late imperial age? Frederick Roberts was born in India in

1832, the son of Abraham Roberts and great-grandson of the famous eighteenth-century Waterford architect, John Roberts. His father brought the family to live in Clifton, Bristol, when Frederick was just two years old, although Abraham continued to pursue a military career in India.

Frederick joined the Bengal artillery in 1851, arriving in India the following year. He saw active service during the Indian Uprising of 1857–8 and was awarded the highest military honour, the Victoria Cross, for bravery. In 1858, suffering from poor health, he took leave and travelled to Waterford. It was there that he met and married Nora Bews. The couple returned to India together, but of their three children who survived infancy, their only son died in the Second Boer War in 1899, with the posthumous award of a Victoria Cross. Frederick Roberts's eventual earldom passed to his two daughters, neither of whom had a surviving heir.

I could find no indication of any earlier marriage to an Indian woman when I searched the India Office records at the British Library. It would have been surprising if such a marriage or similar domestic arrangement were to have existed, in the short period between 1852 and 1858, for Roberts was ambitious and establishing himself in his army career. At this stage of the British colonial project, a marriage between a young British officer and an Indian woman of any class would have been frowned upon by the authorities.

Some years ago, at a temporary exhibition at a museum in Cape Town, South Africa, I saw early film video footage of Roberts on his horse, no doubt recorded at the time of the Second Boer War. He spent two periods of time in southern Africa, first briefly serving as governor of Natal and commander-in-chief in the region, before returning to India, where he was made commander of the Madras Army, and then commander-in-chief of the British Army in India (1885–93).

In 1893, Frederick Roberts was made commander-in-chief in Ireland, leaving India for good. Roberts's legacy to Ireland includes what is perhaps Dublin's most eccentric military grave. As commander, he was also master of the Royal Hospital Kilmainham, a retirement home for soldiers, where he had lodgings and stabled his horse, Vonolel, named after a Lushai (Assam) chief whose people he defeated. When Vonolel died, Roberts arranged for the well-travelled creature, which carried him on a famous march from Kabul to Kandahar, to be buried in the walled garden, complete with a poetic headstone expressing hope that the pair would be reunited in heaven.[2]

Today, serving military personnel are not supposed to voice publicly their views on government policy or be seen to take a political stand. Roberts had no such inhibitions or scruples. From the late 1860s, he was highly vocal in expressing his opinions, perhaps most notably in his call for conscription in early twentieth-century Britain. Anticipating the First World War, he was concerned about the potential catastrophe that would unfold if Britain were to rely on conscripts hastily recruited at the outbreak of war against the German Empire. While others insisted there was no threat of war, he correctly assessed that many potential conscripts would be malnourished and in poor health.

If I had ever hoped to be linked ancestrally to a freedom fighter struggling against colonialism, he was clearly not the man. Posts as commander-in-chief of the British Army in southern Africa, India and Ireland, and eventually, in 1901–4, of the whole British Army worldwide, confirm an unyielding commitment not just to the military, but to British imperialism. But worse was to come.

Following the British defeats in the early stages of the Second Boer War, Roberts took command of British forces in southern Africa where, tragically, his only son had just died. Together with his chief-of-staff Lord Kitchener, he aimed to revitalise the British military efforts. Part of their strategy was the burning of Boer farms and the internment of civilians in concentration camps. As the National Army Museum acknowledges today: 'Conditions there were initially appalling and over 26,000 people – many of them children – perished from hunger and disease'.[3] Did this mean my grandfather Walter Roberts believed we were related to the architect of these early twentieth-century concentration camps? Perhaps this was why Walter had never previously mentioned any connection to the man before Esmé set sail for England.

Frederick Sleigh Roberts's strategies are clearly shocking today, but they were also highly controversial at the time. The authorities needed to win over public opinion for the war effort. It seems that then, as now, propaganda played an important role. The Second Boer War coincided with a considerable increase in newspaper readership and literacy rates (in large part to the development of mass schooling in England and Wales, following the 1870 Elementary Education Act). From the start there was notable public aversion to war in southern Africa, but British newspapers played a key role in moulding public opinion in favour of military action, depicting the Boers as treacherous villains and brutal savages who were only too ready to insult and harm women and children.

A twenty-first-century biographer of Frederick Roberts concedes that Rudyard Kipling's admiration for the commander

coloured later assessments of his achievements but still finds
reason to emphasise his generosity:

> Small, wiry, and an excellent horseman, Roberts possessed
> that invaluable quality of generalship, good physical health,
> as well as great personal charm and kindliness. Fluent and
> persuasive on paper, he was not quick in debate, and he was
> not basically an original thinker, preferring to move forward
> on the basis of previous experience. The popular image of
> the little, simple, upright soldier, the *chevalier sans peur et
> sans reproche*,[4] owed more to Rudyard Kipling's hero-worship
> (as in his poem 'Bobs') than to reality. His surviving papers
> reveal a more complex character – ambitious, manipulative,
> on occasions devious, and with a strong political awareness.[5]

The tendency for 'charm and kindliness' for which Roberts
was known may have been extended to his own troops, and
to his horse, but it did not generally apply to those British
subjects in colonial territories. Quite the reverse. In case
my judgement is criticised as merely reflecting modern
sensibilities, it should be borne in mind that some of his con-
temporaries, particularly in Ireland, had severe reservations
about his character and actions. When Roberts was awarded
the honour of freeman of the city of Waterford in 1893, many
citizens welcomed it, but others expressed strong opposition,
writing to the mayor of the city, alleging he was responsible
for excessive cruelty and the collective punishment of Afghan
civilians a decade or so earlier.[6]

Frederick Sleigh Roberts was a man of the late Victorian
period, an age when racist ideas were being cemented. By the
time he came of age, in the 1850s, it was becoming more and

more unusual for British officers to marry or set up home with Indian women, although the practice remained common among regular soldiers. My grandfather, however, had not claimed direct *descent* from Frederick, merely that we were related in some way to him. The mystery lay in an earlier generation.

When I first started looking at the family relationships of both Frederick Sleigh Roberts and his father Abraham, I was not looking carefully at how some things are recorded and others are wiped from family records. If, like Frederick Roberts, you are made an earl, a peer of the realm, and have the right to sit in the House of Lords, the second chamber of parliament, there may well be strong reasons why you might want others to forget, or at least overlook, particular facts.

I then turned my attention to Frederick Sleigh Roberts's father, Abraham Roberts (1784–1883), and researched his two marriages: the first, to Frances Isabella Ricketts in Mogdapore in West Bengal in July 1820 and, after Frances's death, to Frederick's mother, Isabella Bunberry. Frances and Abraham had three children, each of whom was therefore a half-brother or sister to Frederick.

A deliberate cover up?

After his father's death in 1873, Frederick Roberts had direct access to Abraham's family papers but, after writing his memoirs, he destroyed them.

Why did he do this?

There seemed to be a missing period of some fifteen years in relation to Abraham's domestic life in India. He had arrived as a young man, aged twenty, and he did not marry Frances until a decade and a half later. Those years gave him ample time to have married an Indian wife, or have had a similar domestic arrangement, and to have had a family. This was a common pattern in the early nineteenth century for British officers.

I found an entry for Abraham Roberts in the *Oxford Dictionary of National Biography*:

> In 1809 [Abraham] Roberts had two sons and a daughter. The eldest son was called William; his mother was Indian; her name is now unknown, and whether she was Roberts's wife or his mistress is not clear.

So he did indeed have an earlier 'marriage' and another three children.[7]

Baptismal records exist for both William and the other children in the India Office archives held at the British Library. William was baptised in Delhi in May 1810, and lived in Oudh. This suggests that Abraham Roberts almost certainly acknowledged all three of his children by this first wife, an Indian woman whose name is now lost to history.

It seems likely to me that in destroying his father's papers, Frederick Sleigh Roberts wished to remove all trace of this family.

Abraham's family ties

Frederick Sleigh Roberts may have had access to his father's papers, but he didn't have access to those of his uncle, Thomas, Abraham's brother, who lived in Waterford. Nor could he destroy his father's will or the letters that Captain Thomas Roberts had written to his son[8] – confusingly also called

William Roberts, the same name as my three times great-grandfather – in India. The letters confirm the existence of Abraham's first, Indian, family and also reveal that, in the 1840s, Abraham acknowledged and supported his adult children[9]. It seems Abraham's brother Thomas and other family members back home in Ireland were more than ready to correspond, and to exchange gifts, with two of Abraham's children by his Indian wife, his son William and his daughter Anne, treating them to all intents and purposes in a similar way to other cousins.

Young Freddy

The letters first mention 'Freddy' in April 1844, when we learn that his father, Abraham, is aboard ship at Spithead in the Solent, having arrived from India, intending to go to London 'to do something' for the eleven-year-old Freddy and for his stepson, Hamilton Maxwell. A few weeks later, Thomas Roberts informs his own son William that 'Freddy – is going to Eton – a most expensive seminary – but where he will meet the Sons of the first people of the Kingdom – which in after life is sometimes useful'. Freddy's connections and indeed those of his father were, as his uncle anticipated, to stand him in good stead in his career.

In September 1846, Thomas writes to say that fourteen-year-old Freddy is to go to the East India Company Military Seminary (later the Royal Military College) at Addiscombe and the following month he confirms that he is already installed there. In 1851, we learn that Abraham is to set off for India and that Freddy, having completed his cadetship, and 'passed for the artillery' will soon follow his father to India to serve as his aide-de-camp.

The letters not only give us account of young Freddy's progression through his training, but also some insights into his character. In 1852, when Thomas's son William complains that his cousin Freddy, now a young soldier aged twenty, has not bothered to call on him in India, Thomas observes:

> I am not surprised to find that Fred had not paid you a visit, young chaps now a days are apt to think too much of themselves, particularly wearing epaulettes – but no matter & you were as well without his reacquaintance.

It seems Thomas judges his nephew to have an excessively high opinion of himself, and that as a military officer (wearing epaulettes) Freddy is more interested in the company of other military men than in maintaining a relationship with his cousin, who he perhaps considers to have very little to offer him in term of useful connections.

This seems a credible and accurate early assessment of Frederick Sleigh Roberts, one which is confirmed from a reading of his own book *Forty One Years in India*, which was published when he was in his sixty-fourth year and was no doubt thinking about his legacy.[10] His own account of his life confirms he is far more interested in his military network than maintaining cordial relations with any member of his family, other than his wife Nora.

William, Abraham Roberts's eldest son

By the time Freddy embarked on his career in India, in 1852, his half-brother and Abraham's eldest son also named William was a seasoned soldier, having served in the king of Oudh's army for a number of years, rising to the rank of colonel. Captain Thomas Roberts, having a number of Williams in the family, including his own son, generally distinguishes him from others by calling him 'India William'. This does not appear to be a derogatory term, since he also uses 'London William' to refer to another relative.

The first we hear of Abraham's eldest son William is in a letter that reports that 'India Will' is of the opinion that the king is unlikely to recruit further Europeans but that 'there appears no fear of India Wm losing his place'.

In 1843, we have one of the few comments from Abraham's perspective about his eldest son's situation, and these relate to his mixed Indian and European heritage. On 25 June, Thomas writes that: '[Your Uncle Ab] said that his Son Wm had made a great many Enemies – and being of "colour", was against him', so Abraham relayed to his brother the discrimination his mixed-heritage son had encountered. William was not only a casualty of the shifting political relationship between the East India Company and the local rulers, but also a casualty of the every-day racism that was finding renewed expression and vigour among Europeans in India by the 1840s, and causing those of mixed Anglo-Indian heritage to be marginalised. Significantly, his father, a senior Indian army officer, is all too aware of this.

Abraham Roberts's relationship with his children

An enduring relationship between Abraham Roberts and his children by his Indian wife can be inferred from his brother's

Thomas's letters, and the two brothers seem to have themselves maintained a close relationship, despite the physical distance between them and the infrequency of Abraham's visits to England and Ireland, particularly during the first three decades of his service in the East India Company's military force, when travel between India and the British Isles was slower than after the Suez Canal was built.

William and his sister Anne are already in their thirties when we come across them in the letters, whereas Freddy is just entering adolescence. There is no indication that any of them – William, Anne or their brother John – spent any part of their childhoods in Ireland or England, whereas Freddy, the son of his third marriage, was taken to England when still a toddler. Abraham returned to India to pursue his career.

William and his siblings, by contrast, were probably brought up in a household where Abraham and their mother were both present during their early years. The documents suggest that Abraham successfully maintained a relationship with his first three children, even after their mother disappeared from the scene when they were all under twelve years of age and their father had married Frances Ricketts. It's possible that Frances acted as stepmother to them for some years.

Abraham ensured that Freddy had the chance to be educated at Eton and the Company Military Seminary at Addiscombe, whereas no such provision had been made for his eldest son William, who had also elected to pursue a military career two decades earlier. We know that children of Indian and Anglo-Indian mothers were sometimes educated in Britain and sometimes in India, with fairer-skinned children often travelling to Europe and darker ones receiving their education in India. But any decision relating to

William's education may have equally been influenced by income. Abraham does not appear to have been a wealthy man during his youth, although as a Company officer he would have benefitted from the spoils of war, or loot, if and when a wealthy Indian ruler was conquered in a campaign in which he was involved. This is confirmed by his brother Thomas when he writes on 28 August 1843 that 'we will be anxious to know if the report is heard from by all be true, that they [the East India Company forces] have taken Kytul and that the prize money will be enormous', noting that if the story is true, 'Uncle Ab may well retire on his share'. Thomas's letter confirms the expectations of those at the centre of Empire, of riches through loot; it was regarded as normal that Company men would be able to help themselves to the riches of conquered Indian subjects.

Abraham left something to each of his surviving sons and daughters in his will. Those residing in India each receive an annuity for life: Anne gets 600 rupees per annum; William 444 rupees per annum; and John's widow 150 rupees per annum. It was common for men such as Abraham to leave money to their 'natural' children, when referring to those born out of wedlock but, interestingly, neither William, Anne nor John is *named* as a son or daughter in the will.

Squaring the circle

There is no simple geometrical solution to the puzzle of Freddy Roberts's exact relationship to my family. But it seems likely that it lies with his father Abraham and his three children by a now unknown Indian mother.

Lieutenant-General, later General, Sir Abraham Roberts was an East India Company officer who served for nearly fifty years in India. Abraham was a contemporary of my three times great-grandfather, William Roberts, the former slave and founding pastor of the Unitarian church in Madras. It is quite likely that this William Roberts and Abraham Roberts, son of a Waterford rector, might well have met in Madras. Abraham entered the service of the East India Company in 1804 and in March of the following year arrived in India, where he was posted to the Bengal European Regiment. William, the Unitarian pastor, records in his letters how he met with Company military officers, and how he took opportunities to discuss theological questions with them. Pastor William Roberts had travelled to London and Boulogne, to China and various places along the Bengal coast, had become acquainted with life in London, and his work as butler to William Harington, a prominent Madras civil servant, would have guaranteed that he acquired the skills to communicate with young officers such as Abraham Roberts of Waterford.

Abraham's first wife – whom he married sometime between 1805 and 1809 – is likely to have been one of William Roberts's three daughters. The oldest would have been of marriageable age soon after Abraham arrived in India. I believe this woman, my great-great aunt, is likely to have been the 'unknown first wife' who married Abraham Roberts, long before Freddy was born. Part of the confusion in resolving the Roberts lineage is due to the fact that Abraham Roberts married another Roberts – the daughter of William Roberts, aka Thiruvenkatam. I will give this woman a name, both to give her a degree of dignity and to help me tell the story. I call her Hannah. She was born probably around 1794 about the time William (Thiruvenkatam) was working in the Harrington household as a butler. Hannah was the child of William Roberts's first marriage. By the time Hannah married Abraham, her mother (again a woman whose name has been lost) was dead, and her father had remarried to a woman named Mary.

Abraham Roberts probably sought to marry Hannah around 1808, when she was about fourteen years old. While this seems extremely young today, it was common practice for women to marry young in the early nineteenth century. Abraham would have been about twenty-four years old. While the *Oxford Dictionary of National Biography* asserts that we do not know whether she was Abraham's wife or concubine, this is due to the fact that no record of the marriage has been found. This is not entirely surprising. Generally speaking, it was Anglican marriages that were reported and recorded on the East India Register. Were they formally married? William Roberts would no doubt have expected his daughter Hannah Roberts to be married in a Unitarian ceremony, although the Unitarian chapel itself was not built until 1813. I cannot imagine that William would have readily allowed his daughter to live with Abraham Roberts without what he regarded as the 'sacrament' of marriage.

From what we know of the Waterford Roberts, it seems likely they too would have preferred their son Abraham to marry, rather than take a mistress, in India. Marriage held different meanings in the nineteenth century than it does today. Any marriage outside of the Anglican church might have held a different meaning for William and his daughter Hannah Roberts on the one hand, and Abraham Roberts on the other. While Abraham acknowledged all three of his children from this relationship, through to his death in 1873, and provided for them in his lifetime and beyond through his will, he never used the term 'natural children', which would have suggested he considered them illegitimate. Maybe not mentioning them as his sons and daughters in 1873 was out of deference to the sensibilities of his second and third families, and particularly to his much loved and probably rather spoilt youngest son, Freddy, who clearly seems to have preferred to write Hannah and her children out of the family history. By the 1870s, marriages between Europeans and Indians were predominantly the preserve of working-class people, and Abraham would have been well aware of this.

This isn't the only reason we do not know Hannah's real name. Her own father, a Unitarian pastor and a progressive of the early nineteenth century who adopted many of the ideas of the European Enlightenment, failed to mention his daughters by name in his letters, although his sons, Theophilus, Joseph and William Roberts Jr were all named. It seems that although influenced by Enlightenment ideas and an avid reader of new texts, women's rights – as articulated by his contemporary, the English feminist writer Mary Wollstonecraft, whose books he would certainly have found at Johnson's bookshop – do not appear to have been something that engaged his thinking.

Finally, I think it important to stress that we might have enjoyed the memory of Hannah Roberts's real name if Freddy had not wished to curate history to suit his reputation as Earl of Kandahar, Pretoria and Waterford. Freddy seems to have gone out of his way to destroy any of his father's records that might link the Waterford Roberts family to Abraham's Indian wife and family. Frederick Sleigh Roberts has a lot to answer for.

He might have been ashamed of this relationship with an Indian family, but one existed. I am not exactly proud to have a relationship with him either.

From left: back row: Esmé, Maurice, with Tiny and Roland Barker.
Front row: Audrey with Rolana Barker, Hemel Hempstead, 1954.
We stayed with the Barkers when we visited Singapore in 1965.

Epilogue

At Hatfield House, Hertfordshire, 1955. From left: Kitty, Audrey, Esmé.

To answer the question I posed myself when I began this book, 'Where are you from?', I've journeyed back across seven generations, investigating the stories of family members in vastly different social circumstances. My short answer to this question still remains 'Britain', for this is where I grew up, and first tried to make sense of the world.

Yet a simple answer feels incomplete. I believe there's so much more to heritage, identity and belonging – for everyone – than can be captured in a single word, and this is especially true for those whose family histories have been framed and shaped by empire, and for anyone whose personal or recent family story includes migration.

My second question was 'Where am I *really* from?' I'm not from Chennai or Singapore, and I've never visited Miri, the town in Sarawak (Malaysia) where my mother was born, but I feel that I'm carrying a shared memory of these places, encoded deep within me. I have a sense of belonging to these places too. It is a multiple belonging that has little to do with politics or nationhood, but which is somehow rooted in the criss-crossed histories of these places with each other, and with the country where I live.

This seems more than simple nostalgia. The stories I've been told, and the new ones I've uncovered in my research, give me a special relationship to these places, almost a kinship, in many ways ephemeral and intangible. What have I inherited?

Well, I have been inspired by my great-great-great-grandfather William Roberts, not least because the project he began, the Unitarian church in Vepery, Chennai, that he founded in the late eighteenth century, has survived into the twenty-first and is still serving some of the poorest people in that neighbourhood. But also because he was, by any standard, a remarkable person, unfazed by those in power and ready to challenge accepted orthodoxies. He was open to learn from anyone, including women and men in humble circumstances. But even before I learned the details of his story, I feel that his legacy had been passed down our family to me.

I have always been encouraged to stand up for justice and to speak out for what I believe to be right. I was taught that learning comes from being open to different people and cultures. Yet, from an early age, I also realised that not everything was as it should be.

To survive, and thrive, it was important for me to figure out the difference between appearances and reality, to handle everyday indignities and racist remarks, and recognise that people could be inconsistent and that teachers might make claims that were untrue. These experiences have helped shape the person I am today. They have enabled me to be bold and to ask critical questions.

I feel a sense of belonging in many places, drawing both on my own experiences and on what I have inherited, my family's histories.

Facing the past

Looking at my family history has meant understanding the complexity of the European colonial past.

When I first arrived in Chennai in 2018, stepped inside the former Anglican St Mary's Church and wandered close to the site of the Fort St George garrison buildings, overlooking the Coromandel coast, and saw the fabric of the church and the plaques on its walls, all recalled the trade and military conquest of early British colonial era. I brought with me the hundred-year-old stories of my grandparents in that same city, wanting to find out more about my family from the records housed there.

These stories had been told and retold in different places,

first in Madras and later in Sarawak, then Singapore and finally in England, as each generation moved east and then west across the then British Empire. The storytelling was done by the women of the family – my mother Esmé, my grandmother Hilda, and Hilda's stepmother Lydia. So it seems that I come from a long line of storytellers, but I took on the task of filling in the gaps with a careful process of fact-checking and archival research.

I found that my family's story intersects with the story of millions of others. After leaving Chennai, I travelled to Kandy in Sri Lanka. When I told my university colleagues there of my visit to India and my encounter with Pastor Ruth at St Mary's, they made links with the history of their own country. They took me to the tea plantations of Nuwara Eliya to learn about the living conditions of Tamil workers whose ancestors were brought there by British planters in the colonial era. The Sri Lankan scholars, the women working as union leaders on the plantations and I each had vastly different social circumstances. But I learned that while our family histories differed, we each carried a sense of a colonial past and a colonial legacy.

A tangible colonial legacy

A shared colonial history links many British citizens from across Asia as well as people from former British colonies in Africa and the Caribbean and others in Britain today. During lockdown, as I unearthed more documents related to my mother, I spoke to a friend whose own mother, Theresa, arrived in Liverpool from Jamaica, just four years after Esmé. Each of the two women has a unique story and particular personal experiences, settling in different parts of the country, finding work, establishing a home and bringing up children. Yet, as young women of colour in 1950s Britain, they faced common challenges.

Britain is the country around which so many of us have circled, and this is the country we have shaped and formed, too.

Every generation of the men in the Roberts family from the 1780s until the late nineteenth century travelled to London, the metropole. William Roberts came several times, first as a recently freed slave and later as a butler to a European family. His son Joseph spent time studying at a Unitarian college in England, and his grandson, Samuel (my great-grandfather) came on furlough towards the end of his career, where he served as a clerk in the Indian colonial administration. While none of my nineteenth-century ancestors settled in England, other Indians and Anglo-Indians did so, and they made an impact on the communities in which they lived.

We can measure the impact of Britain and its empire by looking at its cities that grew wealthy from global plunder, trade and taxation from India and other colonies, and from the rich contents of its museums, collected in the name of science and learning, but often just carelessly looted. Great country houses and estates over the centuries, too, were frequently shaped, directly or indirectly, by the profits of war, piracy and enslavement.[1]

And Britain's colonial heritage within its empire has also left traces. From the seventeenth century onwards, military officers, adventurers, traders and colonial administrators, Portuguese, Dutch, French and other Europeans as well as British, made their homes for longer or shorter periods in India and founded families there. Many of them sent their mixed heritage children to be educated in Europe, and a number settled there. These children were integrated into British society at different levels and, for some, their Indian roots were quietly forgotten. I think many British families who today identify as white would be surprised to uncover mixed heritage in their own past. I wonder if they could answer the question, 'Where are you *really* from?'

Britishness and belonging

The British promise of belonging to the empire with free movement to and from Britain began to fray shortly after the Second World War as anti-colonial movements grew in strength. Although some 700 million people in British territories were granted British citizenship, including the right to live in the UK, it was quite clear that there was little intention of enabling many to access these rights.

The promise of Britishness, instilled in schooling – in fact, instilled in the very culture of empire – turned out to be hollow. Anglo-Indians adopted Christianity, aspects of British culture, including British dress styles and fashions, and they ate broadly British-style meals. The school curriculum in both India and Singapore was so English that, some forty years after he had left school, I recall that my uncle Ralph could recite the counties of England as they were in the 1930s. Members of my family and so many others were born in *British territories*, and Britain was forcibly made the centre of their universe, yet imperial laws, policies and decision-making meant that each generation experienced discriminatory treatment at the hands of the authorities.

The attitude of the 'Mother Country' was made all too clear in 1942 when, in the face of a Japanese invasion, the British authorities evacuated white residents as they fled Singapore and Malaya. They left behind many vulnerable people, like my grandparents and their three British North Borneo-born children, and those who worked for the colonial administration. These people, who saw themselves as British, suddenly learned that they weren't considered British at all.

Coloniser and colonised

My grandparents, Anglo-Indians born in British India at the end of the nineteenth century, were the children of empire. My grandfather Walter lived for most of his life in countries ruled by Britain, until Singapore achieved self-governance in 1959. He died in Singapore just a couple of weeks before it became a fully independent and sovereign state on 9 August 1965. My grandmother lived for a further thirteen years and became, of course, a Singaporean citizen, as did her sons Dudley and Ralph.

As Anglo-Indians in India, my relatives were prevented from accessing certain jobs reserved for Europeans and had limited educational opportunities. Anglo-Indians earned more than Indians, but less than Europeans, for the same work. Sometimes they were treated as almost-Europeans, sometimes as 'natives' – it depended if and when they were useful to the British authorities. In other respects, they were an embarrassment, a group to be mocked and ridiculed, and who felt the impact of social policies designed to differentiate by race and ethnicity. In the early twentieth century, as the authorities squeezed their space in the Indian job market, my family left for Sarawak, where they assisted in the colonisation of this new British territory. In this sense, they were both colonised and coloniser. But the choice was never up to them.

Secrets and lies, and a change of tone

Until the mid-nineteenth century, empire meant that white colonisers of all classes formed intimate and family relationships with the colonised. Frederick Sleigh Roberts, defender of the British Empire and British interests in Afghanistan and South Africa, and who helped quash the 1857 Indian Uprising, was not alone in hiding his family ties to an Indian woman. The adolescent Freddy I came across in his uncle's letters from Waterford, Ireland, was already showing himself to be a singular and stubborn young man, fully capable of rewriting history in his own interests. His racial intolerance and bigotry were commonplace in the latter half of the nineteenth century.

So where am I from? And … where are you from?

I return to these questions through the lens of a mixed heritage woman. As a child growing up in a mixed family in the second half of the twentieth century, like so many others I had to struggle hard against those who thought they could determine my identity for me and tell me who I was. As small children we know very little about our family histories beyond the stories that parents and grandparents tell us, and there is still little to read about mixed heritage families today or about our place in a shared colonial past. Researching this history has not only uncovered things peculiar to my family, it's also highlighted ways in which mixed heritage children and adults are not an aberration: we have always been here.

So I turn those vexed questions around and ask instead: What does it take to belong? Why, in our global age, are we still confusing nationality, race and ethnicity? Where are we all from? Do you *really* know where you are from?

Migration and mixedness are the norm and have long been so.

That is why I say, when I am asked: 'I am from here. How about you?'

Chambersbury JMI School, Hemel Hempstead, 1958.
Audrey in middle row, 6th from right.

Acknowledgements

I am grateful to the Hosking Houses Trust for the residency at Church Cottage which allowed me the time away from everyday responsibilities and a busy itinerary to complete this book, and especially to Sarah Hosking, both for your imagination in creating this opportunity and your generous hospitality.

I benefitted immensely from the peace of Literature Wales's Writers' Retreat, Nant Cottage, and from the company and conversation of many wonderful women I met at Tŷ Newydd Writing Centre. Special thanks to Miriam Williams, Mariel Jones, Margaret Jones and Pamela Petro for your welcome, your hospitality, and sharing your love of reading and writing.

I also enjoyed a residency in the inspiring surroundings of Cove Park in Scotland and thank Alexia Holt and all those at this beautiful arts centre for your support and encouragement.

I am deeply indebted to Cliona Purcell who very generously shared her transcripts of the Thomas Roberts letters in the keeping of Waterford Treasures Museum, and her knowledge of various members of the Waterford Roberts family. Likewise, Raja Mylvaganam provided valuable insights into the family of William Roberts of Madras for which I am especially grateful. Thank you both for your research and for taking the time to talk to me about mine.

Thanks to Dr Sumita Adam from Chennai; Jon Bagust of Edinburgh Unitarian Church; Abhi Janamanchi of Cedar Lane Unitarian Universalist Church, Bethesda, Maryland; Rev Harrison Kingsley of Chennai Christian Unitarian Church; and Rev Ruth Kiruba Lily Elizabeth of St Mary's Church, Chennai for helping me make connections.

Many friends and colleagues have offered support and encouragement during the course of writing and I am especially grateful to Madee Bagshaw, Rohini Corfield, Joan Cowley, Jenny Douglas, Kjersti Draugedalen, Hala Evans, David Forster, Viv Golding, Beate Goldschmidt-Gjerløw, Betty Jennings, Raminder Kaur, Alan Lester, Suzanne Overton-Edwards, Marietou Seye, Jo Shipley, Marta Stachurska-Kounta, and Hugh Starkey for your conversation, feedback, questions, insights, and practical support in keeping me on track.

I could not have written this book without the support of members of my own family: my dear late mother Esmé, on whose family stories I draw; my late father Maurice who I came to know better in the writing of this book; Christine and Darrell Fieldhouse who welcomed me into their home and shared family documents, photos and reminiscences about family life in Madras; Cheryl Weston, who has fielded so many questions; Charlie Osler, Chay Osler, Tahnee Osler and Luisa Minghella, for your advice and encouragement; and last but not least, Louis Osler Eguchi, who very early on in this project commented: 'I've always wondered who I really am'.

Finally, my very sincere thanks to Lennie Goodings at Virago for running with this project and for being a fabulous editor twice over; to Zoe Carroll and all at Virago for supporting this book through production; and to Howard Watson for careful, considerate and courteous copyediting.

Bibliography

Anderson, Valerie (2011), 'The Eurasian problem in nineteenth century India' Unpublished PhD thesis. University of London School of Oriental and African Studies (SOAS), Department of History.

Anderson, Valerie (2020), *Race and Power in British India*, London: Bloomsbury.

Anthony, Frank (1962), *Britain's Betrayal in India: The Story of the Anglo-Indian Community*, London: Simon Wallenburg Press.

Bear, Laura (2007), *Lines of the Nation: Indian Railway Workers, Bureaucracy, and the Intimate Historical Self*, New York: Columbia University Press.

British and Foreign Unitarian Society (1816–1838), Extracts from William Roberts's letters, 1816–1838. London: BFUS.

Caplan, Lionel (2001), *Children of Colonialism: Anglo-Indians in a Postcolonial World*. London: Berg.

Chee, Tong Suit (1972), *The Brethren Story: 150 Years of History in Singapore*, Singapore: Brethren Network Fellowship.

Cheong, Koon Hean (2019), *Seeking a Better Urban Future*, Singapore: World Scientific Publishing Co., https://doi.org/10.1142/11246.

Chhabra, Heeral (2015), 'Schools for European and Eurasian children in India: making of the official policy in colonial India and its contemporary significance', *Policy Futures in Education* 13(3): 321.

Dalrymple, William (2019), *The Anarchy: The Relentless Rise of the East India Company*. London: Bloomsbury.

Ditchfield, G. M. (2011), 'Jeremiah Joyce', *Oxford Dictionary of National Biography*, https://doi.org/10.1093/ref:odnb/15152.

Goh, Sin Tub (2017), 'The Sook Ching', *BiblioAsia* 12(4), January–March, https://biblioasia.nlb.gov.sg/vol-12/issue-4/jan-mar-2017/the-sook-ching.

Gough, Kathleen (2008), *Rural Society in Southeast India*. Cambridge University Press.

Gove, Richard H. (2007), 'The great El Niño of 1789–93 and its global consequences: reconstructing an extreme climate event in world environmental history', *The Medieval History Journal* 10 (1&2): 75–98.

Hancox, Dan (2021), 'The secret deportations: how Britain betrayed the Chinese men who served the country during the war', *Guardian*, 25 May, www.theguardian.com/news/2021/may/25/chinese-merchant-seamen-liverpool-deportations.

Hancox, Dan (2022), 'Chinese seafarers were coerced into leaving UK after war, Home Office admits', *Guardian*, 2 August, www.theguardian.com/world/2022/aug/02/chinese-seafarers-were-coerced-into-leaving-uk-after-war-home-office-admits.

Hickman, Katie (2019), *She-merchants, Buccaneers & Gentlewomen: British Women in India 1600–1900*, London: Virago.

Irschick, Eugene F. (1989), 'Order and disorder in colonial South India, Modern Asian Studies', 23(3), 459–492. Doi:10.1017/S0026794X00009513.

Lester, Alan (2022), *Deny and Disavow: Distancing the Imperial Past in the Culture Wars*, London: Sunrise.

McNally, Frank (2015), 'Suir things – An Irishman's diary about Frederick Roberts and his famous Waterford family. Soldiers and painters', *Irish Times*, 1 October, www.irishtimes.com/opinion/suir-things-an-irishman-s-diary-about-frederick-roberts-and-his-famous-waterford-family-1.2373293.

Muthiah, S. (2015), 'Madras miscellany: A corner for storytellers', *Hindu*, 1 August, www.thehindu.com/features/metroplus/madras-miscellany-a-corner-forstorytellers/article7489521.ece.

Mylvaganam, Raja (2014), 'The Life of a Tamil Convert: William Roberts Proselytising in the Wake of the Enlightenment', in Esther Fihl and A. R. Venkatachalapathy (eds), *Beyond Tranquebar: Grappling across Cultural Borders in South India*. Hyderabad: Orient Blackswan.

National Army Museum (NAM) (n.d.), 'Frederick Roberts: Bobs', www.nam.ac.uk/explore/frederick-roberts-bobs.

National Army Museum (NAM) (n.d.), 'Malayan Emergency', www.nam.ac.uk/explore/malayan-emergency.

National Army Museum (NAM) (n.d.), 'What was National Service?', www.nam.ac.uk/explore/what-was-national-service.

National Library Board (NLB) Singapore e-Resources (n.d.), 'Emergency is Declared in Singapore', *History SG*, https://eresources.nlb.gov.sg/history/events/a8f32f00-dd7f-4384-abc0-e21e9f79507f.

Neild, Susan M. (1979), 'Colonial urbanism: the development of Madras city in the eighteenth and nineteenth centuries', *Modern Asian Studies* 13(2): pp. 217–246. doi: 10.1017/S0026749X00008301.

Newsinger, John (2013), *The Blood Never Dried: A People's History of the British Empire*, London: Bookmarks Publications.

Oldfield, John (2021), 'Abolition of the slave trade and slavery in Britain', British Library, 4 February, https://www.bl.uk/restoration-18th-century-literature/articles/abolition-of-the-slave-trade-and-slavery-in-britain.

Ong, Chuit Chung (1997), *Operation Matador: Britain's War Plans Against the Japanese 1918–1941*, Singapore: Times Academic.

Otto, Brent Howitt (2015), 'Navigating race and national identity for Anglo-Indians in the struggle for rights and recognition in colonial Calcutta, 1821–1830', *International Journal of Anglo-Indian Studies* 15(1): 13–33, www.international-journal-of-anglo-indian-studies.org/index.php/IJAIS/article/view/6/2.

Patnaik, Utsa (2012), 'Some aspects of the contemporary agrarian question' *Agrarian South: Journal of Political Economy* 1(3): 233–54.

Piccini, Jon & Money, Duncan (2021), '"A fundamental human right"? Mixed-race marriage and the meaning of rights in the postwar British Commonwealth', *Comparative Studies in Society and History*, 63(3), 655-84.

Roberts, Frederick Sleigh (1898), *Forty-One Years in India*, London: Richard Bentley.

Robson, Brian (2011), 'Roberts, Frederick Sleigh, 1st Earl Roberts (1832–1914)', *Oxford Dictionary of National Biography*, https://doi.org/10.1093/ref:odnb/35768.

Sanghera, Sathnam (2020), *Empireland: How Imperialism Has Shaped Modern Britain*, London: Penguin.

Saravanan, V. (2010), 'Agrarian policies in the tribal areas of Madras presidency during the pre-survey and settlement period, 1792–1872', *Indian Journal of Agricultural Economics* 65(2): 261–76.

Seng, Loh Kah (2006), 'Beyond rubber prices: negotiating the Great Depression in Singapore', *South East Asia Research* 14(1): 5–31.

Singapore National Archives, oral history interview: Alex Abishegadaden, March 1994, www.nas.gov.sg/archivesonline/oral_history_interviews/record-details/637463ee-1160-11e3-83d5-0050568939ad?keywords=alex+abisheganaden&keywords-type=all.

Sleeter, Christine (2015), 'Multicultural curriculum and critical family history', *Multicultural Education Review* 7(1–2): 1–11, https://doi.org/10.1080/2005615X.2015.1048607.

Tiang, Jeremy (2017), *State of Emergency*, Singapore: Epigram

United Nations (1948), *Universal Declaration of Human Rights* www.ohchr.org/en/universal-declaration-of-human-rights.

Visram, Rosina (2002), *Asians in Britain: 400 Years of History*, London: Pluto Press.

Zeheter, Michael (2015), *Epidemics, Empire, and Environments: Cholera in Madras and Quebec City, 1818–1910*, Pittsburgh: University of Pittsburgh Press.

Notes

Chapter 1

1. Sathnam Sanghera (2020), *Empireland: How Imperialism has Shaped Modern Britain*, London: Penguin.

Chapter 2

1. In 1967 the US Supreme Court ruled, in the case of *Loving v. Virginia* that such laws were unconstitutional under the equal protection and due process clauses of the Fourteenth Amendment. The case arose after Richard Loving, a white man, and Mildred Jeter, a woman of mixed African-American and Native American ancestry, travelled in June 1958 from their homes in Central Point, Virginia, to Washington, DC to be married. The couple returned to Central Point, where they lived with Mildred's parents, while Richard, a construction worker, began building them a home of their own. In July 1958, police entered the Lovings' bedroom in the early hours of the morning and arrested them for violating the state's ban on interracial marriage. At a hearing in a Virginia state court in January 1959, the couple pleaded guilty to having violated the state code, which prohibited a 'white' person and a 'colored' person from leaving the state to be married and returning to live as man and wife. The judge sentenced the Lovings to one year in jail but suspended the sentence on the condition that the couple leave the state immediately and not return as man and wife for a period of twenty-five years. The Lovings filed a suit in a Virginia state court in November 1963, seeking to overturn their convictions on the grounds that the Virginia law was inconsistent with the Fourteenth Amendment. The case was rejected and was then accepted for review by Virginia's Supreme Court of Appeals, which upheld the constitutionality of the state laws. The Lovings then appealed the case to the US Supreme Court, which heard the case in April 1967. In a unanimous decision, the Supreme Court overturned their convictions. On behalf of the court, Chief Justice Earl Warren's opinion was that freedom to marry is one of the 'basic civil rights of man'. The

ruling had the effect of invalidating laws against interracial marriage in fifteen other states.

2. Dan Hancox (2021), 'The secret deportations: how Britain betrayed the Chinese men who served the country during the war', *Guardian*, 25 May, www.theguardian.com/news/2021/may/25/chinese-merchant-seamen-liverpool-deportations. The decision was made at a Home Office meeting in 1945. It was never discussed in parliament and was kept secret from the press and public. They had taken huge risks for the UK, for 3,500 merchant vessels were sunk by Nazi U-boats and more than 72,000 lives were lost on the Allied side.

3. Dan Hancox (2022), 'Chinese seafarers were coerced into leaving UK after war, Home Office admits', *Guardian*, 2 August, www.theguardian.com/world/2022/aug/02/chinese-seafarers-were-coerced-into-leaving-uk-after-war-home-office-admits.

4. *Hansard*, House of Commons, 28 March 1950, vol. 473, col. 337.

5. *Singapore Free Press*, 5 July 1949, 9 July 1949; *Malaya Tribune*, 5 November 1949, 11 November 1949, https://eresources.nlb.gov.sg/newspapers.

6. National Army Museum, www.nam.ac.uk/explore/what-was-national-service. National Service began in 1947 and continued for well over a decade, being gradually phased out in the late 1950s. According to the National Army Museum, 'unofficially, it was also decided not to conscript the vast majority of black and Asian British men. Despite high levels of immigration in the mid-1950s, no black or Asian men were commissioned and only a few hundred black and Asian soldiers served in the ranks throughout the years of National Service.' There was no conscription from Northern Ireland, for fear of Nationalist unrest. More than 2 million men were called up to the armed forces, serving in one of Britain's garrisons in Europe and around the world.

7. Navy, Army and Airforce Institute or NAAFI is an organisation that provides shops, a canteen and other recreational facilities for British servicemen, either at home or overseas, wherever they happen to be stationed.

8. The age of majority, when a person is recognised as an adult and can marry without their parents' consent, was twenty-one years. The 1969 Family Law Reform Act would reduce the age of majority in England and Wales to eighteen.

9. Singapore National Archives, oral history interview: Alex Abishegadaden, March 1994, www.nas.gov.sg/archivesonline/oral_history_interviews/record-details/637463ee-1160-11e3-83d5-0050568939ad?keywords=alex+abisheganaden&keywords-type=all.

10. Tarring and feathering was an act of mob violence. An individual was coated in tar and then covered with feathers. It was a form of torture, not just designed to humiliate but also to inflict pain, since the subsequent removal of the tar would cause severe damage to the skin.

11. Rosina Visram (2002), *Asians in Britain: 400 Years of History*, London: Pluto Press.

12. Visram 2002.

13. Jon Piccini and Duncan Money (2021) '"A fundamental human right"? Mixed-race marriage and the meaning of rights in the postwar British Commonwealth'. *Comparative Studies in Society and History*, 63(3), 655-684. doi:10.1017/S0010417521000177, p. 659.

14. United Nations (1948), www.ohchr.org/en/universal-declaration-of-human-rights.

Chapter 3

1. Alan Lester (2022), *Deny and Disavow: Distancing the Imperial Past in the Culture Wars*, London: Sunrise, p. 174.

Chapter 4

1. Singapore joined the Malaysian Federation in 1963, marking the island's full independence from colonial rule. The other members of the federation were Malaya and the former British colonies of North Borneo and Sarawak. Following tensions within the Malaysian Federation and Singapore's formal expulsion, Singapore broke away and declared itself an independent republic on 9 August 1965.

2. Loh Kah Seng (2006), 'Beyond rubber prices: negotiating the Great Depression in Singapore', *South East Asia Research* 14(1): 5–31.

3. Koon Hean Cheong (2019), *Seeking a Better Urban Future*, Singapore: World Scientific Publishing Co., https://doi.org/10.1142/11246.

4. The Christian Brethren movement began in Britain in the early nineteenth century, and the focus was on Bible study, prayer, worship and witness. The movement later divided into two groups, the closed or exclusive Brethren and the open Brethren. The Singapore Brethren, from the second, open group, was established by Eliza and Philip Robinson, who came from Australia in 1857 and founded the Robinsons company in the city. In September 1866, they built a meeting house in Bras Basah Road, which they named Bethesda. The church had both an English-speaking and a Chinese-speaking congregation from the 1860s. See Tong Suit Chee (1972), *The Brethren Story: 150 Years of History in Singapore*, Singapore: Brethren Network Fellowship.

5. Chuit Chung Ong (1997), *Operation Matador: Britain's War Plans Against the Japanese 1918–1941* (Singapore: Times Academic).

6. William Dobbie, quoted in the *London Gazette* (1948), Supplement 38215, 20 February, p. 1250, www.thegazette.co.uk/London/issue/38215/supplement/1250.

7. Junior Cambridge exams were normally taken at age sixteen, when students completed secondary school. Exam papers were sent to the UK to be marked and graded. Students who did well would then remain at school for a further two years to take more specialised Senior Cambridge examinations. The Junior Cambridge exams were the equivalent of O levels (later GCSEs) and the Senior Cambridge were the equivalent of A levels, and success could lead to a place at college or university.

8. Japan acknowledged that 6,000 had died, but former Singapore prime minister Lee Kuan Yew estimated it was as many as 70,000. BiblioAsia, the Singapore National Library, includes this first-hand account by a survivor, Goh Sin Tub, who was a young boy at the time: Goh Sin Tub (2017), 'The Sook Ching', *BiblioAsia* 12(4), January–March, https://biblioasia.nlb.gov.sg/vol-12/issue-4/jan-mar-2017/the-sook-ching.

9. National Library Board (NLB) Singapore e-Resources (n.d.), 'Emergency is Declared in Singapore', *History SG*, https://eresources.nlb.gov.sg/history/events/a8f32f00-dd7f-4384-abc0-e21e9f79507f.

10. National Army Museum (NAM) (n.d.), 'Malayan Emergency', www.nam.ac.uk/explore/malayan-emergency.

11. NAM.

12. John Newsinger (2013), *The Blood Never Dried: A People's History of the British Empire*, London: Bookmarks Publications, p. 218.

13. Jeremy Tiang (2017), *State of Emergency*, Singapore: Epigram.

Chapter 5

1. Valerie Anderson (2011) 'The Eurasian problem in nineteenth century India'. Unpublished PhD thesis. University of London School of Oriental and African Studies (SOAS), Department of History, p. 146.

2. Princely states were ruled by Indian princes but in the nineteenth century were increasingly controlled by the British authorities.

3. Quebec, Ontario, Nova Scotia and New Brunswick.

4. Valerie Anderson (2020), *Race and Power in British India*, London: Bloomsbury.

5. This what Valerie Anderson (2011) found when looking at the case of railway employees a generation earlier, in the 1880s, p. 251.

6. Anderson 2011, p. 247.

7. Anderson 2011, p. 241.

8. F. Anthony (1962), *Britain's Betrayal in India: The Story of the Anglo-Indian Community*, London: Simon Wallenburg Press.

9. Laura Bear (2007), *Lines of the Nation: Indian Railway Workers, Bureaucracy, and the Intimate Historical Self*, New York: Columbia University Press.

10. Born in the early eighteenth century, Isabella was married in Madras to a senior East India Company official, Edward Croke (1690–1769), governor of Fort St David and Lord Liverpool's great-grandfather. The fact that it is now difficult to confirm Isabella's Indian or Eurasian background is unsurprising, given that later generations of elite British families were coy about their Indian ancestors.

11. Brent Howitt Otto (2015), 'Navigating race and national identity for Anglo-Indians in the struggle for rights and recognition in colonial Calcutta, 1821–1830', *International Journal of Anglo-Indian Studies* 15(1): 13–33, www.international-journal-of-anglo-indian-studies.org/index.php/IJAIS/article/view/6/2.

12. Minute of Lord Canning, Viceroy of India, on Education, 1860, quoted in Heeral Chhabra (2015), 'Schools for European and Eurasian children in

India: making of the official policy in colonial India and its contemporary significance', *Policy Futures in Education* 13(3): 321.

13. George Cotton, quoted in Chhabra 2015, p. 321.

14. Heeral Chhabra (2015), 'Schools for European and Eurasian children in India: Making of the official policy in colonial India and its contemporary significance', *Policy Futures in Education* 13(3): 3.15.

15. Anderson 2011, p. 155.

Chapter 6

1. Susan M. Neild (1979) 'Colonial urbanism: the development of Madras city in the eighteenth and nineteenth centuries', *Modern Asian Studies* 13(2): pp. 217–246. doi:10.1017/S0026749X00008301.

2. Kathleen Gough (2008) *Rural Society in Southeast India*. Cambridge University Press. Until the thirteenth century, under the Chola kings, 'the Vellalars were the dominant secular aristocratic caste ... providing the courtiers, most of the army officers, the lower ranks of the kingdom's bureaucracy, and the upper layer of the peasantry' (p. 29).

3. William Roberts (1833).

4. Raja Mylvaganam (undated) 'The life of a Tamil convert William Roberts proselytising in the wake of the Enlightenment'. https://www.academia.edu/7191290/The_Life_of_a_Tamil_Convert_William_Roberts_Proselytising_in_the_Wake_of_the_Enlightenment.

5. Eugene F. Irschick (1989), 'Order and disorder in colonial South India', *Modern Asian Studies*, 23(3), 459-492. doi:10.1017/S0026749X00009513 p. 460.

6. Richard H. Gove (2007) 'The great El Niño of 1789–93 and its global consequences: reconstructing an extreme climate event in world environmental history'. *The Medieval History Journal* 10 (1&2): pp. 75–98.

7. Raja Mylvaganam (undated).

8. William Roberts (1818) 'A Letter to Unitarian Society of London from William Roberts A Native of Madras' published as: *A Letter to The Unitarian Society for Promoting Christian Knowledge and the Practice of Virtue by the Distribution of Book by A native Unitarian Christian of Madras to which is prefixed An Introduction by The Rev. Thomas Belsham*, London: by Richard and Arthur Taylor.

9. John Oldfield (2021), 'Abolition of the slave trade and slavery in Britain', British Library, 4 February, https://www.bl.uk/restoration-18th-century-literature/articles/abolition-of-the-slave-trade-and-slavery-in-britain.

10. Utsa Patnaik (2012), 'Some aspects of the contemporary agrarian question', *Agrarian South: Journal of Political Economy* 1(3): pp. 233–54.
William Dalrymple (2019), *The Anarchy: The Relentless Rise of the East India Company*, London: Bloomsbury.

11. Lascar comes from the Hindi and Persian word *lashkar*. The Portuguese in India used it to mean soldiers, and later it was applied to sailors.

12. R. Visram (1986), *Ayahs, Lascars and Princes: The Story of Indians in Britain 1700–1947*, London: Pluto.

13. Roberts 1818, p. 4.
14. Roberts 1818, p. 5.
15. Roberts 1833, p. 6.
16. Built in Rotherhithe, Kent, and launched in 1772, the *Bessborough* was a three-deck ship with a gundeck measuring just under 144 feet (44.6 metres) in length and slightly less than 39 feet (11.6 metres) in breadth. The hold was just over 15 feet (4.6 metres) in depth: 'British Merchanteast indiaman "Bessborough" (1772)', *Three Decks – Warships in the Age of Sail*, https://threedecks.org/index.php?display_type=show_ship&id=29067.
17. A hulked ship is one that has had its rigging and possibly internal equipment removed. Many wooden ships of this period once decommissioned in this way served longer as hulks than as ocean-going vessels. A hulk might be used as a warehouse or refitted as a floating prison.
18. Roberts 1818, p. 7.
19. Visram 1986, p. 13. See also K. Hickman (2019), *She-merchants, Buccaneers & Gentlewomen: British Women in India 1600–1900*, London: Virago.
20. Quoted in Visram 1986, p. 13.
21. Roberts 1818, pp. 7–8.
22. *Public Advertiser*, 2 December 1786, no. 16391, in Visram 1986, pp. 18–19.
23. *Public Advertiser*, 5 December 1786, no. 10393, in Visram 1986, p. 19.
24. Roberts 1818, p. 8.
25. Roberts 1818, p. 9.
26. Homegrown Staff (2021), '300 Years Ago, India's Very First Bible was Translated into Tamil by a German Missionary', 8 June, *Homegrown*, https://homegrown.co.in/article/60515/the-story-of-indias-very-first-bible-translated-into-tamil-in-1714-by-a-german-missionary.
27. Roberts 1818, pp. 10–11.
28. Unitarianism had become a denomination in England some twenty years earlier after Theophilus Lindsey organised meetings with Joseph Priestley, going on to found the first Unitarian congregation, Essex Street Church, in London.
29. Roberts 1818, p. 11.
30. Almost certainly the William Harrington who was appointed to the Madras civil service in 1777 and who spent the rest of his life in the city, after whom Harrington Road is named: S. Muthiah (2015), 'Madras miscellany: A corner for storytellers', *Hindu*, 1 August, www.thehindu.com/features/metroplus/madras-miscellany-a-corner-forstorytellers/article7489521.ece.
31. Roberts 1818, p. 12 ; Mylvaganam (undated).
32. Roberts 1818, p. 12.
33. Roberts 1823, p. 6, quoted in an unpublished biographical essay by Raja Mylvaganam, drawing on extracts from various of Roberts's letters, 1816–1838, published in the annual reports of the British and Foreign Unitarian Society.
34. Roberts 1818, p. 13.
35. Roberts 1818, pp. 17–18.
36. V. Saravanan (2010), 'Agrarian policies in the tribal areas of Madras

presidency during the pre-survey and settlement period, 1792–1872', *Indian Journal of Agricultural Economics* 65(2): 261–76.

37. M. Zeheter (2015), *Epidemics, Empire, and Environments: Cholera in Madras and Quebec City, 1818–1910*, Pittsburgh: University of Pittsburgh Press.

38. G. M. Ditchfield (2011), 'Jeremiah Joyce', *Oxford Dictionary of National Biography*, https://doi.org/10.1093/ref:odnb/15152.

39. Roberts 1818, pp. 14–25.

40. Roberts 1818, p. 15.

41. Roberts 1818, p. 16.

42. Roberts 1818, p. 15.

43. W. Roberts (1830), p. 18 from extracts from various of Roberts's letters, 1816–1838, published in the annual reports of the British and Foreign Unitarian Society. Quoted in unpublished biographical essay by Raja Mylvaganam.

44. Roberts 1833, p. 15.

45. Roberts 1836, p. 13.

46. Roberts 1837, p. 20.

47. Roberts 1837, p. 21.

48. Roberts 1838, p. 15.

49. Roberts 1838, p. 15.

50. Roberts 1838, p. 15.

51. Roberts 1838, p. 16.

Chapter 7

1. Christine Sleeter (2015), 'Multicultural curriculum and critical family history', *Multicultural Education Review* 7(1–2): 1–11, https://doi.org/10.1080/2005615X.2015.1048607.

2. Frank McNally (2015), 'Suir things – An Irishman's Diary about Frederick Roberts and his famous Waterford family. Soldiers and painters', *Irish Times*, 1 October, www.irishtimes.com/opinion/suir-things-an-irishman-s-diary-about-frederick-roberts-and-his-famous-waterford-family-1.2373293.

3. 'Frederick Roberts: Bobs' (n.d.), National Army Museum, www.nam.ac.uk/explore/frederick-roberts-bobs.

4. Translated as: the knight without fear and beyond reproach. This was the reputation of the French knight Pierre Terrail of Bayard (*c.* 1476–1524) who served King Charles VIII of France.

5. Brian Robson (2011), 'Roberts, Frederick Sleigh, 1st Earl Roberts (1832–1914)', *Oxford Dictionary of National Biography*, https://doi.org/10.1093/ref:odnb/35768.

6. According to the Waterford City Archives, while the majority of residents approved of the City Corporation's award, some 'advanced nationalists' objected to it being bestowed on a judicial murderer. A letter from one Michael Field read: 'Some years ago the British Government in India . . . sent Genl Roberts into the country [Afghanistan] to chastise these wild people. The result was that some were found guilty and a batch of 200, and other lots of lesser numbers, were ordered to be tied together and

have Inflammable Oil poured on and set fire to, which was duly done. And this is the man that Waterford is about to present the freedom of the city'. Waterford City Archives, ref. no. P6/5, https://waterfordireland.tripod.com/controversy.htm.

7. Brian Robson (2004), 'Roberts, Sir Abraham (1784–1873)', *Oxford Dictionary of National Biography*, https://doi.org/10.1093/ref:odnb/23741.

8. Captain Thomas's correspondence with his son William (covering the years 1841–52) is archived at the Waterford Treasures Museum. Cliona Purcell, a researcher at the museum has transcribed these letters and the material I quote here comes from her transcription which she has generously shared with me. She has also written a blog in which she discusses the family life of British officers in the early 19th century, and particularly that of Abraham Roberts of Waterford. https://waterfordtreasures.wixsite.com/wattreasuresblog/post/concubines-and-lady-wives-the-family-life-of-the-british-officer-in-the-early-days-of-the-raj

9. I have a digital copy of the text of Abraham Roberts's will from a genealogy report of his grandfather John Roberts from Family Tree Maker online. I have not been able to check it against an original document.

10. F. S. Roberts (1898), *Forty One Years in India*, London: Richard Bentley.

Epilogue

1. Corrine Fowler (2000), *Green and Unpleasant Land: Creative responses to rural England's colonial connections*, Leeds: Peepal Tree Press; Andrea Major (2014), *Slavery, Abolitionism and Empire in India, 1772–1843*, Liverpool: Liverpool University Press.